Lawrence's genius is unquestioned, but he is seldom considered a writer interested in comedy. This collection of essays by distinguished scholars explores the range, scope and sheer verve of Lawrence's comic writing. Comedy for Lawrence was not, as his contemporary Freud insisted, a mere defence mechanism. The comic mode enabled him to function parodically and sarcastically, radically to undermine those forms of authority from which he always felt estranged. Lawrence's critique of the modern failure of the mystic impulse is present in all the comic moments in his writing, where it is used to create an alternative cultural and social space. Lawrence used humour to distance himself from the dominant orthodoxy surrounding him, from the material of his fiction, from his readers and finally from his own often intensely serious preoccupations. This book revises the popular image of Lawrence as a humourless writer and reveals his strategic use of a genuine comic talent.

Lawrence and comedy

Lawrence and comedy

Edited by

Paul Eggert
University College ADFA

and John Worthen
University of Nottingham

Published by the Press Syndicate of the University of Cambridge
The Pitt Building, Trumpington Street, Cambridge CB2 1RP
40 West 20th Street, New York, NY 10011-4211, USA
10 Stamford Road, Oakleigh, Melbourne 3166, Australia

First published 1996

Printed in Great Britain at the University Press, Cambridge

A catalogue record for this book is available from the British Library

Library of Congress cataloguing in publication data

Lawrence and comedy/ edited by Paul Eggert and John Worthen
    p.   cm.
Includes index.
1. Lawrence, D. H. (David Herbert), 1885–1930 – Humor.
2. Humorous stories, English – History and criticism.
3. Comic, The, in literature. I. Eggert, Paul, 1951– .
II. Worthen, John.
PR6023.A93Z645 1996
823′.912–dc20 95-26677 CIP

ISBN 0 521 56275 9 hardback

SE

Contents

Note on contributors

Paul Eggert

is Associate Professor in English at the Australian Defence Force Academy, University of New South Wales, in Canberra. He edited *The Boy in the Bush* and *Twilight in Italy* for the Cambridge University Press Edition of the Works of Lawrence, and is General Editor of the Academy Editions of Australian Literature series.

John Worthen

is Professor of D. H. Lawrence Studies at the University of Nottingham, a member of the Board of the Cambridge University Press Edition of the Works and Letters of Lawrence, Advisory Editor for the Penguin Edition of the Works of Lawrence and author of the first volume of the Cambridge Biography of D. H. Lawrence (1991).

Howard Mills

is Senior Lecturer in the University of Kent at Canterbury and joint author of *D. H. Lawrence's Non-Fiction: Art, Thought and Gender* (1988).

John Turner

is Senior Lecturer at the University College of Swansea and editor of *The Trespasser* (1994) in the Penguin Edition of the Works of Lawrence.

Lydia Blanchard

is Professor of English at Southwest Texas State University at San Marcos and has been editor of the *D. H. Lawrence Review*.

Holly Laird

> is Professor of English at the University of Tulsa and has published *Self and Sequence: The Poetry of D. H. Lawrence* (1988).

Paul Poplawski

> is Lecturer at Trinity College, Carmarthen, and author of *Promptings of Desire: Creativity and the Religious Impulse in the Works of D. H. Lawrence* (1993).

Mark Kinkead-Weekes

> is Emeritus Professor of English at the University of Kent at Canterbury, editor of *The Rainbow* in the Cambridge University Press edition of Lawrence and of *Women in Love* in the Penguin edition and author of the second volume of the Cambridge Biography of D. H. Lawrence.

John Bayley

> is Emeritus Professor of English at the University of Oxford and Fellow of St Catherine's College; he has published widely on Lawrence.

Acknowledgements

These essays draw extensively upon the Cambridge Edition of the Works and Letters of D.H. Lawrence (General Editors J.T. Boulton and Warren Roberts): those texts are the copyright of the Estate of Frieda Lawrence Ravagli, and we are grateful for the permission of the Literary Executor, Laurence Pollinger Ltd, and Cambridge University Press for permission to quote copyright material.

We wish to thank the editors of *The D.H. Lawrence Review* for permission to reprint a much revised version of the essay by Lydia Blanchard which appeared as 'D.H. Lawrence and his "Gentle Reader": The New Audience of *Mr Noon*' in vol xx (1988), 223–35.

Our thanks are also due to Dieter Mehl – in whose company the idea of this volume first materialised – and to Andrew Brown, Kevin Taylor, Ray Ryan and Lindeth Vasey of Cambridge University Press.

Cue-titles

(The place of publication, here and throughout the volume, is London unless otherwise stated.)

(i.) James T. Boulton, ed. *The Letters of D. H. Lawrence.* Volume I. Cambridge: Cambridge University Press, 1979. (All seven volumes of the *Letters* edition are cited in the text by volume and page number.)

(ii.) George J. Zytaruk and James T. Boulton, eds. *The Letters of D. H. Lawrence.* Volume II. Cambridge: Cambridge University Press, 1981.

(iii.) James T. Boulton and Andrew Robertson, eds. *The Letters of D. H. Lawrence.* Volume III. Cambridge: Cambridge University Press, 1984.

(iv.) Warren Roberts, James T. Boulton and Elizabeth Mansfield, eds. *The Letters of D. H. Lawrence.* Volume IV. Cambridge: Cambridge University Press, 1987.

(v.) James T. Boulton and Lindeth Vasey, eds. *The Letters of D. H. Lawrence.* Volume V. Cambridge: Cambridge University Press, 1989.

(vi.) James T. Boulton and Margaret H. Boulton, with Gerald M. Lacy, eds. *The Letters of D. H. Lawrence.* Volume VI. Cambridge: Cambridge University Press, 1991.

(vii.) Keith Sagar and James T. Boulton, eds. *The Letters of D. H. Lawrence.* Volume VII. Cambridge: Cambridge University Press, 1993.

Nehls   Edward Nehls, ed. *D. H. Lawrence: A Composite Biography*. 3 volumes. Madison: University of Wisconsin Press, 1957–9.

*OED*2   *The Oxford English Dictionary*. 2nd edn, prepared by J. A. Simpson and E.S.C. Weiner. 10 volumes. Oxford: Clarendon Press, 1989.

～ Introduction

Paul Eggert

In the mid-1950s F. R. Leavis called Lawrence 'one of the great masters of comedy' but failed to develop the claim, intent as he was on eliciting a body of truths about the life-enhancing, religious and normative potential of Lawrence's writings. In the reconstruction of values which attended the cold-war, industrialist and existentialist climates of the period, *that* particular Lawrence – once established, and answering felt needs – held good for a couple of decades.[1] The construction still deserves respect as testimony to the way in which Leavis and others powerfully responded to energising qualities they discovered in Lawrence's writings. But the result was to construe those qualities as redemptive values of which post-1960s generations of readers, differently attuned, would feel little need. However, the intellectual relativism of the late twentieth century is helping us to recognise another Lawrence. Understanding the place of comedy in his works – particularly those of the 1920s, generally cast as poor relations of the 'great' works of the 1910s – will be central. This, the first book devoted to the subject of Lawrence and comedy, is intended as a contribution to the project. Inevitably this collection of essays, all but one freshly written for the volume and previously unpublished, will not exhaust it; the present Introduction sketches the background and points towards further possible lines of enquiry.[2]

I

The earnestness of the Lawrence-figure we have inherited leads many people, understandably, to assume that 'Lawrence' and 'comedy'

1

are self-contradictory terms. This is a misconception which even a little reflection on Lawrence's prose of the 1920s readily displaces. These writings are usually seen as a restless attempt on Lawrence's part, after the disillusionments of life in wartime Britain, to find another or primitive civilisation with alternative values. The approach is congruent with Leavis's Lawrence and usefully answers in some respects to elements of the writing; but it leaves out Lawrence's changed and changeable mode of address to his subjects. The first publication of *Mr Noon* in 1984 underlined this failure of attention; it made inevitable the present, more wide-ranging re-evaluation of the Lawrence narrator's new self-consciousness, the facetious play with his audience, the badgering wit, the flippant rhetoric, the mock-heroic stances in his poems.

These were not present in the writing of the 1910s. Lawrence's comedy was a more familiar and less challenging thing; whether joyful, drolly embarrassing or intense, it was always securely distanced. Witness Tom Brangwen's speech on marriage at Anna's wedding in *The Rainbow*. It comes shortly below the account of the 'angels' which children *will* get up their noses. Witness also Lawrence's admission in *Twilight in Italy*, in 'The Theatre', of his absurd vulnerability to the emotive appeal of Lucia di Lammermoor-type heroines; the description in 'The Lemon Gardens' of the Signor di Paoli's attempts to fasten the door-spring; and the brittle, sardonic embarrassments in 'The Christening'.[3] It was not that, in his personal life, Lawrence did not have a funny side. He did – as John Worthen's biographical account below of his irrepressible powers of mimicry, and Mark Kinkead-Weekes's account of his uncensored mockery in private letters, make abundantly clear.[4] But he did not find extensive use for it in his writings. He gave up his experiment with writing comedies of manners (*The Merry-go-Round*, *The Married Man*, *The Fight for Barbara*, 1910–12) just as he turned to write the final version of *Sons and Lovers*. The definition of character in terms of external event, class and manners, and the social affirmation of endings (even if ironic) necessary to comic drama must have felt restrictive to a writer galled by the 'visualised' (i. 511) realism that Duckworth's reader, Edward Garnett, wanted him to write.[5] Finishing *Sons and Lovers*, he returned briefly to playwriting. In a letter of 12 January 1913 to Garnett he defended a play he had just written (*The Daughter-in-Law* – 'neither a comedy nor a tragedy') as 'quite objective . . . laid out properly and progressive' (i. 500–1). Despite the Oedipal and working-class air of entrapment, a line of strong if gloomy comedy flows through the homespun female wisdom of Mrs Purdy and Mrs Gascoyne. Their dialect nevertheless acts to distance them from the middle-class audience Lawrence must have had in mind as he wrote the letter; 'I *do* think this play might have a chance on the stage', he added (i. 501).

Women in Love, written 1916–17 with revisions in 1919, proved to be the turning point. It was the last novel in which Lawrence could still believe (against the evidence) that he could address an audience capable of attending seriously to the philosophical and historical reach of his cultural diagnoses. Even here, he built into the work the mocking voice of Ursula. In his essay, Howard Mills traces a process of 'mischief and merriment' and shows how the 'dangerous flamy sensitiveness' of the novel's humour, if given its due weight, tells sharply against Birkin. John Bayley remarks, in his chapter on Lawrence and Larkin, that for both of them 'the point about life and fun was immediacy. Nothing can be preserved, and nothing should be.' Birkin's intellectuality according to Mills is, in Blake's words, an attempt to 'bind . . . a joy, and the winged life destroy'. Ursula's is not, of course, the only voice of mockery in the novel: Gudrun is wickedly satirical about Birkin, as is Halliday. While the mockery gives a vertiginous edge to the writing, the question of how far the ironic undoing applies only to Birkin's preachifying manner as against how far it extends to his analysis of the novel's present in relation to extreme poles of creation and corruption remains an open one.

Lawrence's attitude toward his audience, if already changing in *Women in Love*, changed decisively thereafter. In some basic way, he lost belief in it. He was still exposing himself as a deeply committed analyst of cultural forces in the early versions of *Studies in Classic American Literature* published in the *English Review* in 1917–19. But by late 1922 when he revised the essays for book publication, an astringently mocking disposition had replaced the earlier one. Throughout the twenties, variations on this comic stance would remain in a tense, epidermal relationship to irrupting, thematic elements evolving from the earlier writings. Comedy served as the means by which the pressing seriousness could be kept momentarily at bay; the narrator's comic stances are temporary, dangerous, prickly, cunning. They enact a natural but simultaneously controlled irresponsibility, Bayley claims, to which critics are now just beginning to accommodate themselves, having tried to save Lawrence from himself for too long.

The comic stances do not wisely point up the follies of a third party nor provide the reader with a secure position above the comic-serious fray. The narrator engages in self-mimicry (more typically Lawrentian, Worthen maintains, than we have yet been prepared to grant); he mocks or appropriates voices – or dialogically marshalls them, as George Hyde has shown in relation to *The Lost Girl*. Although he does not say so, the process Hyde describes is curiously midway between modernist and postmodernist; the work of art never settles for long enough to become a finished artifact, and the reader's expectations are trifled with: 'At every stage [in *The Lost Girl*], Lawrence's text draws attention to its own coming into being, its "mode of production", by means of a gesturing, self-dramatising narrator who, like a music-hall entertainer, enacts the disconcerting switches of code that frustrate and disorient passive readerly expectations.'[6] Such expectations may be appropriate to Arnold Bennett's provincial realism (which, Hyde shows, Lawrence is mocking in his portrayal of Woodhouse), but they do not make sense of *The Lost Girl*'s deliberate discontinuities in tone and address.

Reacting in part to some derogatory reviews of *The Lost Girl*, Lawrence turned the second part of *Mr Noon* into a 'furious comedy': in her essay in this volume, Lydia Blanchard shows how the novel's 'gentle reader' is goaded by an irritable narrator into reaction. In becoming 'ungentled',[7] the reader loses caste as anonymous audience member seated safely above the fray, and must instead participate 'in the thick of the scrimmage' – as Lawrence would characterise it in a letter to the Italian critic Carlo Linati (v. 201). Obviously, we need to attend differently than we are used to do if we are to do justice to this kind of art. That is also the burden of Holly Laird's essay on *Birds, Beasts and Flowers*. She shows that the poetic sequences have been misread, with individual poems treated as crystallisations of the unique otherness of the various creatures. This is to ignore what she argues is the essentially mock-epic nature of the narrating poet's encounters and to glide over the range of ironic tones directed outwards and at himself.

II

On 12 February 1915, in a letter to Bertrand Russell, Lawrence wrote: 'I am ashamed to write any real writing of passionate love to my fellow men. Only satire is decent now' (ii. 283). We have seen that it took a few years before he acted on this belief; the 'passionate love' is something he would rather have expressed. Catherine Carswell, reviewing *Phoenix* in 1936, regretted the eventual effect: '"Never yield before the barren" was one of his articles of conduct, and satire was a yielding because a waste of life ... Some of the items [in *Phoenix*] ... have a bright slanginess that is unpleasing.'[8] Not everyone agreed (Leavis, for instance, did not in his review for *Scrutiny*); and indeed Lawrence's reviews retain a 'mocking vivacity', as Leavis called it,[9] that at the time must have been surprising to some people, given the conventions of the literary essay by the gentleman-scholar who would characteristically seek to formulate an authoritative position in relation to the subject-in-hand by exploring and measuring its characteristics against a shared climate of assumptions.[10] In his short essays and reviews in the 1920s, however, Lawrence had learned to exploit the potential of informal, tentative, quirky, spoken-voice writing. As a vehicle of thinking, it allowed him to free-wheel, brake hard, shout abuse from the windows, and even acknowledge the 'traffic cop'.[11] Typically in the reviews and essays, satirical, exasperated or disillusioned voices generate tension or heat – but with a comic edge. The serendipity of the form helped him to introduce his binary oppositions and, half-playfully, yet very seriously, apply and develop them, even as his antics quote or foreground voices which his satirical one trips up or mocks.[12] Comedy, in other words, was by no means only a defence mechanism: it freed Lawrence up, released voices in him, allowed him to function parodically, sarcastically – to be protean. Take this for instance – the response of a man who could visit Paris and be unimpressed:

Oh, those galleries. Oh, those pictures and those statues of nude, nude women: nude, nude, insistently and hopelessly nude. At last the eyes fall in absolute weariness, the moment they catch sight of a bit of pink-and-white painting, or a pair of white marble fesses [buttocks]. It becomes an inquisition; like being forced to go on eating pink marzipan icing. And yet there is a fat and very undistinguished bourgeois with a little beard and a fat and hopelessly petit-bourgeoise wife and awful little girl, standing in front of a huge heap of twisting marble, while he, with a goose-grease unctuous simper, strokes the marble hip of the huge marble female, and points its niceness *to his wife*. She is not in the least jealous. She knows, no doubt, that her own hip and the marble hip are the only ones he will stroke without paying prices, one of which, and the last he could pay, would be the price of spunk.[13]

One feels Lawrence working himself up into a lather ('nude, nude, insistently and hopelessly nude'; 'points its niceness *to his wife*'). The writing is seriocomic in its deliberate staginess. Lawrence wants to generate the ideological energy that will make his plea for the retaining of a lost, instinctual aristocracy seem urgently needed, an inevitability. The passage is from his 'Paris Letter' which he wrote in 1924 for the iconoclastic magazine, *Laughing Horse*, run by his friend Willard Johnson in New Mexico. But equally in his book reviews, Lawrence was apt to pounce on evidence of postwar emotional self-consciousness. In his review of *A Second Contemporary Verse Anthology* he describes its 'sounds' as 'sweetly familiar, linked in a new crotchet pattern' and finds this disappointing in a volume that touted itself as 'the spiritual record of an entire people'. He quotes, and then he demolishes:

> Why do I think of stairways
> With a rush of hurt surprise?

> Heaven knows, my dear, unless you once fell down.

His seriocomic exasperation opens the door to an alternative: 'Man is always, all the time and forever on the brink of the unknown.'[14] And then he has his favoured theme and he is away.

In other essays – such as those on the novel of 1923–5[15] – we, as readers, are imperiously addressed or satirically implicated as he splinters the discursive air, pricking us with its arrows, rather than adopting a disinterested third-person position in which we can guiltlessly join. Comedy and seriousness combine at nearly every step in this endeavour. At other times he vituperates or insults us; but, in counterbalance, we can feel him enjoying a deliberate working-up of venom:

> Amon, the great ram! Mithras, the great bull! The mistletoe on the tree. Do you think, you stuffy little human fool sitting in a chair and wearing lambswool underwear, and eating your mutton and beef under the Christmas decoration, do you think then that Amon, Mithras, mistletoe, and the whole Tree of Life were just invented to contribute to your complacency?
>
> You fool! You dyspeptic fool, with your indigestion tablets! You can eat your mutton and your beef, and buy sixpenn'orth of the golden bough, till your belly turns sour, you fool. Do you think, because you eat beef, that the Mithras fire is yours? Do you think, because you keep a fat castrated cat, the moon is on your knees? Do you think, in your woollen underwear, you are clothed in the might of Amon?
>
> You idiot! You cheap-jack idiot![16]

This is not ranting, although at first it can be mistaken for it. It is comedy but not comedy that is mean to amuse or assuage. Rather, as a form of knowing, comedy is part of the tissue of the case he is making about a modern failure of the mystic impulse. It is tempting to isolate the message from its comic vehicle, but Lawrence does not. If we acknowledge the controlled, comic fibrillation in his writings, especially of the 1920s, we will have a better chance of getting him right.

III

It must be said that the changing relationship of narrator with audience in Lawrence's works which I have been describing scarcely meshes at all with classic accounts of comedy, laughter and wit – although Mikhail Bakhtin's theory of laughter, as I show below, does offer some assistance. Northrop Frye distinguished between the Old Comedy of Aristophanes and Menander, still in touch with ancient rituals of death and revival, and the New Comedy in the plays of

Plautus and Terence adapted by Molière and Jonson. In New Comedy, Frye comments:

> As the hero gets closer to the heroine and opposition is overcome, all the right thinking people come over to his side. Thus a new social unit is formed on the stage, and the moment that this social unit crystallises is the moment of the comic resolution ... The freer the society, the greater the variety of individuals it can tolerate, and the natural tendency of comedy is to include as many as possible in its final festival.[17]

Despite the social reconciliation of its endings, Shakespearean comedy – still in touch with the drama of medieval folk ritual – only partially accepts this movement.[18] It 'begins in a world represented as a normal world, moves into the green world [of the forest], goes into a metamorphosis there in which the comic resolution is achieved, and returns to the normal world' (p. 80). In addition, elements of the older patterning of death and rebirth in the yearly cycle occur in all the comedies.

Bakhtin comments of the Renaissance that laughter was respected as affording access to 'certain essential aspects of the world',[19] but by the seventeenth century its function was corrective and its characters are of the lower or corrupt orders of society. Tragedy, in contrast, dealt with kings and heroes. But by Congreve's time at the end of the seventeenth century, the ludicrous – 'ridiculing Natural Deformities, Casual Defects in the Senses, and Infirmities of Age' – was less welcome: 'I could never look upon a Monkey', he confesses, 'without very Mortifying Reflections.'[20] Preconceptions about stage decorum gradually prevailed, so that by the early nineteenth century Charles Lamb was having to defend comedy on the grounds that it has 'no reference whatever to the world that is. No good person can justly be offended as a spectator, because no good person suffers on stage.'[21] For Baudelaire, writing in 1855, laughter is 'the consequence in man of his own superiority'. It is therefore 'Satanic ... one of the numerous pips in the symbolic apple'.[22] This made it no less interesting to him, but he was acknowledging that the contemporary climate of opinion was set against the vulgarities of comedy.

Later in the century George Meredith was able to defend witty comedy
(e.g. of the Restoration stage), even though grosser forms of comedy
engendering contempt remained, for him, simply out of the question.
Nevertheless he discussed the group functioning of comedy at its lower
levels, thereby recognising its continuing, neoclassical function as a corrective: 'Taking them generally, the English public are most in sympathy
with this primitive Aristophanic comedy, wherein the comic is capped
by the grotesque, irony tips the wit, and satire is a naked sword. They have
the basis of the comic in them – an esteem for common sense. They cor-
dially dislike the reverse of it.'[23]

At the end of the century Henri Bergson found a way of defending
laughter. He saw it acting as a social discipline, restraining eccentricity:
'rigidity is the comic, and laughter is its corrective'; laughter 'appears to
stand in need of an echo . . . [it] is always the laughter of a group'.[24] For
this vitalist philosopher, laughter was also a spiritual corrective for auto-
matism or mechanical uniformity. The latter represent the refractory
tendency of matter with which the soul must always wage battle, for 'a
really living life should never repeat itself' (p. 82). Comedy confirms
rather than discovers: it 'depicts characters we have already come across
and shall meet with again . . . It aims at placing types before our eyes'
(p. 166). It is 'not disinterested as genuine art is. By organising laughter,
comedy accepts social life as a natural environment; it even obeys an
impulse of social life' (pp. 170–1). Bergson makes a useful distinction
between the comic person and the wit. The latter does not forget himself
as a good actor will: 'We always get a glimpse of [him] behind what he
says and does. He is not wholly engrossed in the business, because he
only brings his intelligence into play' (p. 129). In Bergson's terms, the
1920s Lawrence is more the wit than the comic. Although in *The Boy in
the Bush* he can enjoy an innocent laugh at the boy who complains that
'They've frowed away a perfeckly good cat' (a dead one that could have
been skinned),[25] and although he could dramatise the comic confusions
of the Ellis baby being forced to swallow castor oil after having been (as it
turns out, unjustly) suspected of eating possibly poisonous narcissus
bulbs, Lawrence rarely allows us to laugh with him in easeful joy. These
situations seem heavily dependent on his joint author for that novel,

Mollie Skinner. More usually, Lawrentian comedy is on edge, for other things are simultaneously and pressingly at stake *in* the comedy. John Bayley quotes a good example from 'The Captain's Doll': Hepburn's conversation with Hannele about the mistake he made 'undertaking to love'[26] – said, or shouted, on the noisy, swerving bus as they return from their excursion to the glacier.

Freud's *Jokes and their Relation to the Unconscious* of 1905 was written for a professional audience of like mind and background.[27] Its confident manner of shared cultural reference makes this clear; and there is frequent recourse to the first-person plural. When Freud explains comedy of movement (e.g. in pantomime), he says we register it as an excess expenditure of energy – that is, as a deviation from a norm we have long ago internalised as sufficient for the action in question. Freud's argument throughout relies on a calculus of pleasure and pain. The calculus idea naturalises, by implicitly universalising, the discharge of unconscious or pre-conscious inhibitions involved in the joke and, more broadly, in the comic. The discharge is seen by Freud as a form of 'psychical economy'. Jokes, like dreams, give us access to a source of pleasure available in childhood, but later complicated and baffled by the dictates of reason and civilised standards of conduct. Jokes (i.e. jokes made rather than just repeated) and dreams, according to Freud, are alike in this way.[28] Thus hostile jokes allow satisfaction of revengeful impulses towards 'our enemy which we could not, on account of obstacles in the way, bring forward openly or consciously . . . the joke *will evade restrictions and open sources of pleasure that have become inaccessible*. It will further bribe the hearer with its yield of pleasure into taking sides with us without any very close investigation' (p. 103). Freud's model assumes an audience on the same side as the joke-teller. Lawrence's 'hostility', however, is partly towards his material (e.g. respectability, the claustrophobic aspects of family life), but partly also towards his readers. His sense of an audience was not secure in the way that Freud's or even George Eliot's was; the relationship shifts and twists. Usually in the 1920s, Lawrence was only momentarily and illusorily confederate with his audience.

Although Lawrence denounced Freud's archaeological model of the psyche (the conscious mind as a layer above 'that sack of horrors', the unconscious[29]), it may have some useful explanatory power here. The parallelism of jokes and dreams as work of the unconscious explains their unpremeditated surprisingness. There is something of this in the serendipity, adventitiousness and opportunism of Lawrence's comic-serious prose manoeuvring. As a novelist, he had found a way of mini-mising the usually self-censoring inhibitions produced by publishers' and readers' expectations for the novel form. This was clearly not the work of Lawrence's *un*conscious: his writing was undoubtedly a con-scious effort. But it was of a kind that left him in closer communication with underlying moods and sensitivities, prepared to chance his arm in giving them expression and less inhibited by the standards of 'civilised' argumentation and imagination that contemporary critics prized.

IV

Perhaps this observation helps explain the recent interest amongst Lawrence critics in the writings of Bakhtin. He believed that a man never coincides with himself: my description below of the 'provisionality' of Lawrence's writing in the Australian novels is a meditation on this idea. In fact, Baudelaire had already said something like it. In his account of laughter, he worked through the implications of the saying that '*The Sage laughs not save in fear and trembling*' because he 'recognises a certain secret contradiction between his special nature as Sage and the primor-dial nature of laughter' (pp. 449–50). It is interesting therefore that, as John Worthen shows in his essay below, Lawrence loved playing cha-rades but also sensed their dangers for himself. To laugh is to be someone else: the more developed forms of laughter involve a deferral of laughter, but the grosser forms are (developing on Freud) an evacuation or relief – and therefore, as Julia Kristeva remarks, a disruption of the symbolic order in which the Sage operates.[30] But this cannot be fairly applied to Lawrence without qualification: despite attempts in the 1950s and 1960s to turn him into a late-Victorian sage, Lawrence was not one. His writing out of chameleon moods and his comic sharpnesses refute the assump-tion.

Bakhtin's account of the equally disruptive carnivalesque can be illuminatingly applied to Lawrence's novels of the 1920s. In his book on Rabelais, written in 1940 but not published till 1965, Bakhtin describes the tradition of folk laughter in the market-place festivals that grew up in the Middle Ages, disjoint from the humourless official theological culture – when in Roman times the two levels had intermingled. Carnival, Bakhtin says,

> does not know footlights, in the sense that it does not acknowledge any distinction between actors and spectators . . . Carnival is not a spectacle seen by the people; they live in it . . . carnival celebrated temporary liberation from the prevailing truth and from the established order; it marked the suspension of all hierarchical rank, privileges, norms, and prohibitions . . .

For Bakhtin modern satire is the antithesis of 'the people's festive laughter': the 'satirist whose laughter is negative places himself above the object of his mockery, he is opposed to it . . . The people's ambivalent laughter, on the other hand, expresses the point of view of the whole world; he who is laughing also belongs to it'.[31] In his comedy, Lawrence-as-narrator never occupies either of the two positions Bakhtin describes for long. He can be radically out of sympathy with the popular culture of his time, and thus a 'satirist'. But he is soon implicated in the ideas he is pursuing, changed by the questions he is asking.

His humour – something like that of today's oppressed and minority groups – feeds off the pressure imposed by a dominant culture. To bear the pressure, a compensatory or grim or wicked humour is necessary for such groups, creating cultural space for vital and aggressive styles of social criticism to function. So it was with Lawrence. In his analysis below of linguistic elements in *St. Mawr*, Paul Poplawski provides a new basis for examining the deliberateness of Lawrence's social satire. He shows how the Manbys, for instance, are 'distanced from their own agency as subjects' by Lawrence's careful deployment of passive and intransitive verbs, and how, more generally, there is a systematic blurring of 'the immediacy and specificity of actions and events . . . as if their very reality were being thrown into question'.

Another of Bakhtin's emphases – the relation of laughter to the under-world and to death (based on Lucian's 'image of Menippus laughing in the kingdom of the dead'[32]) – may offer help in future studies of Lawrence's use of comedy. His need to draw on images of other worlds – green worlds, in a sense – which might vitalise the present one gave him an interest in the world of the dead. It haunts his works of the 1920s (e.g. Count Dionys, Jack Grant, Don Ramón, the Man Who Had Died) and draws on images of ancient Egypt and Mexico. Menippean laughter – which can face, even efface, the dead – is never far away. In the 'London Letter' which he wrote in January 1924 after a depressing winter in London,[33] Lawrence responded to the Christmas 1923 number of the *Laughing Horse* which Willard Johnson sent him from New Mexico. In his commentary accompanying the printing of the Navajo 'Song of the Horse', Johnson had stressed the laughing neigh of the Indians' mythical turquoise horse in its diurnal route across the sky. Lawrence was evidently roused. His 'Dear Old Horse: A London Letter' reads:

> It would be a terrible thing if the horse in us died for ever: as he seems to have died in Europe. How awful it would be, if at this present moment I sat in the yellow mummy-swathings of London atmosphere – the snow is melting – inside the dreadful mummy-sarcophagus of Europe, and didn't know that the blue horse was still kicking his heels and making a few sparks fly, across the tops of the Rockies. It would be a truly sad case for me.

In concluding that man must again become like the centaur, Lawrence enumerates its qualities:

> First of all, Sense, Good Sense, Sound Sense, Horse Sense. And then, a laugh, a loud, sensible Horse laugh. After that, these same passions, glossy and dangerous in the flanks. And after these again, hoofs, irresistible, splintering hoofs, that can kick the walls of the world down.[34]

In this Introduction I have stressed Lawrence's comic stances in relation to his subject matter and his audience; its emotional underpinning we see here is ultimately anarchoapocalyptic, something Lawrence does not in the least wince from. John Turner's analysis of the hysterical laughter in *Aaron's Rod* is of especial interest here. Turner's essay lends some intriguing justification to John Middleton Murry's evaluation of the novel in a contemporary review as the most important of Lawrence's to date. For Lawrence, Turner argues, it epitomised the postwar period, to which (however) hysterical laughter and rage were the only honest responses: Murry on the other hand praised, as he would, Lawrence's newfound 'serenity'.[35]

Stressing the comic dispositions of Lawrence's writings does not mean that Lawrence can never be held to account for what he wrote, only that we must take much more care in examining both how he wrote and the different impulses from which he wrote. Whether or not Bakhtin's ideas are invoked, the aim of listening for contrary voices in Lawrence's work is always in danger of being recruited to an older habit of thinking: the comic deflations, the parodying, the wildness and wickedness *can* be made to demonstrate some concept of 'essential sanity', thus sanitising the extremism of Lawrence's thinking. What has to be remembered is that between 1916 and 1925 Lawrence became both passionate imperson-ator, committed disrupter and tensely-comic deflator. His comically protean yet deeply committed and fully extended impieties became pos-sible only because he was no longer seeking to imitate authoritative forms. Recognition of this comic focus casts, too, a different light on Lawrence's own pieties, on those forms of seriousness which have tradi-tionally attracted critical commentary but which also alienated large numbers of readers. The present volume on Lawrence and comedy offers, its editors hope, a new way of thinking about Lawrence's writing in the middle part of his career, even though we have included only one essay on a short novel and nothing on his last two major novels, *The Plumed Serpent* and *Lady Chatterley's Lover*. We believe there is enough here to offer a new departure: we offer it, however, with no confident sense of what the point of arrival will be, nor what will be found on this newly foreign shore.

Notes

1 F.R. Leavis, *D.H. Lawrence: Novelist* (Chatto & Windus, 1955), p. 13. He concludes that

the insight, the wisdom, the revived and re-educated feeling for health, that Lawrence brings are what, as our civilization goes, we desperately need...when I think of the career that started in the ugly mining village in the spoilt Midlands, amidst all those apparent disadvantages, it seems to me that, even in these days, it should give us faith in the creative human spirit and its power to ensure fullness of life.   (p.15)

2 Lydia Blanchard's essay is a much revised version of 'D.H. Lawrence and his "Gentle Reader": The New Audience of *Mr Noon*', *D.H. Lawrence Review*, xx (1988), 223–35. Earlier essays on aspects of the subject of comedy include: Leo Gurko, '*The Lost Girl*: D.H. Lawrence as a "Dickens of the Midlands"', *PMLA*, lxxviii (1963), 601–5; R.P. Draper, 'Satire as a Form of Sympathy' in *Renaissance and Modern Essays*, ed. G.R. Hibbard (Routledge, 1966), pp. 189–97; Richard Wasson, 'Comedy and History in *The Rainbow*', *Modern Fiction Studies*, xiii (1967–8), 465–77; Donald Gutierrez, 'Lawrence's *The Virgin and the Gypsy* as Ironic Comedy', *English Quarterly*, v (1972–3), 61–9, reprinted in his *Lapsing Out: Embodiments of Death and Rebirth in the Last Writings of D.H. Lawrence* (Rutherford, NJ: Fairleigh Dickinson University Press, 1980); Gerald Doherty, 'A "Very Funny" Story: Figural Play in D.H. Lawrence's *The Captain's Doll*', *D.H. Lawrence Review*, xviii (1985–6), 5–17; John Bayley, 'Lawrence's Comedy and the War of Superiorities' in *Rethinking Lawrence*, ed. Keith Brown (Milton Keynes: Open University Press, 1990), pp. 1–11; George Hyde, 'Carnivalising the Midlands: *The Lost Girl* and *Mr Noon*', *Essays in Poetics*, xv (1990), 55–70; and the special issue of *Études lawrenciennes* (vi, 1991) on DHL and humour with essays by Keith Cushman ('The Serious Comedy of "Things"', pp. 83–94), Jacqueline Gouirand ('Ironie et satire dans la fiction du Nottinghamshire des annés 20', pp. 39–52), Adrian Harding ('Self-parody and Ethical Satire in *The Rainbow*', pp. 31–8), Ginette Katz-Roy ('Lyrisme et humour dans la poésie de D.H. Lawrence', pp. 13–29), Jean-Pierre Pichardie ('Une brassé d'orties ou le guirlande de Britannia', pp. 95–102), Martine Ricoux-Faure ('Lawrence fait la comédie', pp. 5–11), Nicole Tartera ('De l'humour à la satire sociale, ou les facettes de l'esprit Lawrencien', pp. 53–68) and Thérèse Vichy ('L'ironie dans *The Woman Who Rode Away*', pp. 69–81).

3 *The Rainbow* (1915), ed. Mark Kinkead-Weekes (Cambridge: Cambridge University Press, 1989), p. 130; *Twilight in Italy and Other Essays*, ed. Paul Eggert (Cambridge: Cambridge University Press,

1994), pp. 139–41, 114–15, 122–3; both *Twilight* accounts are revisions of material written in 1913; and *The Prussian Officer and Other Stories*, ed. John Worthen (Cambridge: Cambridge University Press, 1983), pp. 172–80.

4 See also a limerick by DHL which Warren Roberts records as item C213.5 (*A Bibliography of D. H. Lawrence*, 2nd edn, Cambridge, Cambridge University Press, 1982), and DHL's response to John Middleton Murry's *The Life of Jesus Christ* – a four-page book, *The Life of J. Middleton Murry by J. C.* (privately printed, 1930 – Roberts, *Bibliography*, item A51). The complete text reads: 'John Middleton was born in the year of the Lord 1891? It happened also to be the most lying year of the most lying century since time began, but what is that to an innocent babe!' (p. 3). DHL's signings of his first editions also have their moments: George Lazarus's copy of *Amores* (1916) has: 'D.H. Lawrence/his own copy/not given to anybody'; and in Lazarus's copy of *Psychoanalysis and the Unconscious* (1921), he wrote 'Signed, errors and all/D.H. Lawrence'.

5 For a discussion of the comedies, see Susan Carlson Galenbeck: 'A Stormy Apprenticeship: Lawrence's Three Comedies', *D.H. Lawrence Review*, xiv (1981), 191–211.

6 Hyde, 'Carnivalising the Midlands', p. 59.

7 The word is Earl Ingersoll's in 'D.H. Lawrence's *Mr Noon* as a Postmodern Text', *MLR*, xxxvi (1990), 304–9 *passim*.

8 *Spectator*, 27 November 1936, pp. 959–60.

9 'The Wild, Untutored Phoenix', *Scrutiny*, vi (1937), p. 353: Leavis valued the 'lively ironic humour' of DHL's reviews as witnessing 'the play of a supremely fine and penetrating intelligence' (pp. 353–4). Cf. A. Desmond Hawkins's review in the *Criterion*: 'His sense of humour was not notably subtle, but it certainly was vivid' (xvi, 1937, pp. 748–52); Hawkins pointed out to the 'uproariously funny review of Professor Sherman, and a game of repartee . . . with an anthology of contemporary verse' (p. 749).

10 E.g. Clifton Fadiman's review of *Phoenix* in the *New Yorker*:

[T]here remains much in the argumentative Lawrence which does not date, and this is almost as bad, for while it is nonsense, it is dangerous nonsense . . . He reaches reaction not by the road of domination but by the road of anarchism. His unrestrained worship of the 'individual' (never defined, but apparently someone exactly like D.H. Lawrence) leads him to abhor all collective and social restraints, to scorn science, to laugh at the idea of progress, and finally to state flatly that economic and social adjustment is not worth striving after.   (17 October 1936, pp. 82–3)

Cornwell's *The Savage Pilgrimage: A Narrative of D.H.Lawrence* (Secker, 1932) sets its course against such conventionalising response.

11 'The Novel', *Study of Thomas Hardy and Other Essays*, ed. Bruce Steele (Cambridge: Cambridge University Press, 1985), 188:18–20.

12 Joan Peters, for instance, shows in a forthcoming essay that DHL's essays on the novel should be read as doubly voiced and that Bakhtin was wrong to say that 'Authoritative discourse can not be represented – it is only transmitted' (Mikhail Bakhtin, *The Dialogic Imagination*, ed. Michael Holquist, Austin: University of Texas Press, 1981, p. 344).

13 'Paris Letter' was published in April 1926; reprinted in *Phoenix: The Posthumous Papers of D.H.Lawrence*, ed. Edward D. McDonald (New York: Viking, 1936), p. 120.

14 Ibid., pp. 322–3.

15 In *Study of Thomas Hardy*, ed. Steele.

16 'Aristocracy' (written 1925) in *Reflections on the Death of a Porcupine and Other Essays*, ed. Michael Herbert (Cambridge: Cambridge University Press, 1988), 371:40–372:13.

17 'The Argument of Comedy' (1949), anthologised in *Comedy: Developments in Criticism*, ed. D.J. Palmer (Macmillan, 1984), pp. 75–6.

18 Cf. DHL's play, *The-Merry-go-Round*, which can be seen as a reworking of *As You Like It*.

19 *Rabelais and his World*, trans. Helene Iswolsky (Cambridge, Mass.: MIT Press, 1968), p. 66.

20 In Palmer, *Comedy*, p. 40.

21 Ibid., p. 55.

22 Baudelaire, 'On the Essence of Laughter, and in General, on the Comic in the Plastic Arts', anthologised in *Comedy; Meaning and Form*, ed. Robert W. Corrigan (San Francisco: Chandler, 1965), pp. 454–5, 453.

23 *The Idea of Comedy* (1877), reprinted in *Comedy*, ed. Wylie Sypher (New York: Doubleday Anchor, 1956), pp. 39–40. Sir Philip Sidney had made a similar point:

our comedians think there is no delight without laughter; which is very wrong ... we scarcely do [delight] but in things that have a conveniency to ourselves or to the general nature; laughter almost ever cometh of things most disproportioned to ourselves and nature. Delight hath a joy in it, either permanent or present. Laughter hath only a scornful tickling.

(*An Apology for Poetry*, 1595; ed. Geoffrey Shepherd, Manchester, Manchester University Press, 1973, p. 136).

24 Bergson's treatise, *Laughter* (1899), in Sypher, *Comedy*, pp. 74, 64.

25 D.H. Lawrence and M.L. Skinner, *The Boy in the Bush* (1924), ed. Paul Eggert (Cambridge: Cambridge University Press, 1990), 43:23–4.

26 In *The Fox, The Captain's Doll, The Ladybird*, ed. Dieter Mehl (Cambridge: Cambridge University Press, 1992), 149:19–20.

27 Vol. viii of the *Complete Psychological Works of Sigmund Freud*, trans. James Strachey (Hogarth Press, 1960): the 'jokes' of the title translates the German *der Witz*, meaning both jokes and wit.

28 Jokes and dreams differ in that 'A dream still remains a wish, even though one that has been made unrecognizable; a joke is developed play' (ibid., p. 179); Julia Kristeva adds that jokes, unlike dreams, are a form of 'socialization of psychic activity' (*Revolution in Poetic Language*, trans. Margaret Waller, New York, Columbia University Press, 1984, p. 222).

29 In DHL's Introduction to *Psychoanalysis and the Unconscious* (Harmondsworth, Penguin, 1975), p. 207.

30 Cf. Kristeva on this point: *Revolution*, pp. 222–5.

31 Bakhtin, *Rabelais*, pp. 6, 10, 12.

32 Ibid., p. 69.

33 See e.g. (iv. 542–3, 544–5, 546). Witness the images of entrapment in his essay, 'On Coming Home' of December 1923 (in *Reflections on the Death of a Porcupine*, ed. Herbert, pp. 175–84) and his letters of the same month. The 'Paris Letter' (see above) was written not long after the 'London Letter'.

34 Published in *Laughing Horse*, no. 10, May 1924.

35 Murry's review in the *Nation and Athenæum* (12 August 1922) hailed the novel as 'the most important thing that has happened to English literature since the war' (p. 655).

1

Drama and mimicry in Lawrence

John Worthen

I

The subjects of mimicry and self-mimicry tell us a great deal about Lawrence, not only biographically, but about the kind of interest in drama and the dramatic which he took. This is a side of his life (and his writing) which has been mostly ignored, though the biographical record is full of it. Biographers do not in general know what to do about it, any more than literary critics do. The subjects of mimicry and self-mimicry offer, however, a useful way into some of the patterns of his writing: specifically the kind of performance artistry he employed as a novelist between 1916 and 1923. I shall first describe Lawrence's involvement with the theatre in his early years; then explore his own behaviour as a performer and as a mimic, and how his contemporaries viewed his mimicry; and then show how ideas of theatre and self-mimicry can help to illuminate his own writing performances.

II

The young Lawrence's overt relationship with the theatre and with ideas of the dramatic is surprising for both its intensity and its variety. He read, went to and wrote plays from the very start of his adult life and in his early years was arguably as fascinated by the theatre as he was by prose fiction – he wrote his first three plays (*A Collier's Friday Night, The Widowing of Mrs. Holroyd* and *The Merry-go-Round*) a year before his first novel was published. If we simply examine a period which happens to be reasonably well documented – March 1912 to January

19

1913 – we find an astonishing variety and intensity in his involvement with drama and the dramatic. On 17 March 1912, he and Frieda Weekley (later Frieda Lawrence) saw Shaw's *Man and Superman* in Nottingham, and at the end of May they went to a passion-play in Bavaria (i. 411); they also saw Ibsen's *Ghosts* in Munich sometime during the summer. During April, too, Lawrence had been reading plays: Chekhov's *The Seagull* and *The Cherry Orchard*. He also wrote his fourth full-length play, *The Married Man*, which he based on experiences he had had at the end of March. Towards the end of July, he began writing 'a comedy' which he never finished and about which we know nothing beyond the fact that he said 'I am amusing myself' writing it (i. 427). We know rather more, however, about the journey from Bavaria to Italy which he and Frieda made in August; and we (naturally) find that they went to the theatre while staying in the south German town of Bad Tölz for a single evening. Late in November or early in December, too, in spite of living as economically as they could in the tiny village of Villa, beside the Lago di Garda, they went to see Verdi's *Rigoletto* in Saló, at the southern end of the lake. Between these visits, Lawrence had gone on reading plays and thinking about them: Strindberg's *Miss Julie* and two other plays in October, Edward Garnett's play *The Trial of Jeanne D'Arc* in November. And at the end of October, as an extraordinary kind of busman's holiday from writing *Sons and Lovers*, Lawrence wrote his comedy *The Fight for Barbara* in three days.[1] Nor did he stop thinking about the theatre, either, comparing Strindberg and Ibsen in November (i. 465).

And then, in December, an unlooked-for opportunity to see even more plays (and incidentally to improve his Italian) turned up: the Compagnia Drammatica Italiana Adelia Di Giacomo Tadini – a touring troupe of actors – came to the theatre in Gargnano, next to Villa. The Lawrences, as distinguished local residents, were given the key to a theatre box by their landlord, Signor Pietro di Paoli, and on 28 December they saw a very different version of *Ghosts* from the one in Munich. Lawrence then saw D'Annunzio's play *The Light under the Bushel* on 6 January 1913 and Silvio Zambaldi's comedy *The Wife of the Doctor* on the 9th; while on 16 January he would see *Hamlet* – as *Amleto*.[2] And sometime during the first fortnight of January he also wrote what was argu-ably his own finest play: *The Daughter-in-Law*. By the start of 1913, when he completed *The Daughter-in-Law*, he had written not only twenty short-stories and three novels but six full-length plays. And during the rest of his life he also wrote plays, though not with the intensity of his early years: *Touch and Go* in 1918 and *David* in 1925. He also left unfinished two dramatic fragments, *Altitude* in 1924 and *Noah's Flood* in 1925.

III

What seems to have appealed to the young Lawrence in drama and the dramatic were, to begin with, the sheer emotional power and potential of the actor and the stage. More than any other literary form, drama could act directly upon its audience and provoke the loss of an audience's everyday self, of its self-consciousness and its inhibitions. No reader of Lawrence's letters, for example, will easily forget his description of going to see Sarah Bernhardt in *La Dame aux Camélias* on 15 June 1908, and her extraordinary effect upon him: though it must be said that the letter to Blanche Jennings in which he describes Bernhardt's awesome power is a thoroughly controlled and self-consciously artistic piece of writing, as it hymns her power to make one lose one's self-control and one's inhibi-tions. That, however, is a paradox I shall find myself repeating.

> Oh, to see her, and to hear her, a wild creature, a gazelle with a beauti-ful panther's fascination and fury, laughing in musical French, screaming with true panther cry, sobbing and sighing like a deer sobs, wounded to death, and all the time with the sheen of silk, the glitter of diamonds, the moving of men's handsomely groomed figures about her! She is not pretty – her voice is not sweet – but there she is, the incarnation of wild emotion which we share with all live things, but which is gathered in us in all complexity and inscrutable fury. She represents the primeval passions of woman, and she is fascinating to an extraordinary degree. I could love such a woman myself, love her to madness; for all the pure, wild passion of it. Intellect is shed as flowers shed their petals... (i.59)

Lawrence actually wrote that letter ten days after seeing Bernhardt. A less controlled response appeared in a letter he sent his friend Jessie Chambers the day after the performance, in which she remembered him saying 'that the play had so upset him that at the end he rushed from his place and found himself battering at the doors until an attendant came and let him out ... He added "I feel frightened. I realize that I, too, might become enslaved to a woman"' (i. 56). His immediate response had thus been to say 'no, this kind of letting oneself go is highly dangerous': and the weekend after seeing the performance, he actually re-enacted it to Jessie's family to show them 'how Sarah Bernhardt died in the last scene. He looked quite worn out with emotion.'³ Ten days later, however, in that set-piece letter, he was insisting that one must indeed give oneself up to emotion: 'Intellect is shed as flowers shed their petals.' But both responses pay tribute to the power of the stage performance to move the spectactor uncontrollably. Lawrence felt himself both frighteningly possessed by that power – and eager to employ it himself artistically, as in the letter to Blanche Jennings, or in plays he wrote himself: or in every-day life.

Acting out what had moved him so powerfully – and thus repeating the experience of being in the power of others, while simultaneously taking over and controlling the experience, bringing it within his own verbal control and affecting others with it as he had himself been affected – this was the young Lawrence's first response to theatre and drama.⁴ Performance fascinated him when he was young; it gave him a chance to lose himself in some action or some other person, so that Jessie Chambers would record of a Shakespeare performance that 'Lawrence identified himself with the play, and for the time being lived in its atmosphere.'⁵ But, simultaneously, the experience of performance enabled him to stand back from that very experience, judging it coolly. After going to see Shakespeare's plays as an intellectual adolescent, his immediate reaction had, interestingly, not only been to discuss them but to act them out himself, to try out their power – again, to the Chambers family.

It was, however, characteristic of him to introduce a specifically comic component as well as a serious one into his recreations, thereby illustrating rather beautifully how detached he was from his own feelings, as well as caught up in them. Jessie Chambers, again, described what she saw:

> He went through Hamlet's soliloquy afterwards in our kitchen – 'To be, or not to be ...' And it was the same when we had seen *Macbeth* – 'Is this a dagger I see before me, the handle towards my hand ...?' grasping at an imaginary dagger. It was his characteristic blending of the serious with the comic. Of course we laughed at him, but the two aspects were plainly visible.[6]

As that extract suggests, drama characteristically produced in Lawrence neither the total identification which he chooses to dramatise in his description of Bernhardt (where he is concerned to show off his pride in himself for abandoning his intellectual detachment), nor a purely cool and intellectual appreciation, but some self-contradictory combination of both – including a comic realisation of the inadequacies both of drama and of himself. Realising an action in its concrete dramatic form, and simultaneously recognising where he himself stood in relation to it – very often outside it, where malice and mimicry would be a natural response to it – was something which became normal in Lawrence's own written and unwritten comic performances, and specifically in his early playwriting. Whereas his first four novels were in different ways all experiments in tragedy, three of his first six plays were explicitly 'comedies' – *The Merry-go-Round, The Married Man* and *The Fight for Barbara* – and a fourth implicitly a comedy too (*The Daughter-in-Law*): while he had also, of course, worked on a 'comedy' in the summer of 1912. This demonstrates how ready Lawrence-as-dramatist was to write about the way people were exposed, shown up and seen through: how prepared he was to employ those resources of wit and malice which he also regularly used in performances in his private life, but which he almost completely kept out of his early prose fiction.

IV

And it is specifically upon Lawrence as performance artist – in life, but also in drama and in fiction – that I shall now concentrate. We know about Joyce, reciting limericks in his cups: about Beckett, remorseless about illness and affliction: about Eliot, playing possum and practical jokes: but much less about Lawrence, entertaining his friends with performances so funny that (David Garnett once said) they laughed 'until laughing was an agony'. What has inhibited this recognition, more than anything else, has been the notion – deriving from a number of sources but specifically from Norman Douglas and T.S. Eliot – that Lawrence had no sense of humour:[7] in the popular imagination he is still (I quote the *Daily Telegraph* of June 1991) a humourless 'bearded bore'. David Garnett, however, said that Lawrence 'was the only great mimic I have ever known; he had a genius for "taking people off" and could reproduce voice and manner exactly. He told you that he had once seen Yeats or Ezra Pound for half an hour in a drawing-room, and straightway Yeats or Pound appeared before you . . .'[8] All his life, Lawrence not only imitated people: he also presented polished and at times complex comic turns to his friends: report after report of such occasions survives in the biographical record. As late as 1927, Lawrence was still doing his turn of Florence Farr reciting W.B. Yeats to the minimal music of the psaltery which Garnett had seen Lawrence perform back in 1912, and which Lawrence had probably first witnessed in 1909. He would chant, monotonously,

> 'You who are bent and bald and blind.' Paused, then stretched his thin hands over his knees delicately, as if an instrument lay there, plucked an imaginary string and whined 'Pi . . . ing . . . wa . . . ang.' Deepening his voice 'With heavy heart' staccato ping-wang, 'and a wandering mind.' And he ping-wanged so violently to show the state of his mind that our hoots of laughter swept him with us . . .

Accounts of such occasions, however, do more than simply remind us of Lawrence's accomplishment in the fields of the dramatic and the comic. His performances, like his mimicry and a good deal of his writing, were often a good deal wilder, and show him cultivating a delight in malice and a fascination with the grotesque. Frieda remembered him telling her about his experiences in Cambridge with Bertrand Russell and the other Fellows of Trinity, in March 1915: 'he had had a shock. When he told me about it, he acted for me how after dinner they walked round the room the other professors with their hands on their backs and discussed the Balkans in a professional way and they really knew nothing, L. said. But he was bitter about their deadness.'[9] And it was again Frieda who never forgot the revivalist meetings she saw him doing in 1912 – or the 'frenzy' of the participants:

> There was the revivalist parson. He would work his congregation up to a frenzy; then, licking his finger to turn the imaginary pages of the book of Judgement and suddenly darting a finger at some sinner in the congregation: 'Is *your* name written in the book?' he would shout.
>
> A collier's wife in a little sailor hat, in a frenzy of repentance, would clatter down the aisle, throw herself on her knees in front of the altar, and pray: 'O Lord, our Henry would 'ave come too, only he dursn't, O Lord, so I come as well for him, O Lord!' It was a marvellous scene! First as the parson then as the collier's wife Lawrence would make me shake with laughter.[10]

In 1926, Rolf Gardiner watched Lawrence imitating the 'Singhalese dervishees or devil-dancers' he had seen in Ceylon. But Lawrence did not just demonstrate the steps of dances: a reserved and not a particularly well man, he suddenly gave, to Gardiner's astonishment, 'an imitation of their frenzy, quite terrifyingly, his piercing blue eyes popping right and left out of his pale face as he twisted like a cobra, shuffling in his carpet slippers like one possessed by demons'.[11]

That fascination with frenzy and its non-intellectual dramatic power – the extraordinary, dangerous, alien side of his comic turns – had actually been a mark of the performances he had been giving since his adolescence. May Chambers (Jessie's sister) recalled how, playing charades, 'In the word *fanatic*, he went up in the attic dressed like an old crone to fetch down her lazy son. His shrill, withering vituperation made me shiver ... "You acted a bit too well," we told Bert. "You *became* a fanatic."' Even while still a respectable chapel-going Congregation-alist, he would mercilessly mimic the local members of the Christian Endeavour class 'repeating in turn "The servant of the Lord is like a well-filled house . . . ."'[12] Richard Aldington, in the late 1920s, also experienced Lawrence recollecting Ceylon – but, this time, its fearful 'medley of fantastic noises': 'he once asked me if I had heard the night noises of a tropical jungle, and then instantly emitted a frightening series of yells, squawks, trills, howls and animal "help-murder" shrieks'. As late as 1929, when he was dying, his friend Frederick Carter noted how remarkable his feeling still was 'for the natural grotesque which exists in character', and how 'His malice gave the piquancy and sauce to his tale, touching it with a gleam of that deliberate exaggeration in fact, which makes revelatory the penetration of true caricature.'[13] Lawrence would on occasion act out his grotesques in ways that made people wonder – just as they would later about his writing – how much of his performance was in fact controlled enactment and how much uncontrolled possession. '"Repent!" he had shouted with blazing eyes and wild gesticulations as he preached. "Judgement. The last day! Hellfire for everyone!"'[14] Richard Aldington remembered how, in 1919, 'in that state of animosity which comes to a man when he finds himself alone against the world', Lawrence 'was literally "satirical"', reminding Aldington of 'a wild half-trapped creature, a satyr'. Mimicking his Congregational minister on one occasion when young, he became genuinely frightening. David Chambers recalled how

> We were returning from Chapel on a summer evening . . . Lawrence
> was in a dark mood and by the time we had reached the Warren he
> began to inveigh against the Chapel and all it stood for and especially
> against the minister, the Reverend Robert Reid, for whom we all had a
> great respect. Lawrence poured a stream of scorn and raillery upon
> the poor man, made fun of his ideas, and mimicked his way of
> expressing them: it was a fierce, uncontrollable tirade, an outpouring
> of long pent-up rage that left us all silent and rather frightened. We
> had never seen him in such a mood before. He seemed to be beside
> himself.[15]

Brigit Patmore, who knew Lawrence very well, once insisted that 'Lorenzo's imitations aren't *acting* – they're . . . they're inspired, they're demoniacal possessions.'[16]

V

Such performances are particularly interesting in coming from a writer who spent much of his life in solitary confinement with pen and paper. They were one of the very few ways in which – away from his writing – Lawrence was prepared to engage in performance. The absurdity of the grotesque sanctioned his exhibitions, and the comedy tended to emerge as frenzy, possession, hilarity and satire: and from there seems at times to have been redeployed in his writing.

But even his performances were by no means always solitary exhibitions. He regularly orchestrated charades and other performances with his friends: Enid Hilton observed, even when he was young, 'His love of playing charades, which he did with intensity . . . the game allowed full use of imagination, character creating and building.'[17] We can see how the charades and playlets of his adult life permitted even wilder, more extravagantly comic explosions of energy and wit which drew on the energies of a group performing together: itself a kind of paradigm of the functioning of a comic novel.

It may well have been so as to escape the fatal inhibitions of self-consciousness – to which he was such a prey in his early years – that Lawrence always seems to have insisted, if possible, on involving the people with him in the performances he set up and stage-managed: he emphatically did not want an audience of onlookers who would watch as he himself would have watched. So, for example, David Garnett recalled how, in Icking with the Lawrences in 1912, 'In the evenings we all three of us acted complicated nonsense charades, without an audience.' Guests visiting Ottoline Morrell at Garsington Manor in the winter of 1915 – among them Bertrand Russell – found Lawrence involving them too: 'One afternoon he organised a play and made everyone act. He was Othello, in a straw hat and long magenta Arab robe.' It was an event in which the whole group had to participate, and in which Lawrence therefore could also join, effortlessly and unselfconsciously being the group's inspiration, as he had so often been at the Chambers' farm ten years earlier. Dorothy Brett, at a party in London that same winter of 1915, though finding the charades he was organising great fun – 'You trotting round the room riding an imaginary bicycle, ringing the bell, crying in a high falsetto voice, "Ting-a-ling-a-ling!" and running over us all' – tried to get out of her acting role – a refusal 'about which there is much squabbling and much laughter'. Catherine and Donald Carswell, a few years later, would also have much preferred to be an audience, but were not allowed to: 'One evening we tried charades, in which Lawrence excelled, having invented a special kind of his own. But I am the worst of performers, and Donald is not much better, so that we failed in playing up, while we could not be spared to act as audience.'[18] What mattered to Lawrence was the group of people acting and performing together, he himself drawing them out in the common pursuit of 'the natural grotesque'. But the best surviving account of such an occasion – one which took place in London in the winter of 1917, and which in many ways suggests the creation of a fictional episode – exists only in the form which the American poetess Hilda Doolittle (H.D.) gave it in her *roman à clef*, *Bid Me to Live*, in which distinctive versions of Lawrence, Frieda, Richard Aldington, Arabella Yorke, Cecil Gray and others appear. I have taken the liberty here of supplying the names of the characters which her account disguises.

There was Lawrence, saying 'We'll do a charade, you be the tree of life, Hilda.'

Adam and Eve were Richard and Arabella of course. Gray was the angel at the gate. It was the end of madness. It was the beginning. Gray was the angel, a joke with an umbrella. 'Take your umbrella,' shouted Lawrence, 'Grigio, you be the angel with the flaming sword,' and they had screamed as Gray had posed with the umbrella, static and calm, the angel at the gate.

'Dance,' said Lawrence, 'you dance' he said to Hilda.

'But I'm the tree,' she said, 'or what am I?'

'You are the apple-tree,' said Lawrence, 'you dance. Now Adam and Eve, you come along here and Frieda, you be the serpent,' he said, 'you growl and writhe.'

'Serpents don't growl,' said Frieda. But she obligingly plumped herself flat on the floor and wriggled on the blue carpet. They have shoved aside the table. There they all were, and Captain Jack White screamed from the day-bed, 'what can I be, old Lorenzo?'

'You be the audience, you be the chorus of the damned: come on, Eve.'

Eve snatched a branch of laurel from the jar by the Spanish screen.

'Excellent, Arabella, come along, Richard.'

'What are you?' said Richard, 'what's left for you? Oh, I see, old Lorenzo of course is Gawd-a'-mighty.'

Lawrence took up a Jehovah-like pose by the fire-place; he chanted from an imaginary scroll, 'Women, I say unto thee...'

'But that's not Jehovah, get back to Genesis,' shouted Richard.

'Well, dance anyhow,' said Lawrence, 'the Tree has got to dance, dance, hand them the apples,' and the chorus of the damned shouted from the day-bed while Frieda writhed her Teutonic serpent pattern on the carpet.[19]

The dancing, the shouting, the writhing: these performances were clearly not only *funny* but in a stronger and older sense *comic*. They channelled high and at times overwrought spirits: Dionysiacally they both revealed and released inhibitions. Mabel Luhan, in Taos in 1924, saw the same: 'he loved charades – and he was so gay and witty when he was playing! He could imitate anything or anybody. His ability to identify himself intuitively with things outside himself was wonderful...' But she went on to make a point about Lawrence which she – an exceptionally self-conscious person herself – was in a good position to make: 'He loved to act and was perfectly unselfconscious about it. We used to imitate each other in the syllables we were acting out and I wish you could have seen him and Frieda being Tony and me in the front seat of the car...! We used to laugh until we were tired.'[20] The point about Lawrence's unself-consciousness in these performances is crucial. A man as self-conscious and untouchable as Lawrence especially enjoyed such occasions, and Mabel Luhan could not help noticing it. It is also clear, however, that Lawrence was not only identifying himself 'intuitively with things outside himself', as Mabel Luhan liked to imagine. The satire on herself and her husband Tony 'in the front seat of the car' must have been done with controlled wit and observation, and probably with a good deal of malice: it certainly wasn't simply the intuitive reproduction Mabel preferred to think it was.

VI

This is especially interesting because it is clear that, in one sense, Lawrence as mimic, play and charade director was directly paralleling his work as a novelist and comic writer. He resembled, in fact, no one so much as Charles Dickens in his capacity for mimicry, in his fascination with the dramatic, in the frenzied energy he would pour into performances, in his natural tendency to act out in his fiction performances of the human grotesque and in his manipulation, as a fictional narrator, of his comic characters. Just as Lawrence struck David Garnett as the best mimic he had heard – so Dickens, too, struck everyone who knew him as the most accomplished mimic they had ever known. Acting out an old woman, for example, he reproduced (according to a friend) 'her manner of speech, her ways, her excuses etc.... to the very life. He could imitate, in a manner that I have never heard equalled, the low population of the streets of London in all their varieties'.[21] Dickens was also once famously observed at work by his daughter Mamie who (as a special treat) was allowed to be in his room while he was writing.

> I was lying on the sofa endeavouring to keep perfectly quiet, while my father wrote busily and rapidly at his desk, when he suddenly jumped from his chair and rushed to a mirror which hung near, and in which I could see the reflection of some extraordinary facial contortions which he was making. He returned rapidly to his desk, wrote furiously for a few moments, and went again to the mirror. The facial pantomime was resumed, and then turning toward, but evidently not seeing, me, he began talking rapidly in a low voice. Ceasing this soon, however, he returned once more to his desk...[22]

Both Dickens and Lawrence were essentially dramatic writers, even in their prose fiction: both regularly enacted their fiction in the theatre of their own minds: both employed dominant and thoroughly manipulative narrators in their prose narratives – narrators who at times we have difficulty distinguishing from the voice of the author: and both particularly enjoyed dramatising the grotesque. Dorothy Brett was living in New Mexico with the Lawrences in 1924 when Lawrence was writing his short novel *St. Mawr*, and she recalled an occasion when – coming in for lunch while in the middle of writing – Lawrence read out loud to her and Frieda what he had written that morning, and literally acted out the narrative from the point of view of its narrator. Dorothy Brett recalled how 'you' – Lawrence –

> are still twinkling with amusement, and you are still living more with them than with us. You read out the scene of the tea-party, of the tart Mrs. Witt, the scandalized Dean and his wife, and the determined Lou. You laugh so much over it, that you have to stop – and we are laughing too. Then you read out Mrs. Witt's defense of the horse when Rico pulls him over and the horse kicks Rico in the face. You read it with such keen joy and pleasure at the final downfall of Rico and the terrible revenge of the horse, that Frieda is horrified; she says that you are cruel and that you frighten her.
>
> But you are too immersed in the people and the story to care what anyone says. With great relish and giggling, you describe Rico's plight. You hate Rico so, that for the moment you are the horse; in fact, you are each person yourself, so vivid are they to you. With each character your voice and manner change: you act the story rather than read it, and we sit entranced, horrified, amused – all by turns, while your lunch gets colder and colder on your plate.[23]

She added 'How rare it is that you read out anything': but she also recorded another occasion, the following summer, when Lawrence again read his work out loud. One wonders how rare such performances really were: it seems that his friends probably did not often observe them because they tended to be private or domestic occurrences. But Frieda saw them all the time. 'He'd read to me, and make me read some of his writing . . . We never quarrelled about his writing except that I had to like what he'd written day by day.'[24] When Lawrence was revising *Sons and Lovers* in the autumn of 1912, for example, Frieda described in a letter how 'he . . . reads bits to me and we fight like blazes over it' (i. 449): before revising *The Widowing of Mrs. Holroyd* in August 1913, Lawrence found himself 'very busy reading the play to Frieda' (ii. 58). When the Lawrences were living in the same house as the Brewsters in Ceylon in 1922, Achsah Brewster recalled how, every night, 'he would

read what he had written during the day' – and the same happened on
Capri in 1926: 'We sit quietly round the stove while you read out to us
some of your most recent poems. . .'[25] On the second occasion which
Dorothy Brett recalled from the summer of 1924, Lawrence had invited
the actress Ida Rauh to take part in a read-through of his new play
David: 'We might have some fun with it, when you come . . . it will be
amusing to read, amongst us' (v. 252). But, in the event, according to
Dorothy Brett (whose memoir of Lawrence addresses him throughout
as 'you'), he read out the whole play himself, 'in the slightly shy, bashful
way you have; and you sing in a soft voice the little songs you have
invented for the play. You live every part. In some subtle way you change
and change about, as the characters alter from men to women, from
young to old. You read till evening. . .'[26] Here Lawrence – without, of
course, a fictional narrator in the dramatic form to oversee the behaviour of his characters – took the parts of *all* his characters: as Frieda
remarked about the writing of *David*, 'Lawrence was these people while
he wrote.' Only one thing marred the reading: an outburst from him in
the middle of one of the songs. Dorothy Brett recorded how he suddenly stopped and said: '"I feel so embarrassed. You all embarrass me. I
cannot go on." . . . But there is no time to finish it: you are too tired by
now, your voice is getting hoarse; so we leave and arrange to come up
again tomorrow.'[27] The self-consciousness was never very far away:
even as an adult, even in the midst of the loss of the watching self in performance.

We can even gain an insight into what his performances of
mimicry must have been like from one of the rare occasions where
Lawrence transcribed into written form, his own mimicry himself, in
a letter in the summer of 1929 while he, his German mother-in-law
and Frieda were at the Kurhaus Plättig, 3000 feet up in the middle of
the Black Forest. Ill and irritable himself, Lawrence found he could
not bear the platitudes of Frieda's mother. A letter to a German friend
gave him the chance to blow off steam by enacting what so irritated
him: and the foreign language (as it often does) made permissible
what would perhaps have been subject to self-censorship if written in
English:

Es ist natürlich furchtbar – nur oben in meinem Zimmer hab' ich es gern. Der Tannenwald ist ganz herum – ganz im Wald, Friedele, merkst du! im grossen, wunderbaren Tannenwald! nein! und die Luft! – und die nette Leut' die so freundlich mit mir reden – ach, wir haben's gut, wir sollen dankbar sein! Wenn ich denke an Männer die in Kohlengruben arbeiten – in grossen Fabriken – !!!! – Natürlich hasse ich jeden Tannenbaum mit giftigen Hassen, so schwarz und hart und steif-haarige. Warum können sie nicht Blätter haben!

[It is of course dreadful – I only like it up in my room. The pine-forest is all around – really in the forest, my little Frieda, do you realise? in the great, wonderful pine-forest! ah! and the air! – and the nice people who so kindly chat with me! – ah, aren't *we* lucky, shouldn't *we* be grateful! When I think of men working in coal-mines – in great factories – !!!! – Naturally I hate with poisonous hatred every pine-tree, so black and hard and stiff-haired. Why can't they have leaves!]

(vii. 387–8)

The fearful accuracy of his parody of the old lady's platitudinous sentimentality is, interestingly, succeeded by his own absurd hatred for the trees and his peremptory demand that they should have leaves. It is as if he realises that he has gone too far with his unforgiving satire of the Baroness, and redresses the balance by presenting his own absurdity. But the letter also gives us an idea of what his mimicry of others must have been like: exact, spiteful and rather frighteningly funny.

The bitter and savage authorial performances accompanying the actual composition of *St. Mawr* – 'you are still living more with them than with us' – may also remind us of Dickens's performance in front of the mirror. The crucial (and enormous) difference between Dickens and Lawrence as actors and performers lay, of course, in the self-consciousness of Lawrence outside the small group to whom he performed (and just occasionally within it, too), and the extraordinarily public talent of Dickens. Lawrence was extremely reluctant to perform in public: to a suggestion that he should give some lectures in America, he replied: 'I ... don't see myself on a platform ... The worst of it is, I am not a public man – not a bit – always have a "Strictly Private" notice in my hat' (iii. 357): while Dickens hugely enjoyed his public performances and public persona, taking to his public readings as some men take to drugs. But the connection between mimicry and the kind of disturbing, grotesque drama and dramatic fiction they wrote was strong in them both: and both created characters who, as Robert Garis powerfully argued in *The Dickens Theatre* (1965), *enact themselves* in ways that are uncanny, at times frightening, to their audience.

VII

The connection between what Lawrence wrote and what he acted out is most closely made, however, by a series of central figures in the novels he wrote between 1916 and 1924. David Garnett noticed of the mimicry and the charades that 'the person whom Lawrence most constantly made fun of was himself':

> He mimicked himself ruthlessly and continually and, as he told a story, acted ridiculous versions of a shy and gawky Lawrence being patronised by literary lions, of a winsome Lawrence charming his landlady, of a bad-tempered whining Lawrence picking a quarrel with Frieda over nothing. There was more than a little of Charlie Chaplin in his acting: but bitterer, less sentimental.[28]

The fiction of Lawrence's middle years, 1916–24, gave rise not just to a number of more explicitly satirical works than before – stories like 'Jimmy and the Desperate Woman' and the short novel *St. Mawr* – but also to a sequence of comic, quasi-autobiographical central figures in the major novels: Rupert Birkin, Aaron Sisson and Rawdon Lilly, Gilbert Noon, and Richard Lovatt Somers, in *Women in Love, Aaron's Rod, Mr Noon* and *Kangaroo*. These fictional characters are not, of course, simple portraits of their creator: they are fictional creations, whose only substantial existence is within the narrative in which they play a part. But readers of *Women in Love*, for example, will recognise Birkin being characteristically Lawrentian in his intensest moments: and readers of *Kangaroo* will not miss the parallel between the biography of the author and the bad-tempered Englishman with a German wife who leaves Europe and visits Australia, to live in a house beside the Pacific Ocean which is a mirror image of the house in which the novel itself was actually written. It seems clear that in his novels between *Women in Love* and *Kangaroo,* Lawrence conducted a series of experiments with central figures who had gone through some of his experiences and possessed some of his own potential, just as he had always used the lives of other people in his fiction: so as to see where they would go and what they might do, given such potential. The autobiographical figures in these novels are a very different kind of autobiographical creation from Cyril Beardsall in *The White Peacock* or Paul Morel in *Sons and Lovers*, who are never subjected to parody and ridicule in the way these later characters always are.

So, for example, we find Rupert Birkin in *Women in Love* being both typically Lawrentian and wildly absurd. It is Birkin who takes off his clothes, rolls in the primroses and embraces the trunk of a birch tree before deciding that he is weary of people and 'loved now the soft, delicate vegetation, that was so cool and perfect' at the end of chapter VIII. And in his philosophical letter to Halliday which the latter reads aloud in the Café Pompadour in chapter XXVIII, Birkin is absurd both for writing such things, and for writing them to people like Halliday and his friends. The witty responses which the café circle make to the letter are perfectly natural. This is Halliday reading the letter:

> "... 'There is a phase in every race ... when the desire for destruction overcomes every other desire. In the individual, this desire is ultimately a desire for destruction in the self'—*hic!*—" [Halliday] paused and looked up.
>
> "I hope he's going ahead with the destruction of himself," said the quick voice of the Russian. Halliday giggled, and lolled his head back, vaguely.
>
> "There's not much to destroy in [Birkin]," said the Pussum. "He's so thin already, there's only a fag-end to start on."
>
> "Oh, isn't it beautiful! I love reading it! I believe it has cured my hiccup!" squealed Halliday. "Do let me go on.— 'It is a desire for the reduction process in oneself, a reducing back to the origins, a return along the Flux of Corruption, to the original rudimentary conditions of being—' Oh, but I *do* think it is wonderful. It *almost* supersedes the Bible—"[29]

But Birkin is by no means the only such central, comic Lawrentian figure in these novels. Aaron Sisson – one half of the quasi-Lawrentian double-act in *Aaron's Rod* – is in a stubborn and murderously bad temper at the start of the novel: he goes out for an evening's drinking, exits the pub drunkenly, and then has no idea what he wants to do.

> The men were dispersing. He should take the road home. But the devil was in it, if he could take a stride in the homeward direction. There seemed a wall in front of him. He veered. But neither could he take a stride in the opposite direction. So he was destined to veer round, like some sort of weather-cock, there in the middle of the dark road outside the "Royal Oak."[30]

And as the novel's narrative itself veers round, casting about for directions in the gloom ('Our story will not yet see daylight' starts chapter IV: the novel contains no daylight scene until the start of chapter VIII[31]), so the central figure at this stage of the novel also veers and wanders: farcically incapable of going home, ridiculously unable to go on with his old family life, comically wondering what he should do with himself and where he should go. 'Comes over one an absolute necessity to move', starts Lawrence's *Sea and Sardinia*, written during the writing of *Aaron's Rod*: but although *Sea and Sardinia* is a travel book, it has no more certain answer to the problem of *where* to travel than Aaron has. Its opening paragraph continues: 'And what is more, to move in some particular direction. A double necessity then: to get on the move, and to know whither.'[32] Aaron is subject to both necessities and has no way of dealing with either. He is saved purely by chance – that is, by narrative device: 'a third exit' catches his eye, and, comic hero as he is, off he goes up it.[33] At the end of the first part of *Mr Noon*, an identical impasse has gripped all three main characters – including the Lawrence-potential Gilbert Noon – who are frozen into immobility within the narrative and may – it is suggested – remain permanently stuck: 'this obtuse-angled triangle ... Emmie, and Childe Rolande, and Mr Noon may sit forever in the Eakrast bedroom'.[34] Only a similar narrative device rescues them and allows Gilbert Noon to move forward into Part II of the novel – but, then, what else *could* rescue them?

In Part II, Gilbert regularly makes a self-important fool of himself: and the narrator takes great pleasure in pointing out what a fool he is. One of the joys of *Mr Noon* for Lawrence – it became as autobiographical a piece as he ever wrote — was almost certainly because it offered him an opportunity to mimic himself 'ruthlessly and continually', as he re-enacted many of his own earlier selves and experiences. He certainly never wrote a novel in which the narrative voice was stronger, more 'Gawdy-a'-mighty' or more impolite to the novel's central characters (Gilbert and Johanna). Moreover, set pieces such as Gilbert's meeting with Joanna's father, or the discovery of Gilbert and Johanna in bed together by the hotel-keeper in Detsch, suggest not only the marvellous performances of self-mimicry which so many of Lawrence's friends recalled,[35] but the complex and comic narrative dislocation caused by a narrator who now – ten years on from the experiences being described – believes in almost nothing of what his central, quasi-autobiographical character believes in. The bitter, sarcastic and all-controlling narrative turns out not to be a guide to any better or superior truth which – as readers – we might learn from, but yet another kind of comic self-mimicry; the self-mimicry of a narrator with all the words but none of the answers. The narrative's bitter mimicry of the comic absurdities of a man in love is the natural consequence of a narrative which has no time for love but is also desperately unsure about what it *does* have time for.

Richard Lovatt Somers in *Kangaroo* apparently has answers to all the problems that Aaron and Gilbert cannot solve. He has made his marriage: and he has got on the move so successfully that he has arrived in Australia. But he has travelled there, we learn, 'with a rabid desire not to see anything and not to speak one single word to any single body—except Harriett, whom he snapped at hard enough'.[36] What price travel, and seeing the world, on such terms? Absurd Richard, even more like his creator than Aaron is, regularly finds himself subjected to the humiliating ignominy implicit in a desire to travel without seeing or speaking.

For a man who has travelled so far, too, Richard's continuing restlessness is comical. It drives him and Harriett to the nearby town of Wolloona, where Richard – just once – is obliged to speak to someone NOT Harriett (all he says is 'Don't bother'). The wind is viciously cold,

Harriett hates it, and they forlornly trail to the beach to try and get out of the wind. There they begin to recover their composure: only to get caught by a wave and to struggle damply up to the dry again:

> Where immediately a stronger blast seized Lovatt's hat and sent it spinning to the sea again, and he after it like a bird. He caught it as the water lifted it, and then the waste of waters enveloped him. Above his knees swirled the green flood, there was water all around him swaying, he looked down at it in amazement, reeling and clutching his hat.[37]

The prose imitates first the grotesqueness of Richard's sudden swoop after his hat 'like a bird' (when he is clearly going to get soaked): and then his standing up to his knees in the middle of a sentence where neither he nor we know exactly what is what ('swaying' is probably the water and 'reeling' is probably Richard – but neither is certain). Harriett's reaction helps us to see her husband with cruel objectivity, as her positively sand-bag solidity contrasts with his comical airiness and fluidity:

> Harriett had fallen on her knees on the sand in a paroxysm of laughter, and there she was doubled up like a sack, shrieking between her gasps:
>   "His hat! His hat! He wouldn't let it go"—shrieks, and her head like a sand-bag flops to the sand—"no—not if he had to swim—" shrieks—"swim to Samoa."[38]

The similes 'like a sack' and 'like a sand-bag' are cruel enough to *her* physical absurdity: but she also brings out beautifully Richard's *apparently* fixed determination (he will chase his hat to Samoa) and his *actual* fluidity (he really doesn't have the least idea of what he is doing or where he is).

The uses of the comic in such a novel are very complex: but they ensure that the hero's experience is as surprising to him as – in its turn – the narration is, to the reader. There can be no certainty either from such a hero or in such a narrative – a narrative which in *Kangaroo* offers fragments, bits (one chapter quotes extensively from extracts from a Sydney morning paper), profound reflections and serious absurdities. In spite of treating the characters like caricatures of themselves, most of the time the narrator – the 'Gawd-a'-mighty' of the comic sketch – is not truly in control, not truly dominant: the kinds of certainty promised by an omniscient narrator would be entirely inappropriate. Instead, the novel (its 'record ... taken down for this gramophone of a novel' as the narrator himself puts it[39]) apparently plays itself: the central figures, sometimes absurd and sometimes profound, move through the narrative without even the possibility of learning from the narrator how they might live better. There is no 'Gawd-a'-mighty' narrator, either in fiction or in life, who might help them or tell them what they should do. The narrative insistences of these novels are, instead, subjected to their readers' derisive refusal to accept them.

VIII

In the comic performances of these heroes and his controlling or – at times – significantly non-controlling 'Gawd-a'-mighty' narrators, Lawrence can in one way be seen as the manipulator and dramatiser of his fictions, exactly as he was of his friends in charades and playlets: as the omniscient primary narrator who finds ways of getting both his characters and his secondary narrator to move under his direction.

But it is also possible to distinguish what he did early on in his career from what he began doing during its middle period, when he had largely given up writing plays but was introducing a new kind of dramatic tension between narrator and character into his fiction. It is easy to see how, in Lawrence's early fiction, the characters are regularly subjected to particularly manipulative direction by their narrator: this is the case in, for example, the insistently and self-regardingly first-person narrative of *The White Peacock*, or the portentously over-written narrative of *The Trespasser*, or the cruelly manipulative narrative of *Sons and Lovers*, or what is at times the stridently purposeful narrative of *The Rainbow*. The characters of these novels inevitably play out the tragedies which their controlling narrator manipulates them into suffering. For example; Cyril Beardsall, first-person narrator of *The White Peacock*, looks at George Saxton when the latter has fatally missed the chance of marriage with Lettie, tells him that 'you thought you were too good to be rejected': "'And nothing else,'" I completed, with which the little, exhausted gunboat of my anger wrecked and sank utterly. Yet no thoughts would spread sail on the sea of my pity; I was like water that heaves with yearning, and is still.'[40] And we thus know the tragic catastrophe of the moment.

The narrator of *Sons and Lovers* similarly sums up the moment into a final formulation when remarking of Walter Morel that he 'had denied the God in him'. There is here almost none of what Wayne Booth most usefully described as a characteristic 'blurring' in Lawrence's mature fiction of 'the borderlines between author's voice and character's voice'.[41] The narrator's voice in these early tragic fictions is single, undivided, not reflecting upon itself.

Something rather similar can be seen to have been true of the charades and playlets Lawrence organised with his friends during these years. We have an account of his being comically disturbed in the winter of 1914 when participants in a play refused to act out the scenario they had been given. John Middleton Murry remembered how the group

> set a play in motion which was a dramatisation of the actual situation between Katherine [Mansfield] and me, and in which Mark Gertler, the painter, was cast for the part of my successor. Not unnaturally I acted my own rôle with considerable conviction; and so did Katherine, for when the third act was under way, she suddenly refused to obey the scenario, which ended in a reconciliation with me, and insisted on staying with Gertler. There was a psychological explosion. Lawrence indignantly interrupted the drama, hustled me aside, and asked me with intense and passionate severity: 'Was I blind?' If not, how did I dare to expose myself. 'It's not as though we didn't love you...'[42]

Murry felt that he had been foolish in allowing such 'truth-telling' games to occur. But the writer of *Sons and Lovers* and *The Rainbow* clearly found deeply disturbing a psychodrama which was growing indistinguishable from real life: as disturbing, perhaps as a novel would be whose characters managed to escape from the control of their narrator. The unexpected lurch into real life of the little Murry play as Katherine departed from the scenario would have offended the early Lawrence's sense of art and narrative as well as of life and friendship.

But one of the things which happened to Lawrence's fiction after *The Rainbow* was that a radically new loosening up of narrative – especially the narrative of the central figure or figures – became a regular mode. The old, responsible, manipulating narrator is dropped; now, facetious and often irresponsible narrators make their entrance: the quasi-autobiographical central figures, caricatured and parodied, bear far more responsibility: what has been seized on as a series of Bakhtinian 'dialogic' voices mediates between the various narrations; and the narrators regularly become as fallible and helpless as the characters are. The parody and self-mimicry to which the later heroes (and the novels' narrators) are subjected, and the comic reversals experienced by the heroes, could not have been effected in novels strictly controlled by omniscient narrators.

This is, interestingly, in line with the way in which Lawrence and his friends increasingly appear to have played out scenarios (charades or playlets) so as to explore possibilities (fictively) through them, rather than to stage prearranged scenarios: and it also links with the fact that Lawrence only wrote one full-length play between 1913 and 1923. His use of the drama was going elsewhere, into fiction where there was at last a genuine interplay between narrative and characters: where dialogue becomes inherent in the kinds of language used. The women in the Adam and Eve scenario of 1917 – especially Frieda, the snake in the grass – were clearly going to be subjected to a harangue from the 'Gawd-a'-mighty' figure starting with a send-up of Christ's 'Woman, what have I to do with thee?'[43] – but they were obviously equally likely to disregard the direction they were being given. Just as the mercilessly mimicked autobiographical central characters of the middle-period novels can, by appealing to our sense of the honestly ridiculous (like Birkin) or to our sympathy (like Gilbert Noon) or just by walking out (like Aaron Sisson) escape the limitations of the narrative which ridicules them, so the characters within the playlets or charades can be seen to be silencing or ignoring their own narrator and creator, or – at the very least – adding to the multiplicity of voices within the fiction.

And, at times, Lawrence's fiction of this period takes on the comic fluidity of the improvised charade illuminated by the wit and malice of uninhibited mimicry: those are precise analogies. The brilliant and revealingly grotesque mimicry of the characters is combined with comic self-mimicry on the part of the narrator, as the narrative wildly – and comically – insists on its central importance and simultaneously abdicates all its responsibility. The fiction becomes far more like improvised charade than it had ever been before; the characters more like dramatic caricatures; and the comedy of the grotesque grows increasingly important.

This can look like carelessness, and has often been represented as such by critics of Lawrence: it can be seen, more normatively, as Lawrence's response – parallel to that of a writer like Bakhtin – to cultural dislocation and to formal narrative experiment. I simply suggest, however, that it represents a fictional development of a kind – and an importance – which we have hardly begun to assess. The great watershed of Lawrence's writing has, for years, been thought to lie between *Sons and Lovers* and *The Rainbow*. The more, however, we consider the kinds of undramatised narrative Lawrence employed in his early fiction, and the sophisticated uses he made of satire, mimicry, drama and comedy in his writing from 1916 onward, the more the crucial division may appear to lie instead between *The Rainbow* and Lawrence's subsequent writing, of which *Women in Love* is perhaps the beginning – though that may still be a heretical thing to say.

Notes

1 See John Worthen, *D.H. Lawrence: The Early Years 1885–1912* (Cambridge: Cambridge University Press, 1991), pp. 458, 576.

2 Ibid.

3 E.T. [Jessie Chambers], *D.H. Lawrence: A Personal Record* (Jonathan Cape, 1935), p. 109.

4 See e.g. Worthen, *The Early Years*, pp. 338–9.

5 E.T., *A Personal Record*, p. 109.

6 Ibid., pp. 108–9.

7 See e.g. Nehls, ii. 14 and T.S. Eliot, *To Criticise the Critic* (New York: Farrar, Straus and Giroux, 1965), p. 25.

8 David Garnett, *The Golden Echo* (Chatto & Windus, 1953), p. 245.

9 Nehls, iii. 99; Frieda Lawrence to Richard Aldington, May [1954], *Frieda Lawrence and her Circle*, ed. Harry T. Moore and Dale B. Montague (Macmillan, 1981), pp. 105–6.

10 Frieda Lawrence, "*Not I, But the Wind...*" (Santa Fe: Rydal Press, 1934), pp. 61–?.

11 Nehls, iii. 83.

12 Ibid., iii. 603; E.T., *A Personal Record*, p. 30.

13 Richard Aldington, *Portrait of a Genius, But...* (Heinemann, 1951), p. 248; Nehls, iii. 413–14.

14 Nehls, iii. 603.

15 Nehls, i. 507; Worthen, *The Early Years*, p. 176.

16 Brigit Patmore, *My Friends When Young* (Heinemann, 1968), p. 82.

17 Enid Hilton, *More Than One Life: A Nottinghamshire Childhood with D.H. Lawrence* (Stroud: Alan Sutton, 1993), p. 10.

18 Nehls, i. 177, 310; Brett, *Lawrence and Brett: A Friendship* (Philadelphia: J.B. Lippincott, 1933), p. 19; Nehls, i. 475.

19 *Bid Me To Live* (Virago Press, 1984), pp. 111–12. DHL (or 'Lorenzo') appears as 'Rico' in the original; Frieda as 'Elsa'; Richard (then married to H.D.) as 'Rafe'; H.D. as 'Julia' (the name Lawrence gave her in his own version of these months in his novel *Aaron's Rod*); Dorothy Yorke, known as Arabella (and just becoming Aldington's mistress), as 'Bella'; Gray (or 'Grigio') as 'Vane' or 'Vanio'; Jack White as 'Ned Trent'.

20 Mabel Luhan, *Lorenzo in Taos* (New York: Knopf, 1932), pp. 68, 190.

21 *Dickens: Interviews and Recollections*, ed. Philip Collins (Macmillan, 1981), i. 11.

22 Ibid., p. 121.

23 *Lawrence and Brett*, pp. 137–8.

24 Frieda Lawrence, 'Introduction' to DHL's *Look! We Have Come Through!*, rev. edn. (Dulverton: The Ark Press, 1971), pp. 10, 12.

25 Nehls, ii. 124; Brett, *Lawrence and Brett*, p. 287.

26 *Lawrence and Brett*, p. 219.

27 *The Correspondence of Frieda Lawrence with Jake Zeitlin, etc.*, ed. Michael Squires (Macmillan, 1991), p. 174; Brett, *Lawrence and Brett*, p. 219.

28 Garnett, *The Golden Echo*, p. 245. The self-mimicry is also an occasional feature of DHL's other writing. There exists a poem with the title 'À La Manière de D.H. Lawrence', which apparently he wrote 'satirising his

own style of poetry'. The red tram-cars of Florence had been replaced by green ones: the poem's last stanza runs:

> ... now they are like cabages
> and people are sad and grim
> all so very mechanical
> oh dear! what's happening to Tuscans!

> (*The Complete Poems of D.H. Lawrence*, ed. Vivian de Sola Pinto and Warren Roberts, rev. edn., Heinemann, 1967, ii. 846, 1034)

At least one well-known Lawrentian obsession – tragic concern over unhappy people who are, like their world, mechanised – is specified: the misspelling 'cabages' is perhaps to celebrate those which had dogged the Florentine printing of *Lady Chatterley's Lover*.

29 *Women in Love*, ed. David Farmer, Lindeth Vasey and John Worthen (Cambridge: Cambridge University Press, 1987), 106:39–40, 107:15–16, 108:11–13; 383:8–384:21.

30 *Aaron's Rod*, ed. Mara Kalnins (Cambridge: Cambridge University Press, 1988), 25:31–6.

31 Ibid., 39:3, 73:7.

32 *Sea and Sardinia* (New York: Thomas Seltzer, 1921), p. 11.

33 *Aaron's Rod*, 25:37.

34 *Mr Noon*, ed. Lindeth Vasey (Cambridge: Cambridge University Press, 1984), 92:29–30, 93:1–3.

35 *Mr Noon*, 168:28–169:32, 152:36–154:31.

36 *Kangaroo*, ed. Bruce Steele (Cambridge: Cambridge University Press, 1994), 19:21–3.

37 Ibid., 274:8, 20–5.

38 Ibid., 274:26–31.

39 Ibid., 280:17–18.

40 *The White Peacock*, ed. Andrew Robertson (Cambridge: Cambridge University Press, 1983), 195:31–4.

41 *Sons and Lovers*, ed. Carl and Helen Baron (Cambridge: Cambridge University Press, 1992), 88:8–9; Wayne C. Booth, *The Company We Keep: An Ethics of Fiction* (Berkeley: University of California Press, 1988), p. 446.

42 John Middleton Murry, *Between Two Worlds* (Jonathan Cape, 1935), pp. 321–2.

43 John ii. 4; see too *Mr Noon*, ed. Vasey, 258:11–34 and Explanatory note on 258:26 (pp. 329–30).

2

Mischief or merriment, amazement and amusement – and malice: *Women in Love*

Howard Mills

I

This essay was a resounding success before it ever got written, in that the very idea of it sent my friends off into peals of laughter. You must have drawn the short straw, they said. Isn't *Women in Love* the one Lawrence thought of calling *Dies Irae*? How about calling your piece *Day of Judgement: Its Lighter Moments*? This made me recall uncomfortably Lawrence's mockery of a poem in a book he once reviewed – a poem which assured us that God 'had his pleasant side'.[1] And I was also aware of how the novel's merriment constantly shades off into mischief and malice.[2]

'Mischief or Merriment' – I take this phrase from the letter Lawrence wrote in 1925 to the Italian critic Carlo Linati, who had complained that Lawrence's fiction was *troppo frenetico!* – too frantic or frenzied; that it lacked artistic detachment. But detachment, replies Lawrence, is just what he never aimed at. For him, 'An author should be in among the crowd, kicking their shins or cheering them on to some mischief or merriment' (v. 201). And the letter itself is full of mischievous merriment: 'I can't help laughing, your article seems such a breathless series of explosions. Do I really seem like that? – all you say?' (v. 200). So that in another alliterating but paradoxical phrase, Lawrence reacts to the critic with amazement and amusement.

That last phrase is actually from *Women in Love* and I'll turn later to its context. But what prompted my essay was not a letter, or a novel, but a photograph. It was taken on the spur of the moment by Catherine Carswell in 1921 and it catches Lawrence between, not amazement and amusement but smiling and laughter. It's all the more delightful and infectious because it's not posed (which is also why it's rather blurred). It catches the laughing Lawrence on the wing (I'm thinking of Blake's little poem about catching the winged joy as it flies). She reproduced it opposite the title-page of her memoir, nicely balancing the title itself with its potentially grim or earnest note – borrowing Lawrence's own phrase for his life, she calls her book *The Savage Pilgrimage*. And I'm especially glad to have that photo because there are few like it. Certainly Mrs Carswell thought her snapshot had rarity-value, for she says: 'It is, I think, a misfortune that by far the most of the photographs and portraits of Lawrence show him as thoughtful – either fiercely or sufferingly so. His usual expression was a kind of sparkling awareness, almost an "I am ready for anything" look which was invigorating to behold.'[3] I agree that, with pictures of Lawrence in merriment, the more would be the merrier. So it's a further misfortune that, when Cambridge University Press reprinted her book in 1981, the photo was left out. The omission reflects the over-solemn way that academia often approaches Lawrence.

I'm encouraged in my impulse to put the balance right by the fact that Mrs Carswell's whole book urges an unsolemn approach. Her Introduction begins by celebrating the diversity of Lawrence's works which, 'with their richness of human admission . . . do away with the charge of morbidity and impotence'. In keeping her determination 'to refrain from approaching the least solemn of men with graveyard graces', she likens him to 'Joey in the Punch and Judy show. He will not "stay put", but bobs up serenely and repeatedly from the grave to mock those who would reduce him to a formula. His unholy ghost will not be pigeon-holed.'[4] 'Morbidity and impotence' are of course the charges which (particularly in the first, uncensored version of her book) she turned right back on the principal 'charger' himself, John Middleton Murry. But very soon after Lawrence's death she had already been prompted to publish a letter that is worth quoting at some length because it helps counteract a still common picture:

> Lawrence was as little morose as any open clematis flower, as little tortured or sinister or hysterical as a humming-bird. . . As to frustration, consider his achievement. In the face of formidable initial

disadvantages and lifelong delicacy, poverty that lasted for three-quarters of his life and hostility that survives his death, he did nothing that he did not really want to do, and all that he most wanted to do he did. He went all over the world, he owned a ranch, he lived in the most beautiful corners of Europe, and met whom he wanted to meet and told them that they were wrong and that he was right. He painted and made things, and sang and rode. He wrote something like three dozen books, of which even the worst page dances with life that could be mistaken for no other man's, while the best are admitted, even by those who hate him, to be unsurpassed. He would have laughed lightly and cursed venomously in passing at the solemn owls – each one secretly chained by the leg – who now conduct his inquest.[5]

And in a superb understatement, she says in her book that 'he was without human dreariness'.[6]

To stress Lawrence's energy, Mrs Carswell lists what he wrote in 'a period of little more than two years':[7] *The Lost Girl, Aaron's Rod, Sea and Sardinia*, the Introduction to Maurice Magnus's Memoirs and *Birds, Beasts and Flowers*. If we extend that list with slightly earlier stories like 'Fanny and Annie' and 'The Captain's Doll' – which Lawrence called 'a very funny long story' (iv. 109) – and from slightly later the final version of *Studies in Classic American Literature* – then we find not only the energetic play of genius but also an increased play of humour. And an intentional play of humour, to judge from essays like the review of Sherman's *Americans* and 'The Future of the Novel' (both 1923) which have humour, even a sense of fun both as their method and as their message.[8] 'On Being Religious' of the same year maintains that 'Either believing in a real God looks like fun, or it's no go at all.'[9] Furthermore several of the fictional works go out of their way to be funny: I mean that comedy isn't incidental to them but the work exists largely as a framework, a pretext, for overtly comic scenes.

That's also the case with at least one chapter of *Women in Love*, which first appeared in that productive period at the start of the twenties although written during the war whose 'bitterness . . . may be taken for granted in the characters'.[10] But before looking at that chapter I need to pause and think about terms.

II

'Comedy', subtle as it may be, is usually easier to identify, openly declares itself as a mode and a tone marked off from others. But while there is overt comedy even in *Women in Love*, I'm more concerned with humour. The word 'humour' *can* be simply a synonym for gentle comedy. But it more often indicates, not a specific playful tone but the whole play of tone: the very play across the light-and-dark spectrum, rather than (to switch metaphors) just playing the notes at the top end of the register – the light and bright and sparkling ones. George Eliot remarked (and the author of *Women in Love* would have nodded vigorously!) that the 'word of all work Love will no more express the myriad modes of mutual attraction, than the word Thought can inform you what is passing through your neighbour's mind':[11] and I fear that *humour* is another such word-of-all-work. It seems analogous, not with sunny brightness or genial mildness, nor even with prevailing climate, but 'simply' with *weather*. Perhaps with the very *changeableness* of weather: we should take a hint about the nature of the novels in which they appear that Birkin is called 'a changer' (*WL* 92:27) and that in the Brangwens 'one could watch the change in their eyes from laughter to anger, blue, lit-up laughter, to a hard, blue-staring anger; through all the irresolute stages of the sky when the weather is changing'.[12] Hardy said that 'flux and reflux – the rhythm of change – alternate and persist in everything under the sky'.[13] *The Rainbow* speaks of the 'quick . . . changeability' of children, a quality which that novel is so good at describing.[14]

That's all very well, but *Women in Love* pushes things to extremes, largely because it describes, not only quick changeability of mood but conflicting feelings experienced simultaneously. A mild example is Gerald's 'amazement and amusement', in 'Gladiatorial' (*WL* 274:36) but that phrase is anticipated in a more volatile scene, on the very first pages. The sisters' faces 'lit up with amusement. "Isn't it an amazing thing," cried Gudrun, "how strong the temptation is, not to [get married]!" They both laughed . . . In their hearts they were frightened.' Then Gudrun makes 'a strange grimace, half sly smiling, half anguish. Ursula was afraid' (*WL* 8:9–13, 28–30). It reminds me of Hazlitt's description of

Macbeth: 'every feeling calls up its fellow-contrary, and thoughts pitch and jostle as in the dark' – and of *King Lear*: 'the imagination is glad to take refuge in half-comic, half-serious comments – just as the mind under the extreme anguish of a surgical operation vents itself in sallies of wit.'[15] Furthermore this novel has dark thoughts about what lies behind smiles or laughs: shared pleasure, or mutual contempt; a release from painful thoughts, or a wish to inflict pain. In 'In the Train', Gerald has by turns 'a queer little smile . . . a look of amusement, calm and curious', a 'good-humoured callousness, even strange, glistening malice' and 'a manly, quick, soldierly laugh' (*WL* 54:33–4, 56:27–8, 59:6–7). Or laughs can be startling and disturbing, like the Baronet's in 'Breadalby' which 'rattled out like a clatter of falling stones' (*WL* 86:38). This is as unsettling a landslide as the 'avalanche' of Paolo's anger in *Twilight in Italy*, a 'white, heavy rage' with 'the cruelty of a falling mass of snow'.[16] Sometimes laughter, anguish and anger are indistinguishable (I think of Eliot's prose-poem 'Hysteria', or his phrase 'the laceration/Of laughter' in 'Little Gidding'.)[17]

III

Let me quote in succession two descriptions, of matters large and small, into which Lawrence throws himself with equal zest. Here's one excerpt:

> . . . there was a burst of sound, and a burst of brilliant light, the moon had exploded on the water, and was flying asunder in flakes of white and dangerous fire. Rapidly, like white birds, the fires all broken rose across the pond, fleeing in clamorous confusion, battling with the flock of dark waves that were forcing their way in.

And here's the other:

> Her soul opened in amazement [that word again]. His voice filled the church! It rang out like a trumpet, and rang out again. She started to giggle over her hymn book. But he went on, perfectly steady. Up and down rang his voice, going its own way. She was help-lessly shocked into laughter. Between moments of dead silence in herself she shook with laughter. On came the laughter, seized her

and shook her till the tears were into her eyes. She was amazed, and rather enjoyed it...

She bent down to prayer in cold reproof of herself. And yet, as she knelt, little eddies of giggling went over her.

– and so on: each passage from which I've excerpted goes on for a couple of pages. The first was Birkin trying to smash the moon while Ursula, in *Women in Love* (*WL* 247:1–5), watches; the second was Anna in *The Rainbow* with a fit of giggling in church.[18] Even my brief and bleeding chunks will remind you that Lawrence describes each with the same zest and detail. He 'enjoyed "doing" ordinary things', observes Mrs Carswell:[19] another early admirer stresses his 'omnivorous interest in all things, from the tiniest object to a vast concept, and his talent for electric, mettlesome descriptions of them'.[20]

'Yes indeed', you may say, 'but don't the excerpts you quoted remind us nonetheless that *Women in Love* is always earnest and intense, whereas *The Rainbow* has room for lighter interludes, even comic relief? So why don't you write about *The Rainbow* and humour? You'd have rich pickings – Tom getting off with the girl at Matlock, Tilly jealous and indignant when Lydia calls to borrow butter, Anna's giggles, her honeymoon (well, "its lighter moments"!) or the adolescent Ursula barricading herself against a 'bedlam' of siblings ("'Mother, she won't answer', came the yell. 'She's dead.'").[21] Why make life difficult for yourself by choosing *Women in Love*?' I have a twofold answer to this.

First, none of those *Rainbow* episodes is straightforwardly humorous, let alone comic relief. They're not interludes, nor is their effect on the characters' lives to give an optimistic lift – several have daunting consequences. Granted, the giggling episode is by definition a collapse into laughter and is infectiously so for the reader. And certainly I want to remind you that Lawrence takes as much trouble over the minutiae of this, the mechanics or so to speak the meteorology of giggling, as he does with, say, the much-commented-on ritual with the sheaves in the same chapter, or the other novel's description of Birkin's moon-stoning which has been commented on too heavily in every sense. Nonetheless that giggling episode isn't just comic, nor it is an interlude. Immediately afterwards, as the couple sit together after family Sunday dinner, Will opens up and talks about his 'close passion', under Ruskin's influence, for churches and church architecture; and Anna listens like a thrilled convert.[22] But the giggles were already a foretaste of her reactions in Lincoln Cathedral [d]uring the first year of their marriage' when, prompted by the gargoyles, 'She laughed with a Pouf! of laughter', and 'mocked, with a tinkle of profane laughter', 'with malicious triumph.'[23] Equally, this destructive impulse in her giggles in church gives them much in common with Birkin's stone-throwing. Both are attempts (involuntary in Anna's case; or accidentally-on-purpose, as Birkin in *Women in Love* would insist on seeing it) to break up some self-contained and self-imposing whole. Anna tries to 'pull herself together' as does the moon, but the disruptive fragmenting giggles are provoked by the self-absorbed Will. No doubt treatises on adolescent psychology will tell us that giggles are an involuntary, displaced expression of sexual feeling; we might think of Angel Clare's orgasmic sneeze when spying on Tess:[24] as Gudrun says to Gerald with 'a smile of obscene recognition', 'All that, and more' (*WL* 243:26, 28). But I read young Anna's as a premonitory outbreak of disruptive scepticism.

And I want next to suggest that, just as the giggling scene has a serious context, the stone-throwing incident is given a humorous context. For although the moon-stoning is *all* that ever gets commented on in 'Moony', it occupies only a couple of pages in a chapter which is as long as 'The Industrial Magnate', and is only one of many contrasting sections of which I will trace the sequence.

(1) First we have Ursula after Birkin escapes from Hermione to France, her deathly feelings echoing those which start two other chapters, 'Sunday Evening' and 'Man to Man': one evening she comes across Birkin. (2) Birkin is throwing stones at the moon's reflection in the pond. (3) They converse, quarrel, are reconciled and she nestles 'as if submissively' (*WL* 252:18). (4) The next day 'Suddenly he found himself face to face with a situation. It was as simple as this: fatally simple' (*WL* 252:37–8). He meditates intensely on the 'awful African process' (*WL* 254:3) and its white northern counterpart, then sees 'the remaining way. And he must run to follow it. He thought of Ursula...he must go to her at

once. He must ask her to marry him. They must marry at once . . . He must set out at once and ask her, this moment. There was no moment to spare' (*WL* 254:32–9). So off he hurries, through a Beldover that 'looked like Jerusalem to his fancy' (*WL* 255:3). (5) And what happens when he gets to her home in Somerset Drive? She's out – gone to change her library books. And her dad, he's 'just doing a bit of work in the shed' (*WL* 255:15). But they have a bit of a talk, starting naturally enough with the chapter's title-motif of the moon. If I now indulge myself with a couple of longish quotations, it's simply to show how Lawrence, in this usually clipped and compressed novel, indulges himself here.

> "The weather's not so bad as it has been," said Brangwen, after waiting a moment. There was no connection between the two men.
>
> "No," said Birkin. "It was full moon two days ago."
>
> "Oh! You believe in the moon then, affecting the weather?"
>
> "No, I don't think I do. I don't really know enough about it."
>
> "You know what they say?—The moon and the weather may change together, but the change of the moon won't change the weather."
>
> "Is that it?" said Birkin. "I hadn't heard it."
>
> There was a pause. Then Birkin said:
>
> "Am I hindering you? I called to see Ursula, really. Is she at home?"
>
> "I don't believe she is. I believe she's gone to the library. I'll just see."
>
> Birkin could hear him enquiring in the dining-room.
>
> "No," he said, coming back. "But she won't be long. You wanted to speak to her?"
>
> Birkin looked across at the other man with curious calm, clear eyes.
>
> "As a matter of fact," he said, "I wanted to ask her to marry me."
>
> A point of light came on the golden-brown eyes of the elder man.
>
> "O-oh?" he said, looking at Birkin, then dropping his eyes before the calm, steadily watching look of the other: "Was she expecting you then?"
>
> "No," said Birkin.
>
> "No?—I didn't know anything of—of this sort was on foot—." Brangwen smiled awkwardly.
>
> Birkin looked back at him, and said to himself: "I wonder why it should be 'on foot'!" Aloud he said:

"No, it's perhaps sudden." At which, thinking of his relationship with Ursula, he added—"but I don't know—"

"Quite sudden, is it?—Oh!" said Brangwen, rather baffled and annoyed.

"In one way" replied Birkin, "—not in another."

(WL 255:32—256:25)

Ursula isn't back very promptly and the two men have plenty of time to quarrel, or rather for Will to get increasingly exasperated at Birkin's fastidious and languid aloofness.

"I suppose," said Brangwen, "you know what sort of people we are?— What sort of a bringing-up she's had?"

"'She'," thought Birkin to himself, remembering his childhood's corrections, "is the cat's mother."

"Do I know what sort of a bringing-up she's had?" he asked simply. He seemed to annoy Brangwen intentionally.

"Well," he said, "she's had everything that's right for a girl to have— as far as was possible, as far as we could give it her."

"I'm sure she has," said Birkin.

Which caused a most perilous full-stop. The father was becoming exasperated. There was something naturally irritant to him in Birkin's mere presence.

"And I don't want to see her going back on it all," he said, in a clanging voice.

"Why?" said Birkin.

This monosyllable exploded in Brangwen's brain like a shot.

"Why!" he repeated. "Why don't I? Because I don't believe in your new-fangled ways and your new-fangled ideas—in and out like a frog in a gallipot. It would never do for me."

Birkin watched him with steady, emotionless eyes.

(WL 257:1—21)

You can see why Birkin later (WL 274:11) says this confrontation came about by 'accident—or mischief' (mischief or mischance – or accidentally-on-purpose again), and you can see how Lawrence milks for maximum mischief and merriment. The turning-point in this comedy is Ursula's return in one of her bright, vague, absent moods which infuriates both men (one of the novel's many sudden switches in alliances), Birkin saying 'we'll leave it for the time being' and Will in 'bitter, rancorous anger' (*WL* 261:22, 8–9). There are more switches to come in this chapter (Ursula re-allies herself in 'easy female transcendency' with Gudrun, then 'turned in spirit towards Birkin again') which I'll pick up later in this essay.

'Amazement and amusement' is the phrase Lawrence uses to describe Gerald's reaction to 'the fiasco of the proposal' (*WL* 266:3). (It further illustrates Birkin's 'quick changeability' that he hurries from the Brangwens' home as abruptly and 'blindly' as he hurried to it, and 'went straight to Shortlands'. It further illustrates Lawrence's mobility of tone that, after the men have wrestled naked, Birkin recounts the 'farce' at the Brangwens', *WL* 266:3, 9, 5.) But there will be readers in whom any amusement at the non-conversation between Birkin and Brangwen is checked by comparing the portrayal of Will in *The Rainbow* with what seems to be the narrator's as well as Birkin's view of Will here. Birkin's reflection 'How curious it was that this was a human being!' (*WL* 255:20–1) is even more withering than Goneril's in *King Lear*: 'O, the difference of man and man!'[25] What most divides readers of this book, especially with chapters like 'A Chair', is the extent to which its comedy depends on misanthropy. But my prior point about the humour of this conversation of Will and Birkin's, whether hilarious or distasteful, is its relative length – relative, that is, to other sections of the chapter, and to its thematic significance or advance of the plot. Its expansiveness verges on self-indulgence in what Mrs Carswell calls the 'uncanny mimicry' by this potential 'Dickens of the Midlands'.[26]

And yet it *does* have a function in the structure of the chapter. But that structure is a comic one, of Birkin's crisis, choice, epiphany and let-down. It is as if Birkin, like Tom in *The Rainbow*, had exclaimed 'That's her' and felt that 'it was ordained so' – but even more deflatingly that Tom 'had to come down from this pleasant view of the case'.[27] And come down from the self-centred, male view: the humour of 'Moony' is directed at self-absorption, male as well as female. But in order to explore further this humorous criticism of Birkin, it will be helpful to step back and develop some points of comparison with a nineteenth-century novel that influenced *Women in Love*.

IV

In that other novel is an incident which reminds me, by its very phrasing, of Birkin's abrupt visit to Ursula ('He must go to her at once'). The heroine, torn between two possible futures (in her case, with husband or lover), turns her thoughts to her son, 'recollecting [his] existence for the first time that morning' and asking after him 'with sudden eagerness'. Now

> She had an aim in life. And she must act . . . There was no time to lose – she must act quickly, before they took him away from her. She must take her son and go away. Here was the one thing she had to do now. She must be calm, and get out of this torturing situation. The idea of decided action, binding her to her son, of going away with him somewhere immediately, made her feel calmer.
>
> She dressed quickly, went downstairs and with resolute steps walked into the drawing-room.[28]

But what follows in *this* novel is far from comic anticlimax. If the heroine's son doesn't fit her 'pleasant view of the case', it's because he's 'bewildered', 'scared' as well as 'delighted' by her abrupt visit (*AK* 312). Far from her feelings or professions of feelings being humorously deflated, we've been told explicitly but compassionately at the very start of this incident that the 'role of the mother living for her child, which she had assumed during the last few years', was 'partly sincere, though greatly exaggerated' (*AK* 311).

That mother is Tolstoy's Anna Karenin. And the most obvious parallel to that episode and even more to her later, illicit visit to her son, is not Birkin's visit to Ursula in 'Moony' but Frieda's clandestine visit to her children in actual life.[29] But a pre-echo of Birkin's impulsiveness can be heard in Tolstoy's portrayal of Levin. Birkin's vision of Beldover as a New Jerusalem as he hastens to propose to Ursula recalls Levin's ecstatic solipsism as he waits to clinch his engagement to Kitty: 'what he saw that morning', says Tolstoy, 'he never saw again', and everything 'seemed not of this earth' (*AK* 428).

The contrast in tone is of course as marked as the similarity of situation. Tolstoy makes Levin's high spirits as infectious to readers as Lawrence makes Anna's giggling. 'Moony', on the other hand, is doubly dismissive: Birkin is a ghost who 'drifted . . . swiftly' to the Brangwens' house and leaves after the proposal-fiasco in a 'blithe drift of rage', while what was 'like Jerusalem to his *fancy*' is to Lawrence 'walled-in' with 'straight, *final* streets' (*WL* 254:40, 261:28, 255:2–3; my italics: we know well Lawrence's attitude to the *final, perfect* or *complete*). But, as I hope a broader look at the two characters will show, this oscillating sense of similarity-and-difference is the life and soul of any fruitful comparison.

'No two novelists, in being so alike, are in fact so different': this paradox, which Mark Kinkead-Weekes has used of Lawrence and Hardy, also fits Lawrence and Tolstoy.[30] The Russian novelist is another of that handful of predecessors with whom Lawrence engaged in a protracted debate – a mixture of exasperation and admiration – through his essays and letters, and vied with – some would say tried to rewrite – in his own novels.

One strand of the quarrel was his view that Tolstoy, like Hardy, made his characters surrender to social convention: Anna and Vronsky aren't allowed to 'live in the pride of their sincere passion, and spit in Mother Grundy's eye'.[31] So that Lawrence perhaps offers a Revised Version of their story in *Lady Chatterley's Lover*. I would suggest that *Anna Karenin* may be compared as fruitfully with *Women in Love*. Here Lawrence emulates Tolstoy on a range of human relationships (those with friends, sisters and parents as well as lovers) and human activities (including mental and physical work, the demands which the community makes on the individual, and the way individuals use work and social roles to 'side-track from themselves').[32]

When Lawrence's letters and essays talk about Levin rather than Anna and Vronsky, they discuss Levin's attitude to the peasants – his particular philosophy, it is alleged – rather than his philosophising temperament. But that temperament is reflected in Birkin as a fictional adaptation of

Levin, and I think Levin showed Lawrence how to treat Birkin humorously. If I in turn may adapt the Foreword to *Fantasia of the Unconscious*,
both characters have the 'absolute need for some sort of satisfactory
mental attitude towards one's lf and things in general that makes one try
to abstract some definite conclusions from one's experiences'[33] – and
some definite programme for one's future life. Both are whole-hoggers,
both go for what F.R. Leavis – speaking of Tolstoy himself in later life –
called 'the simple answer'.[34] Both are impulsive, and often inept in argument. Both are insistent – Ursula calls Birkin insistent, Gerald thinks
him 'insistent rather than confident' (*WL* 58:8–9). But they are at once
insistent and inconsistent. And this generates a good deal of comedy as
well as varying degrees of sympathy.

Here's a comment on whole-hoggers: 'The only thing she dreaded was
his making up his mind. She dreaded his way of seeing some particular
things vividly and feverishly, and of his acting upon this special sight. For
once he decided a thing, it became a reigning universal truth to him, and
he was completely inhuman.' That is Hermione on Birkin, in the discarded Prologue to the novel (*WL* 499:23–7). It must be one in the few
strands of the version for which that prologue was intended which got
carried through to the published novel. Hence the 'Moony' chapter I've
described, and hence scenes between Birkin and Gerald as 'In the Train'
and 'Man to Man'.

At first glance Tolstoy wins hands down at exploiting this topic for
comedy. Think of his humorous, impartial and generous treatment of
that friendship-of-opposites Levin and Oblonsky, not least on their
opposed ideas about love – love of 'just one woman' versus loving lots of
them. Here's Lawrence:

> "Have you ever really loved anybody?" asked Gerald.
> "Yes and no," replied Birkin.
> "Not finally?" said Gerald.
> "Finally—finally—no," said Birkin.
> "Nor I," said Gerald.
> "And do you want to?" said Birkin.
> Gerald looked with a long, twinkling, almost sardonic look into the
> eyes of the other man.

"I don't know," he said.

"I do—I want to love," said Birkin.

"You do?"

"Yes. I want the finality of love."

"The finality of love," repeated Gerald. And he waited for a moment.

"Just one woman?" he added. The evening light, flooding yellow along the fields, lit up Birkin's face with a tense, abstract steadfastness. Gerald still could not make it out.

"Yes, one woman," said Birkin.

But to Gerald it sounded as if he were insistent rather than confident.   (*WL* 57:30–58:9)

That's certainly critical. But Tolstoy is humorously so:

'Tell me frankly,' he [Oblonsky] pursued, picking up a cigar and keeping one hand on his glass, 'give me your advice.'

'What about?'

'It's like this. Suppose you are married, you love your wife, but you are attracted to another woman.'

'Forgive me, but I really find that absolutely incomprehensible . . . It's as if . . . as incomprehensible as if, after a good dinner here [they are in a smart restaurant], I were to go into a baker's shop and steal a roll.'

Oblonsky's eyes sparkled more than usual.

'Why not? Rolls sometimes smell so good that you can't resist them!'   (*AK* 54)

Then he quotes a relevant stanza of Heine 'with a hint of a smile and Levin could not help smiling himself' (*AK* 54). The talk ends when Levin suddenly 'recollected his own sins and the inner conflict he had lived through. And he added unexpectedly [people always say or do the unexpected in *Anna Karenin*]: "However, perhaps you're right. You may very likely be . . . But I don't know, I really don't know."

"There, you see", said Oblonsky, "you're very much all of a piece. It's both your strong point and your failing. You are all of a piece and you want the whole of life to be consistent too – but it never is. You scorn public service because you want the reality to correspond all the time to the aim – and that's not how it is. You want man's work, too, always to have a definite purpose, and love and family to be indivisible. But that does not happen either. All the variety, all the beauty of life are made up of light and shade."'   (*AK*55–6)

Oblonsky's admonition reminds me of Mrs Carswell's observation that Lawrence relished all the varied daily chores as 'a part of life'.[35] It also reminds me of 'the Queen Bee' scolding the protagonist's intolerance in *Sea and Sardinia*: 'such condemnation! Why don't you take it as it comes? It's all life'.[36] (Anthony Burgess said of *Sea and Sardinia* that its 'remarkable piquancy lies in the wonderful generosity of this eye that misses nothing and its contrast with the Lawrence who so easily gets fed up with everybody'[37] – he means Lawrence the portrayed character who is made fun of by Lawrence the author.)

But . . . Although the friend's dinner 'should have drawn them closer still', Oblonsky ends by feeling 'estrangement rather than *rapprochement*' (*AK* 56). And the same is true not only of Birkin and Gerald after their train tête-à-tête but my feeling about the passages I juxtaposed. For while *Women in Love* makes fun of Birkin it can't in this instance compete with Tolstoy because it deliberately clamps down on that generous representation of 'all life' at which *Anna Karenin* (and *Sea and Sardinia* in its own way) excels.

Let me continue my comparison of these two novels, however, and the balance of humour markedly changes.

V

Although chapters like 'Shortlands', 'Crème de Menthe', 'Breadalby' and the 'Gudrun in the Pompadour' emulate the ensemble-scenes, the confrontations of different social or intellectual 'sets', which abound in *Anna Karenin*, they don't reproduce with Birkin very much of Tolstoy's recurrent humour about Levin as a fish-out-of-water/bull-in-a-china-shop. Levin, for all his impatience and ineptness in discussion, is driven by an urge to define his own individual view about social institutions and social duties: Birkin remains aloof. *His* view is that 'We must drop our jobs, like a shot' once the love question has been settled (*WL* 315:13). On the love question itself, however, the position changes. If for Levin the course of true love doesn't run smooth it's because of Vronsky, then Kitty's illness and shame, and his own wounded pride. As for what 'true love' *is*, that's never in question. We're told early on that the thought of Levin's mother 'was sacred to him, and in his imagination his future wife was to be a repetition of that exquisite and holy ideal of womanhood which his mother had been' (*AK* 109–10). Although it needs some unforeseen give-and-take, his marriage with Kitty shakes down pretty well into that repetition. It's Vronsky who has the real problems. The following passage sounds like many in Lawrence's novel:

> [Anna's] chief preoccupation was still herself – how far she was dear to Vronsky, how far she could compensate to him for all he had given up. Vronsky appreciated this desire not only to please but to serve him, which had become the sole aim of her existence, but at the same time he chafed at the *loving snares* in which she tried to hold him fast.
>
> (*AK* 674; my italics)

You can imagine the reactions to all this of Levin, who could not imagine love for woman outside marriage, and he even pictured a family and then the woman who would give him the family (*AK* 110); at most he would shrug, like Vronsky's friend Yashvin, who says to himself that 'a wife is a worry, but it's worse when she's not a wife' (*AK* 573). But you can imagine the alarm bells ringing for Birkin at Levin's fixed ideal of love. Wife as mother? – like as not *magna mater* before you know what's hit you; mother of your children but also an authentic repro. of your *own* mother?? . . . a home resembling that of your parents?! – all this gets the most withering scorn in *Women in Love*, from the sisters' opening talk onward, and it draws the most fastidious wariness from Birkin. The whole book is about his search for a new form of love, or at least an escape from the old. And it's this search that produces the dialogues which attract Lawrence's finest humour. For instance:

> "And if you don't believe in love, what *do* you believe in?" she asked, mocking. "Simply in the end of the world, and grass?"

He was beginning to feel a fool.

"I believe in the unseen hosts," he said.   (WL 129:23–6)

It sounds as if he'd also like his guest (Ursula has come for tea) to be unseen:

> "But don't you think me good-looking?" she persisted, in a mocking voice.
>
> He looked at her, to see if he felt that she was good-looking,
>
> "I don't *feel* that you're good-looking," he said.
>
> "Not even attractive?"
>
> He knitted his brows in sudden exasperation.
>
> "Don't you see that it's not a question of visual appreciation in the least," he cried. "I don't *want* to see you. I've seen plenty of women, I'm sick and weary of seeing them. I want a woman I don't see."
>
> "I'm sorry I can't oblige you by being invisible," she laughed.
>
> (WL 147:18–27)

Birkin (like Levin on other subjects) is being misled, admittedly goaded by her mocking matter-of-factness, into being his own worst advocate. And he's misled further by the example of the cats, the 'fluffy . . . bit of chaos' brought to heel by the masterful 'manly nonchalance' of Mino (WL 150:30–1, 148:32):

> "It is just like Gerald Crich with his horse—a lust for bullying—a real Wille zur Macht—so base, so petty."
>
> "I agree that the Wille zur Macht is a base and petty thing. But with the Mino, it is the desire to bring this female cat into a pure stable equilibrium, a transcendent and abiding *rapport* with the single male.— Whereas without him, as you see, she is a mere stray, a fluffy sporadic bit of chaos. It is a volonté de pouvoir, if you like, a will to ability, taking pouvoir as a verb."
>
> "Ah—! Sophistries! It's the old Adam."
>
> "Oh yes. Adam kept Eve in the indestructible paradise, when he kept her single with himself, like a star in its orbit."
>
> "Yes—yes—" cried Ursula, pointing her finger at him. "There you are—a star in its orbit! A satellite!—a satellite of Mars—that's what she is to be! There—there—you've given yourself away! You want a

satellite, Mars and his satellite! You've said it—you've said it—you've dished yourself!"

He stood smiling in frustration and amusement and irritation and admiration and love. She was so quick, and so lambent, like discernible fire, and so vindictive, and so rich in her dangerous flamy sensitiveness.

"I've not said it at all," he replied, "if you will give me a chance to speak."

"No, no!" she cried. "I won't let you speak. You've said it, 'a satellite,' you're not going to wriggle out of it. You've said it."

"You'll never believe now that *I haven't* said it," he answered. "I neither implied nor indicated nor mentioned a satellite, nor intended a satellite, never."

"*You prevaricator!*" she cried, in real indignation.

"Tea is ready, sir," said the landlady from the doorway.

They both looked at her, very much as the cats had looked at them, a little while before.   (*WL* 150:25–151:15)

If we follow that passage on to the remaining three or four pages, we see the characters undergoing every change under the sky – from concentration to exhaustion to playfulness, from fond closeness to stiffened withdrawal. And my quotation by itself contains simultaneous contrary feelings: as when Birkin 'stood smiling in frustration and amusement and irritation and admiration and love. She was so quick, and so lambent, like discernible fire, and so vindictive, in her dangerous flamy sensitiveness.'

'Dangerous flamy sensitiveness': this could also be the way to describe Lawrence's humour, his stance, in 'Mino'. The chapter has a sort of 'openness' which is quite different from the 'generous impartiality' I attributed (unoriginally enough) to Tolstoy. This openness of Lawrence's is a dangerous or reckless willingness to entertain the most drastic sardonic thoughts about both sides in the argument. Ursula has the last word; the word is *yes*, and it follows her making him come out with *love* as the last-word-but-one.

She [was] looking down at him with strange golden-lighted eyes, very tender, but with a curious devilish look lurking underneath.

"Say you love me, say 'my love' to me," she pleaded . . . in a strong, voluptuous voice of yielding. . .

She put her arms round his neck. He enfolded her, and kissed her subtly, murmuring in a subtle voice of love, and irony, and submission. . .   (*WL* 154:7–10, 19–23)

– and he obliges, or obeys. We meet again that yellow-lit presence looming over a man at the very end of 'Moony': 'She believed that love was *everything*. Man must render himself up to her: he must be quaffed to the dregs by her. Let him be *her man* utterly, and she in return would be his humble slave—whether he wanted it or not' (*WL* 265:6–9: Lawrence's italics). We've met it earlier, in 'An Island': 'he cried. "Let the old meanings go." "But still it is love," she persisted. A strange, wicked yellow light shone at him in her eyes' (*WL* 130:17–20). What Birkin calls her 'war-cry' of 'Do you love me?' (*WL* 251:29, 32) throws our mind forward to a far-from-humorous moment in 'Snowed Up', when Gudrun

> held her arms round [Gerald's] neck, in a triumph of pity. And her pity for him was as cold as stone, its deepest motive was hate of him, and fear of his power over her, which she must always counterfoil.
>
> "Say you love me," she pleaded. "Say you will love me forever— won't you—won't you?" [And he does.]
>
> She gave him a quick kiss.
>
> "Fancy your actually having said it," she said, with a touch of raillery.
>
> He stood as if he had been beaten.
>
> "Try to love me a little more, and to want me a little less," she said, in a half contemptuous, half coaxing tone.   (*WL* 443:5–10, 18–23)

So Ursula's domination-through-submission is treated with a good deal less than Chaucer's humour on this topic, in the Wife of Bath's Prologue. Even in 'its lighter moments' Birkin's defeat attracts something like the grisly humour of Looloo's 'grievous resignation' at being both caricatured and caressed, parodied and pitied, by Gudrun's kindred spirit Winifred (*WL* 235:40).

But now we come to the reckless swing of extremes in chapters like

'Mino' and 'Moony'. Although Lawrence suggests, in those images of wicked yellow light hanging over Birkin, that he has good reason to see moon as Overbearing Woman and to chuck stones at it, nonetheless Ursula is equally justified in suspecting that all that dragging in of the stars masks a will to power on Birkin's part, an unholy alliance of Nietzschean superman-stuff and Bismarckian power-politics. Indeed his violent moonbashing may be more of a parallel than a contrast with the frenzied rabbit called Bismarck in the next chapter. And Ursula scores a point when she says the cat Mino 'is just like Gerald Crich with his horse—a lust for bullying—... Wille zur Macht'. In one of the most interesting articles on the novel, Richard Drain shows that the later paragraphs of the moon-stoning portray Birkin as 'brutal aggressor' and the moon as

> oppressed victim, desperate to escape, 'tormented': 'flakes of light appeared here and there, glittering tormented among the shadows....' The percussive crashing of the stones, the sense of rhythmic chaos and climactic break-up, recall nothing so closely as the effect of the train upon Gerald's horse when he forces it to stand at the level crossing in an earlier chapter. Birkin, who sides with Gerald then, is in Gerald's role here.[38]

And Drain goes on with a suggested correspondence I at first resisted:

> The chapter title 'Moony' teasingly echoes the earlier 'Mino', and Lawrence's choice of name for the cat wryly suggests that the fitting mate for a would-be human Mino is not an Ursula but a Minette.[39]

That verbal chain exists only in the novel's censored version, which for legal reasons replaced 'Pussum' with 'Minette'. But then Pussum (shades of sex-kitten or pussy-galore) connected equally well with the 'fluffy bit' of feline chaos in the 'Mino' chapter. And Lawrence was quick to make an artistic virtue out of legal necessity, choosing the name Minette to match Mino and Moony, and enabling Gerald to complain to his nothing-if-not-critical friend that 'I can't see what you will leave me at all, to be interested in ... Neither the Minettes, nor the mines, nor anything else.' The 'anything else' includes the money, which he makes from the mines and regrets not leaving with Minette to '[close] the account' (*WL* 97:16–18, 96:30–1).

VI

Wordplay, an authority on the subject shows, 'was a game that Elizabethans played seriously'.[40] So did Lawrence, my previous paragraph suggests; but in *Women in Love* with more seriousness than playfulness or humour of the generous or forgiving Tolstoyan sort. John Bayley remarks that the surprise and generosity of *Anna Karenin* is that it presents two positive cases (three, I'd say) where we might expect a positive and a negative.[41] In pointing out those parallels of mine, *Minette, money, Mino* and *Moony*, I've perhaps given the impression that, where readers like Leavis used to find in *Women in Love* positive and negative examples of human relationships, I find two negatives. It may seem that all my avenues of enquiry, all my hunt for humour, lead to something like Anna Karenin's final question: "Are we not all flung into the world for no other purpose than to hate each other, and so to torture ourselves and one another" (*AK* 797). An obvious answer would be that my sampling of Birkin and Ursula, and my linking (rather than contrasting) of them with Gerald and Gudrun, all come from the first half of the novel, before they allegedly 'come through'. But the answer I prefer is that, in the volatile moods of a confrontation like that in 'Mino' – in its variable human weather which Lawrence treats with variable shades of humour – there are constant irruptions of disarming good humour both on Lawrence's part and on that of his protagonists. Such a moment comes at tea in 'Mino' and breaks into Birkin's 'abstract earnestness', his 'battling with his soul' while Ursula is 'jeering' and 'mocking' (*WL* 145:39, 146:19–20, 147:22). I'll pick up from where my previous quotation from the chapter broke off:

> An interrupted silence fell over the two of them, a moment of breach.
> "Come and have tea," he said.
> "Yes, I should love it," she replied, gathering herself together.
> They sat facing each other across the tea-table.

"I did not say, nor imply, a satellite. I meant two single equal stars balanced in conjunction—"

"You gave yourself away, you gave away your little game completely," she cried, beginning at once to eat. He saw that she would take no further heed of his expostulations, so he began to pour the tea.

"What *good* things to eat!" she cried.

"Take your own sugar," he said.

He handed her her cup. He had everything so nice, such pretty cups and plates, painted with mauve-lustre and green, also shapely bowls and glass plates, and old spoons, on a woven cloth of pale grey and black and purple. It was very rich and fine. But Ursula could see Hermione's influence.

"Your things are so lovely!" she said, almost angrily.

"*I* like them. It gives me real pleasure to use things that are attractive in themselves—pleasant things. And Mrs Daykin is good. She thinks everything is wonderful, for my sake."

"Really," said Ursula, "landladies are better than wives, nowadays. They certainly *care* a great deal more. It is much more beautiful and complete here now, than if you were married."

"But think of the emptiness within," he laughed.

(*WL* 151:17–152:2)

They don't remain free of anger and jeering for long. And in the words of that little poem by Blake I alluded to earlier, the book directs much of its energy to dissecting those who 'bind to themselves a joy, and the winged life destroy'.[42] But there's plenty in the novel to illustrate the other half of that Blake poem:

> He who kisses the joy as it flies
> Lives in Eternity's sunrise.[43]

Perhaps those lines were in Birkin's mind when he reflects, in 'Moony' (*WL* 250:16–19), 'What was the good of talking, any way? It must happen beyond the sound of words. It was merely ruinous to try to work her by conviction. This was a paradisal bird that could never be netted, it must fly by itself to the heart.'[44]

Notes

1 *Phoenix: The Posthumous Papers of D.H. Lawrence*, ed. Edward D. McDonald (New York: Viking, 1936), p. 306.

2 The last word gives an early warning of my divergence from F.R. Leavis, who found 'many different kinds of smile and laughter, though never the cruel, the malicious or the complacent' (*D.H. Lawrence: Novelist*, Chatto & Windus, 1955, p. 13).

3 *The Savage Pilgrimage: A Narrative of D.H. Lawrence* (Martin Secker, 1932), p. 156.

4 Ibid., pp. viii, xi.

5 Catherine Carswell, 'D.H. Lawrence' [a letter to the editor], *Time and Tide*, 11 (14 March 1930), 342; reprinted Nehls, iii. 463.

6 Carswell, *The Savage Pilgrimage*, p. 18.

7 Ibid., p. 148.

8 *Phoenix*, ed. McDonald, pp. 314–21; *Study of Thomas Hardy and Other Essays*, ed. Bruce Steele (Cambridge: Cambridge University Press, 1985), pp. 151–5.

9 *Reflections on the Death of a Porcupine and Other Essays*, ed. Michael Herbert (Cambridge: Cambridge University Press, 1988), 189:1.

10 'Foreword to *Women in Love*', *Women in Love*, ed. David Farmer, Lindeth Vasey and John Worthen (Cambridge: Cambridge University Press, 1987), 485:6–7. Subsequent references to this edition will appear in the text in the form (*WL* 485:6–7).

11 George Eliot, *Daniel Deronda* (Edinburgh: Blackwood & Sons, 1878), p. 224.

12 *The Rainbow*, ed. Mark Kinkead-Weekes (Cambridge: Cambridge University Press, 1989), 9:18–21.

13 Thomas Hardy, *Tess of the D'Urbervilles* (Macmillan, 1928), p. 453.

14 *The Rainbow*, ed. Kinkead-Weekes, 65:38–9.

15 William Hazlitt, *Characters of Shakespeare's Plays* in *The Complete Works*, ed. P.P. Howe (Dent, 1930), pp. 191 and 260. DHL worked hard at heightening these elements in his rewriting of an earlier draft of this episode: see Howard Mills, 'Stylistic Revision of *Women in Love* (The Prologue/The Wedding Chapter)', *Études Lawrenciennes*, no. 3 (Université de Paris X), 1988, pp. 99–108.

16 *Twilight in Italy and Other Essays*, ed. Paul Eggert (Cambridge: Cambridge University Press, 1994), 162:28–32.

17 T.S. Eliot, *The Complete Poems and Plays* (Faber and Faber, 1969), pp. 32, 194.

18 *The Rainbow*, ed. Kinkead-Weekes, 103:31–8, 104:5–6.

19 *The Savage Pilgrimage*, p. 65.

20 Kerker Quinn, 'Lawrence as Critic and Artist', *Yale Review* (June 1937), 847; quoted by Simonetta de Filippis in her Introduction to *Sketches of Etruscan Places and Other Italian Essays* (Cambridge: Cambridge University Press, 1992), p. lxxii.

21 *The Rainbow*, ed. Kinkead-Weekes, 246:34, 247:35.

22 Ibid., 106:3.

23 Ibid., 183:3, 190:13, 15–16.

24 Hardy, *Tess of the D'Urbervilles*, p. 194.

25 Shakespeare, *King Lear*, iv.ii.26.

26 *The Savage Pilgrimage*, p. 69.

27 *The Rainbow*, ed. Kinkead-Weekes, 29:24, 40:20, 1.

28 Leo Tolstoy, *Anna Karenin*, trans. Rosemary Edmonds (Harmondsworth: Penguin Books, reprinted with revisions 1978), p. 311. Subsequent references to this edition will appear in the text in the form (*AK* 311).

29 DHL describes one such incident in a letter to Edward Garnett, 17 July 1914 (ii.199).

30 'Lawrence on Hardy' in *Thomas Hardy after Fifty Years*, ed. L. St. J. Butler (Macmillan, 1978), p. 90.

31 'The Novel', *Study of Thomas Hardy*, ed. Steele, 180:6–7.

32 *Study of Thomas Hardy*, ed. Steele, 24:11–12.

33 *Fantasia of the Unconscious* (Harmondsworth: Penguin Books, 1971), p. 15.

34 '*Anna Karenina' and Other Essays* (Chatto & Windus, 1967), p. 32.

35 *The Savage Pilgrimage*, p. 67.

36 *Sea and Sardinia* (Secker, 1927), p. 146.

37 *Flame into Being: The Life and Works of D.H. Lawrence* (Heinemann, 1985), p. 114.

38 Richard Drain, '*Women in Love*' in *D.H. Lawrence: A Critical Study of the Major Novels and Writings*, ed. Andor Gomme (Hassocks: Harvester, 1978), p. 88.

39 Ibid.

40 M.M. Mahood, *Shakespeare's Wordplay* (Methuen, 1957). p. 9.

41 *Tolstoy and the Novel* (Chatto & Windus, 1966), p. 224.

42 William Blake, *The Poems*, ed. W.H. Stevenson (Longman, 1971), p. 162.

43 Ibid.

44 My concluding sentences are influenced by the last paragraph of Richard Drain's essay (see note 38). While checking references I realised that he also quotes the couplet from Blake which I first use in a different context in the third paragraph of my essay.

～ 3

Comedy and hysteria in *Aaron's Rod*

John Turner

Humor is warm, wit cold,
Wit can be a common scold,
But humor can laugh and do no harm:
For wit is cold and humor warm
    (Witter Bynner; 'O For a Witless Age')[1]

Accusations of humourlessness have always dogged Lawrence, both as a man and writer. Witter Bynner's little poem, inspired by the Lawrence he knew in Mexico, creates the familiar picture of a 'passionate puritan',[2] full of high seriousness and low malice, but lacking the humour which bespeaks a sense of proportion towards ourselves and, towards others, the forgiveness of sins. Philip Heseltine agreed with Bynner: 'no one had a keener sense of the absurdities and weaknesses of others. But of true humour, the humour of God and man as opposed to angel and devil, Lawrence was fundamentally incapable.' Indeed, Heseltine thought, it is more than likely that 'Lawrence's incontestable greatness in some respects, both as man and artist, was directly due to his lack of humour.'

Yet Lawrence's letters show a man much interested in comedy, and committed to comedy in his own work, especially in the novels after *Women in Love* where, with lighter touch, he deliberately set out to reach a wider audience.[3] *The Lost Girl* 'does so amuse me', he wrote (iii. 503); *Aaron's Rod* 'is funny. It amuses me terribly' (iii. 227); whilst *Mr Noon* too, he thought, was 'funny, but a hair-raiser' in which he took 'much wicked joy' (iii. 702, 646). Clearly there is a disparity between Lawrence's sense of his own work and its usual critical reception; and this disparity constitutes a part of my subject here. For the nature of the comic writing in *Aaron's Rod* is inseparably bound up with the question of its author's reputation for humourlessness; as we shall see, a discussion by the one is by its very nature an account of the other.

70

> Why did I laugh to-night? No voice will tell;
> No god, no demon of severe response,
> Deigns to reply from heaven or from hell.
> Then to my human heart I turn at once   [4]

'Why did I laugh to night?' When Keats asked himself that question in 1819, he turned first to a god or 'demon of severe response' for an answer; and when none was forthcoming, he turned to his 'human heart'. But still he found no answer. Laughter, it seems, is a mystery, implicated with our profoundest attempts to image and understand our own humanity. Keats, for all his relish in 'Verse, fame, and beauty',[5] had been sure in his conscious mind that he wanted to die; but suddenly a burst of laughter issuing from deep in his unconscious had discomposed him. Whether happy or cynical (and it may be a measure of Keats's surprise that he does not say which), his laughter had possessed an energy which disturbed him in the ease of his former certainties.

We find a similarly unaccountable and disruptive burst of laughter in chapter III of *Aaron's Rod*:

> Jim suddenly doubled himself up and burst into a loud harsh cackle of laughter. Whoop! he went, and doubled himself up with laughter. Whoop! Whoop! he went, and fell on the floor, and writhed with laughter. He was in that state of intoxication when he could find no release from maddening self-consciousness. He knew what he was doing, he did it deliberately. And yet he was also beside himself, in a sort of hysterics. He could not help himself, in exasperated self-consciousness.[6]

Why did Jim Bricknell laugh that night? Lawrence gives no answer. His novel guards the mystery that baffled Keats; and yet, in Jim Bricknell's laughter, we may find, in negative, an epitome of everything that Lawrence wished to celebrate in *Aaron's Rod*.

Since Lawrence gives us no answer directly, we must approach our question contextually. After the pictures of working-class life in the first two chapters of the novel, chapter III introduces us to five Bohemian sons and daughters of the bourgeoisie. It is Christmas Eve and, after an evening of systematic drinking and desultory flirtation, a common purpose briefly animates them all: to decorate a fir-tree in the garden with candles. In chapters I and II the rituals of a Christian Christmas had only served to confirm the tensions and irritability of everyday working-class family life; and now the dilettantes of Bohemia find the emptiness of their daily lives confirmed as, in a characteristic act of cultural bricolage, they toy with a pagan ritual of tree-worship. Despite a certain vestigial power, such rituals no longer generate the sense of social cohesion.

Nor is it the socially cohesive that interests Lawrence but the eccentric: in his own word, the 'odd' (*AR* 26:3). Aaron in chapter I, the Jewish landlady of the ironically named 'Royal Oak' in chapter II, the Bricknell family in chapter III: all are people who, in their different ways, feel themselves to be alienated from the central practices of their society. What makes Jim Bricknell remarkable amongst these outsiders is the sustained malice with which he observes the goings-on around him. Sardonically, he stands detached even from his own group, watching with the impassivity of a Red Indian. From the start his smile has been fixed upon his face in a mirthless amusement that brings 'a wild tremor' (*AR* 30:11) to the heart of his father and even discomforts his fiancée Josephine Ford. Three times he erupts into laughter. The first is when Robert Cunningham, who is flirting with Josephine, waxes romantic over the ringing of church bells. This causes Jim to roll in his chair 'in an explosion of sudden, silent laughter, showing his mouthful of pointed teeth, like a dog' (*AR* 31:13–15); and the military connotation of 'explosion' here epitomises – as do countless similar metaphors throughout *Women in Love* and *Aaron's Rod* – the analysis that Lawrence will offer of post-war England. The second is when Robert's wife Julia begins her dance in worship of the tree. This brings 'a short, harsh, cackling laugh' from Jim: '"Aren't we fools!" he cried. "What? Oh God's love, aren't we fools!"' (*AR* 32:39–33:2). It seems to be the fellow-contraries of faithlessness and sentimentality in modern life that provoke him here.

His third outbreak of laughter – 'in a sort of hysterics', as we have seen – follows the unexpected arrival of Aaron Sisson, absconding from Christmas with his family. Suddenly the emergent harmony of the candle-lit scene in the garden is disrupted as the young people realise that a stranger has been watching them. Jim the observer now finds himself observed; and it may be that Aaron's working-class origins, clearly declared by his clothes, fill the would-be revolutionary Jim with a renewed sense of the folly of these favoured children of the bourgeoisie. Perhaps he senses that Aaron is about to break away more effectively than any of these young Bohemians can; or perhaps his laughter is no more than a cynical amusement at the universal dissolution of Christian family values. Whatever its final meaning, however, the immediate cause of Jim's laughter is Robert's treatment of Aaron. 'Anything you wanted?' he asks peremptorily (*AR* 33:31), with the authority of one only recently demobbed; and soon he will urge Aaron to get back to his 'wife and kiddies' (*AR* 36:26). Jim's fit of laughter, if provoked by a sense of the folly of the haute bourgeoisie, is also a recognition of their presumption – given the treachery and infidelity of their own lives – in daring to tell the working classes how to live. Jim, it seems, can see through the old world, though he cannot see his own way through to a new; and hence, half-patronisingly and half-admiringly, he takes up Aaron as a possible solution to the problems of his own life.

Jim will behave hysterically again in chapter VIII ('A Punch in the Wind') when he is driven by Rawdon Lilly's taunts to punch him in the wind. Lilly himself had been stung into contempt both by Jim's behaviour – asking Lilly to 'save' him, then flirting with his wife – and by the beliefs that express and justify such behaviour. For Jim, whilst professing himself a believer in the self-sacrifice of Christian love, also admires the treachery of Judas. 'The finest thing the world has produced, or ever will produce—Christ and Judas', he says (*AR* 78:18–19), with a sardonic complacency that manifests the growing impotence of Christianity to articulate and hierarchise ethical experience in a coherent form. Lilly has a new faith to offer, grounded in independence and self-responsibility; but Jim, a wolf who believes in the lamb, is left to stumble from contradiction to contradiction – all in the name of a love which he needs as a child might need it, which he dignifies as self-sacrifice to a higher principle and which he then betrays with relish. It makes Lilly, already enraged by Jim's flirtation and his wife's responsiveness, quite sick: '*You want to be loved*, you want to be loved—a man of your years. It's disgusting—' (*AR* 82:12–14). At this Jim gets up and punches him in the solar plexus. 'I knew

I should have to do it, if he said any more', he says (*AR* 82:24), and sheep-
ishly sits down again. It may seem a spontaneously violent act; but in
Lawrence's narrative the act rings false. 'To Lilly, rigid and physically preoccupied, there sounded a sort of self-consciousness in Jim's voice, as if
the whole thing had been semi-deliberate. IIe detected the sort of
maudlin deliberateness which goes with hysterics, and he was colder,
more icy than ever' (*AR* 83:3–6).

Hysterical in laughter and hysterical in rage: Jim's behaviour epitomises the spirit of post-war England as Lawrence portrays it in *Aaron's
Rod*. 'It is the last of my serious English novels,' he said, 'the end of *The
Rainbow, Women in Love* line. It had to be written – and had to come to
such an end' (iv. 92–3). The opening paragraph of *Aaron's Rod* senses
how 'the violence of the nightmare' of the war has been released into the
general air of England (*AR* 5:6), spreading an infection that will manifest
itself not only in Jim's hysterics but also in the almost unconscious
weeping of Josephine in chapter VII, the war-neuroses of Captain
Herbertson and Angus Guest, and the sobbing of Lottie in chapter XI,
where Aaron detects amidst all her distress 'a luxuriating in the violent
emotions of the scene in hand, and the situation altogether' (*AR*
126:24–5). Such violent feeling has a secret underground life of its own,
like the pit-bank fire that smoulders throughout chapter III or, on the
broader European stage of the second half of the book, like the bomb
that shatters Italian cafe-society in chapter XX. It is compulsive and – in
the perverse fashion which Lawrence associates with hysterical behaviour – pleasurable. Lottie's tearful performance recalls the production of
Aida in chapter V; for everywhere in the novel we find a histrionic society
described in theatrical terms. The clearest example is in the vivid street
'scene' of chapter XIV (*AR* 186:34); but again and again, we see the melo-
dramatic staginess of modern life, with its hysterical passions, and can
only guess by contrast at the possibility of 'a proper world' ritually
united in 'a common purpose and a common sympathy'.[7]

Lawrence seems to use the term 'hysterics' in its popular sense of 'a
convulsive fit of laughter or weeping' (*OED*2). But we should remember
the technical definition of 'hysteria' in contemporary psychoanalysis if
we want to appreciate fully the alternative diagnosis of the characteristic

ailments of his civilisation that Lawrence is offering here; for *Aaron's Rod* is a deliberate attempt to challenge a concept which Lawrence knew to be already under revision in analytic circles as a result of the 'male hysteria' experienced in the First World War.[8] In so far as classical analysis had a comprehensive theory of hysteria, it was believed to originate in the denial of childhood sexual memories; its characteristic defences were repression and dissociation; its characteristic feature was the conversion of mental ideas into physical symptoms for which no organic cause could be found; and its expression in histrionic behaviour was seen as a largely unconscious strategy designed either to attract attention to the sufferer or to distract attention away from the real cause of his or her suffering. Lawrence, however, does not trace the origins of hysterical behaviour either to the repression of sexual memories or, more generally, to the repression of sexual desire. He turns instead to the lack of religious community and religious hope in a contemporary culture that cannot meet the existential crisis facing it; and the word 'religious' here has the idiosyncratic (and unattractively gendered) meaning that Lawrence himself gave it in *Fantasia of the Unconscious*, where it signifies 'the desire of the human male to build a world',[9] to create beliefs, values, artefacts or simply ways of living that are capable of sustaining his sense of wonder in life.

The theme of *Aaron's Rod* is the bankruptcy of the beliefs, values, artefacts and ways of living that are to be found in the world of the early twentieth century. Men (and women too), in attempting to accommodate themselves to outworn cultural ideals, do themselves an inner violence which only serves to breed further violence – a violence of which the war was but one expression and Aaron's 'black dog' another. Here is the vicious circle in which Jim Bricknell, like most of the other characters in the novel, finds himself spinning. He has no 'religion' in Lawrence's sense of the word, and does no work: 'He spent his time wavering about and going to various meetings, philandering and weeping' (*AR* 74:33–5). His tears – in a novel full of tears – are the psychosomatic expression of a dissociation which has set mind against body, conscious against unconscious and self-consciousness against spontaneity. Like the classic hysteric, he inscribes upon his body the suffering of his mind; his psychic hunger creates in him the delusion that he is unnaturally thin so that, at the Lillys' cottage, he devours the best part of a loaf of bread to fatten himself up. But man shall not live by bread alone. 'What do you reckon stars are?', Jim asks in a sepulchral voice, when his laughter dies down (*AR* 34:29). The silence of these infinite spaces, it seems, frightens him; with no religious belief to connect him with the universe and its inhabitants, he languishes in a dissociation which Lawrence thinks typical of his age. 'The emotions that have not the approval and inspiration of the mind are just hysterics' he wrote. 'The mind without the approval and inspiration of the emotions is just a dry stick, a dead tree, no good for anything unless to make a rod to beat and bully somebody with.'[10]

Hence the hysterical nature of Jim's laughter in chapter III, and of his anger in chapter VIII: the unity of his body and mind has broken down, leaving him lost amidst ideas which are no more than self-contradictory rationalisations of perverse and warring desires. Unlike Anna Brangwen's giggling in church in *The Rainbow*, which forms part of her initiation into a new period of her life, Jim's laughter is no rite of passage. It is the laughter of a man who refuses to take responsibility for his own unhappiness. His life, like his father's house, languishes at the end of a cul-de-sac, and his hysterical fit is one of those gifts reserved for men and women whose growth in years brings a withering of hope: 'the laceration/Of laughter at what ceases to amuse'.[11] There is none of the liberating grace of true comedy here: neither laughter nor rage offers him a way out of the dead end of his own life and that of the culture around him. Jim may be drawn to Aaron, but it is no surprise when Aaron silently leaves early next morning; for there is nothing in Jim that might hold out hope to a man who, however unconsciously, has risen to free himself from the nightmare of history.

> Essayez, un moment, de vous intéresser à tout ce qui dit et à tout ce qui se fait ... vous verrez les objets les plus légers prendre du poids, et une coloration sévère passer sur toutes choses. Détachez-vous maintenant, assistez à la vie en spectateur indifférent: bien des drames tourneront à la comédie.
>
> [Try, for a moment, to become interested in everything that is being said and done ... you will see the flimsiest of objects assume

importance, and a gloomy hue spread over everything. Now step
aside, look upon life as a disinterested spectator: many a drama will
turn into a comedy.]　　　　　　　　　　　　(Henri Bergson, *Le Rire*)[12]

Aaron's departure from the Bricknell house is one expression of a need
that Lawrence valorises throughout the whole novel: the need to put
oneself at a distance, physically and psychically, from a world whose
moral and emotional claims have gone dead. Even on the first page of the
novel, Aaron is beginning the long process of withdrawal. Coming
home, late, from a union meeting, he walks up the side path of his house
and into his own backyard. 'There he hung a moment, glancing down the
dark, wintry garden' (*AR* 5:17–18). It is a moment of initiation, in which
the reader too hesitates on the threshold of a family, a working-class
culture and indeed a whole society whose domestic life has become
frozen in what Thomas Hardy called 'the antipathetic, recriminatory
mood of the average husband and wife of Christendom'.[13] Aaron's wife
seems a typical woman of her class: trapped in a marriage that cannot
compensate her for the self-sacrifice it demands, she develops a bitterness that paradoxically enables her to accept it. She is a living proof of
Ibsen's dictum that 'the smoke of sacrifice does not always rise'.[14] Aaron's
response to her nagging is perhaps characteristic of most men in his
culture and is certainly characteristic of Aaron himself: 'A blank look had
come over the man's face, as if he did not hear or heed any more' (*AR*
8:30–1). He assumes a mask that helps him to keep his distance.

The question of the new perspectives brought by distance is crucial to
Lawrence's strategy in *Aaron's Rod*; in chapter after chapter he plays with
unconventional perspectives in order to loosen conventional attach-
ments. Jim's aloofness and Aaron's inaccessibility are used in chapter III
to distance us from the shallow febrility of the young Bohemians; and
chapter v ('At the Opera') places the same young people in a box so close
to the stage that they cannot but see through the illusion of the stage performance. Art, like love, disappoints them; effete as they are, they find
the heroic love celebrated by their nineteenth-century forebears a trans-
parent sham, unable any longer to sustain either an individual sense of
wonder or a communal sense of culture.

The most unsettling perspectives in *Aaron's Rod*, however, occur in chapters IV and XI ('The Pillar of Salt' and 'More Pillar of Salt') as twice, from the security of his garden shed, the unseen Aaron surveys the home he has deserted. 'It was like looking at his home through the wrong end of a telescope', he thought (*AR* 39:12–13). Yet this is the perspective that he needs in order to resist the impingements of family life, with all its insatiable demands upon him. Jealously the outsider must guard his inner space. Later on, in Italy, he finds a new perspective: 'the people seemed little upright brisk figures moving in a certain isolation, like tiny figures on a big stage. And he felt himself moving in the space between. All the northern cosiness gone. He was set down with a space round him' (*AR* 151:39–152:2). Even when the expatriate community presses him close, the old defences still work; the deceptively attractive glimmer on Aaron's face, we read, 'only meant that he was looking on the whole scene from the outside, as it were from beyond a fence' (*AR* 141:29–30). He has come abroad to safeguard the foreignness of his inner self; and – like Lilly in chapter IX, high above Covent Garden and the busy everyday world – Aaron most typically looks out upon this new world from a hotel window in Milan ('XX Settembre') and from a high attic-terrace in Florence ('High Up over the Cathedral Square').

The fictional arabesque that lifts Aaron out of the claustrophobia of a working-class Midlands family and sets him down amidst the spaciousness of Northern Italy involves him in a long process of defamiliarisation which begins by estranging him from his own home and ends by estranging him from himself. 'His mask, his idea of himself dropped and was broken to bits. There he sat now maskless and invisible' (*AR* 163:30–1): by the time he reaches Novara, Lawrence tell us, Aaron resembles Wells's invisible man, visible in his clothing but invisible in his nakedness. The comparison suggests much about the fictional purpose of Aaron's taciturnity; of the characteristic absence of his presence; even of the musicality of his gifts within the essentially verbal form of the novel. For in his remoteness Aaron frustrates our usual idea of a fictional hero. His aloofness from the emotional, moral and political claims made upon him balks our desire as readers to involve ourselves in the novel as we ordinarily involve ourselves in real life. We too become estranged from our everyday concerns; and it is this estrangement that much of the comedy in the book is designed to encourage. For, as Bergson wrote in his essay *Le Rire*, the effectiveness of comedy depends upon its ability to distance our sympathies from the daily goings-on of life. 'Step aside, look upon life as a disinterested spectator: many a drama will turn into a comedy.' Even Bergson's theatrical images parallel Lawrence's own, as he tries to show Aaron in his role as *spectator ab extra*.

The real *spectator ab extra* in the novel, however, is also its creator: Lawrence himself in his role as novelist. It is he who inhabits the ultimate distances of his text and occupies its final perspectives. Yet his presence too is strangely absent; and here lies the clue to the chief difference between *Aaron's Rod* and the traditional comedy of manners which lies behind so much of the book. Often in the nineteenth century – in Austen or James, for instance – the authorial presence had been elusive, hidden within the texture of a comedy that demanded of its readers an intelligence thought to be necessary to the discriminations of true virtue and the establishment of a virtuous society. But in Lawrence the authorial presence does not act as a discipline in this way at all. The imperative of good manners has evaporated altogether; comedy has deserted the service of good conduct and community. Bergson, who had the comedy of manners in mind when writing *Le Rire*, thought the purpose of laughter was to generate social solidarity by ridiculing deviancy; but to Lawrence comedy offered a way to breach that social solidarity. His comedy is not the redefinition of a desirable society but the dissolution of an undesirable one; and hence it often seems an esoteric rather than a communal art, aiming not to recall its readers to common ideals of conduct but to awaken the elect amongst those readers to their full existential liberty. He that hath ears to hear, let him hear.

The novel begins with the comedy of Millicent's breaking the blue ball, the delicate Christmas ornament which had once belonged to her father. She has been performing, acting up, creating – the colloquial expressions say it all – and finally she throws the ball wildly into the air with the clear intention of breaking it. Her gesture is in part an act of revenge against her father; but it is also an act which recognises the nature and the symbolism of the ball itself. Its fragile beauty – which, like

Mozart's art to her father, is a lie to the truth of Millicent's world – arouses her ambivalence; its perfect shape – which, like the happy family Christmas which it symbolises, is a lie to her own sense of the family circle – excites her violence. 'She wanted to break it' says Aaron (*AR* 11:10). It is a natural wish, especially in children, to smash the order of the world which holds them in thrall; it is even a mechanism of change and evolution. Aaron's wife, however, immediately denies that Millicent had meant to break the ball, and Millicent herself in consequence bursts into a flood of tears – the first tears in this tearful book. Such a denial is an attempt by the mother to put herself and her daughter on the side of the angels; and yet to be on the side of the angels means that she must lie to herself, mystify her daughter and condemn the anger which she is placing under taboo to a continued half-life in the guise of hysteria.

Aaron, however, breaches the taboo; he thinks the unthinkable and speaks the unspeakable. 'She wanted to break it'; and he wants to see it when it is broken. His chief feeling seems to be one of relief – a reaction, Lawrence thought, common to people who break taboos.[15] 'So—this was what it was. And this was the end of it. He felt the curious soft explosion of its breaking still in his ears. He threw his piece in the fire' (*AR* 11:16–19). Millicent has a child's ambivalence about possessions, being possessive and destructive by turns; but Aaron, albeit reluctantly, accepts their loss. The blue ball smashes, as his mask will later drop and be broken to bits, and his flute be blown to pieces. The whole of the novel is implicit in the breaking of the blue ball; and the comedy lies not in Aaron's perspective but in Lawrence's, as he contrasts Aaron's ability to consign the past to the flames with his wife's determination to hang on to it for fear of anything new. The comedy lies in the malicious exactitude of Lawrence's observation, as he exposes the obsessive idealism and the hysterical patterns of feeling that chain the future to the corpse of the past. The comedy is mixed, as Aaron himself discovers in telling his life story late at night in chapter xiv: 'A comedy it seemed, too, at that hour. And a comedy no doubt it was. But mixed, like most things in this life. Mixed' (*AR* 194:16–18). There is, in other words, some sympathy present for Aaron's wife and children; but more powerful still is the satire which, by breaching taboo, aims to 'lead our sympathy away in recoil from things gone dead'.[16]

There is a similarly mixed moment at the end of chapter III, when Jim awakes to find Aaron gone and, on the bedroom floor, 'two packets of Christmas-tree candles, fallen from the stranger's pockets' (*AR* 38:11–12). It is a daring and skilful invention on Lawrence's part, dividing the reader's loyalties between contradictory demands. Do we condemn Aaron for his selfishness in forgetting the commission given him by his wife and daughter? Or laugh at the fine carelessness that enables him to walk away from them? Both responses make themselves felt. Certainly Aaron's behaviour is not nice; but then Lawrence seems no more interested in Aaron's niceness than he is in Yvette's in *The Virgin and the Gipsy*.[17] Indeed, it takes a not very nice man to do the things that Aaron does; and these are the things that qualify him as our fictional hero. For surely, as the novel turns away with Aaron from his wife and daughters, our loyalty turns as well. Domestic concerns, important though they are, fall from Aaron as leaves from an autumn tree; and a small pulse of laughter at his carelessly dropping the candles, painful though the moment may be, dismantles still further the taboos that govern the burdensome family morality in the book.

But if we turn away from family loyalties, what shall we turn to? At the end of chapter VIII, after Jim has punched Lilly in the wind, there follows a richly comic scene in which Lilly, the most vocal of men, strives might and main to avoid showing the others that he has been left speechless. The chapter seems set to close with his determination never to see Jim again – 'a devil sat in the little man's breast', we read (*AR* 85:9) – when suddenly Tanny arrogates the last word to herself: 'You shouldn't play at little Jesus, coming so near to people, wanting to help them' (*AR* 85:10–11). Her malice is below the belt and takes the breath away; and yet her words have their truth, encouraging us to undertake a critical review of Lilly's performance here. He too, it seems, like Jim, is not without his contradictions: despite his faith in independence and self-responsibility, and despite his dislike of Jesus, 'he had a certain belief in himself as a saviour' (*AR* 73:23–4). The idealisms and feelings of the past are not so easily shaken off. Yet whereas Jim's contradictions are perverse, leading him to seek happiness where none is to be found, Lilly is more at ease with himself; his variousness, indeed, lies at the root of his creativity. Yet it is not a creativity that excels in comedy. The comedy of chapter VIII is Lawrence's own; and in so far as Lilly is a self-portrait, Lawrence's self-parody shows that it is not to the authority of his ideas but to his vitality as a writer, and particularly as a writer of comedy, that we must trust for the future.

For Lawrence's comedy in *Aaron's Rod* is a way of keeping faith with the future. In March 1921, while still writing the book, he had read Cyril Scott's satire *Blind Mice*, and disliked it for its 'emotional nihilism' – a nihilism he attributed to 'the vulgarity of the common code of virtue' which it upheld and yet whose bankruptcy it portrayed (iii. 691). It was a book quite without hope. '[I]f *only* he'd grinned', said Lawrence, 'even up his sleeve, what a marvellous satire it would have made. But he never grinned' (iii. 733). *Aaron's Rod*, however, is the novel of a man who did grin. If Lawrence had confined himself to satirising Aaron's selfishness or Lilly's hubris by the standards of 'the common code of virtue', he too, like Scott, would have been hankering after a past that had already failed. The house of his fiction would have rested upon pillars of salt, and its guardian angel would have been the spirit of hysteria, hungry like Jim for new life but unable to break free from the chains of the old. But Lawrence's comedy offers itself as an antidote to hysteria. It rejoices in the unpredictability of the future, and sustains our faith in that future not by code or convention but by the author's own elusive presence in the background, grinning in malice or self-mockery, and tirelessly offering us new perspectives for old. Aaron's recalcitrance and Lilly's indomitability may each induce in us an insouciance that is happy to jaunt with the author down the open road of his novel.

> The seriousness of the great God Pan, who grins a bit, and when he gets driven too hard, goes fierce. You are one of the very few people in the world at the moment who are capable of this: this fierce reckless-ness, based on trust, like the recklessness of Pan: trusting deep down to the springs of nature, the sources: and then the laughter.   (iv. 556)

These words of Lawrence to Mabel Dodge Luhan, dating from January 1924, respect the vitality of comedy as a religious power. As Keats turned to God or Demon to explain his laughter, so Lawrence invokes laughter as

one of the dark gods of our nature. Akin to malice and anger, it is one of the
original spontaneous powers of our nature, maintaining us in a spirit of
vital connexion with – and of vital resistance to – the world around us. In
his essay 'Pan in America', written in May 1924, Lawrence traces the death
of Pan to a long history of urbanisation, culminating in the modern
industrial world where our relationships with nature and one another are
largely instrumental in kind; and it is to combat this history that he
invokes the power of Pan. The laughter of Pan, he says, reveals 'the
uncanny derision of one who feels himself defeated by something lesser
than himself':[18] his smile is the smile of one who retains the consolation of
esoteric knowledge and the confirmation of esoteric powers, even amidst
the isolation of defeat. In a wonderful passage of *Aaron's Rod*, Lawrence
invokes that knowledge and those powers in order to repudiate, as best he
may, a modern post-war world where money is the only connection, 'the
only authority left' (*AR* 136:22). The passage in question comes at the end
of chapter XIII, and concludes the history of Aaron's discomfort amidst
the comforts provided by Sir William Franks and his wife in Novara.

The domestic economy of the Franks household is organised upon
principles opposite to those espoused by Aaron, and constitutes a special
kind of temptation to him. Sir William thinks life 'a storing-up of
produce and a conservation of energy', whilst Aaron thinks it 'a sheer
spending of energy and a storing-up of nothing but experience' (*AR*
155:33–6). It is a question of prudence and responsibility: whether a man's
duty is to make provision for his wife and family, or to go his own way and
trust to chance for the future. Sir William Franks has put his faith in
'Providence with a banking account' (*AR* 142:18), and sacrificed much
that was vital in himself to that belief. But once again the smoke of sacrifice does not rise: the old man is fearful of death because he has never
really lived. His wife too, despite her fierce protective will, is haunted by
the nightmare that the people of Novara are about to loot their house. She
works hard to hide the inner poverty brought by wealth and, true to the
habits of her class, uses art to help her. Beethoven, she says, convinces her
of the existence of a personal destiny that will restore to her everything
that she has ever lost. Aaron's temptation is to speculate upon such attitudes: to make music in order to charm money out of the bourgeoisie. But

the novel has other plans for him. His purse will be stolen and finally his flute blown up, in the long history of denudation that began with the breaking of the blue ball. While the Franks cling on to their personal possessions, Aaron acquiesces in the impersonal destiny that is dis-possessing him. Off, off, you lendings: the false self must be stripped away so that a new self may emerge and help to fashion a new historical age.

The temptation to prudence, in other words, has little power over Aaron; if he does his share of 'shoe-licking' while in the Franks' house-hold (*AR* 169:23), he will spit the boot-polish out as soon as he leaves. For beyond the claustrophobic opulence of their house lies the spaciousness of the Italian streets, where a new self can develop the 'almost swaggering carelessness which is Italy's best gift to an Englishman' (*AR* 152:12–13). Beyond their neglected gardens rise 'the tiger-like Alps' (*AR* 150:32), with a fearlessness and ferocity poised to empower the timidity of modern life. Even inside the house there is resistance, born out of the conviviality of a very good supper and the dampening effect of the deference due to wealth and power. When Sir William leaves the dining-room to join the ladies, the natural pride and the vitality of youth, warmed by alcohol, turn all his guests against him. Aaron, Arthur, the Colonel – even the Major, hag-ridden as he is by the nightmare of the post-war world – become increasingly drunk and high-spirited. All men together, and all but Aaron soldiers or ex-soldiers, the four of them lark about as they climb the stairs to where the others are waiting. 'The Colonel, oh awful man, did a sort of plump roly-poly cake-walk, like a fat boy, right to the very door of the sanctum-sanctorum, the library. Aaron was inwardly convulsed. Even the Major laughed' (*AR* 173:16–19).

But worse is to follow, as Lady Franks begins to play Schumann on the piano.

> Everybody listened in sanctified silence, trying to seem to like it. When suddenly our Colonel began to spring and bounce in his chair, sling-ing his loose leg with a kind of rapture up and down in the air, and capering upon his posterior, doing a sitting-down jig to the Schumann *vivace*. Arthur, who had seated himself at the farthest extremity of the room, winked with wild bliss at Aaron. The Major tried to look as if he noticed nothing, and only succeeded in looking

agonised. His wife studied the point of her silver shoe minutely, and peeped through her hair at the performance. Aaron grimly chuckled, and loved the Colonel with real tenderness.   (AR175:36–176:8)

It may be, as Lady Franks said in discussing Beethoven, that art confirmed her in her possessions and filled the gap they hollowed out in her emotional life; but Schumann here reveals a property of art which wholly escapes her possessiveness. His *vivace* arouses in the Colonel a Dionysiac joy that Beethoven himself might have approved, particularly the Beethoven of the seventh symphony in which Wagner saw 'Dance in its highest condition; the happiest realisation of the movements of the body in an ideal form'.[19]

For the comedy here, like carnival for Bakhtin, is a matter of the body – not the body abused, as in hysteria, but the body celebrated as the throne of Pan, Dionysos and all the other dark gods whom Lawrence venerates. The Colonel's wordless little jig, and the silence of the laughter it provokes, insert into the structures of social authority – including the structures of the author's own text – a power whose indeterminate yet contagious vitality establishes (in Bakhtin's words) 'a living contact with unfinished, still-evolving contemporary reality'.[20] It holds out hope of freer energies and richer social forms. Unlike the laughter of Jim Bricknell, which was the laughter of a man in chains, and unlike the smile of Sir William, which was the 'smile of old people when they are dead' (AR 139:31), the Colonel's laughter might really carry us through, out of the wilderness and into the promised – though as yet uncharted – land of the future. It is no accident that Aaron chuckles grimly as he watches the Colonel's jig; for as the Colonel's dance is touched with derision, so is Aaron's chuckle touched with malice. 'Among the creatures of Pan', Lawrence wrote, 'there is an eternal struggle for life, between lives';[21] and so too between the lives of individual people. The differences between Sir William and Aaron are for both men a matter of life and death; and the malice in Aaron's laugh is the power that turns him away from things gone dead, so that he may at last begin to trust in 'the springs of nature, the sources: and then the laughter'.

It is, of course, imaginable that a reader might find Aaron's laughter simply unmannerly; and here we come back to the point at which we began. Any account of Lawrence's comedy is simultaneously an account of his reputation for humourlessness. To accuse Aaron of unmannerliness – and Lady Franks is obviously offended, since suddenly 'Her playing went rather stiff' (AR 176:19) – is to claim the primary importance of consideration for others; while to laugh with him is to admit that there are times when the greater need is to consider oneself and to resist the rights of others. As Aaron sat in the Franks's garden, looking across at the Alps and the city of Novara, 'He felt some finger prodding, prodding, prodding him awake out of the sleep of pathos and tragedy and spasmodic passion' (AR 151:15–16). Pathos and tragedy and spasmodic passion: these are the words in which Lawrence sums up the self-sacrificial ethic of consideration and its corollary, the hysterical private life, which have been his subject in Aaron's Rod – and it is to this world (differently interpreted, of course) that the reader who finds Aaron unmannerly, and Lawrence's writing humourless, would return us. But the finger of the novelist prods Aaron into laughter: a grim chuckle which resists repression, self-sacrifice and hysteria alike. Aaron does not put this into words any more than Lawrence does; but their silence is rich in potentiality. Even in its wordlessness laughter may subvert authority, and become one of the springs of nature from which the future will flow.

Trust in the springs of nature – what Lawrence jocularly called 'Divine Providence' (iii. 594):[22] it is his own method in struggling to write the picaresque life of Aaron Sisson that he would also recommend to us. He that hath ears to hear, let him hear. If Jim Bricknell's infidelities make him untrustworthy, Aaron's do the reverse; for they show a man learning to trust in the springs of his own nature. As Lou Andreas-Salomé once wrote, 'people who are not "faithful" do not necessarily desert one person for another, but are often simply driven *home to themselves* and only then may make their way back to mankind again as though from a free universe'.[23] Aaron's Rod is the story of a man who is driven away from home in order to come home to himself. It is a serious novel, which often grins and, when driven too hard, grows fierce; and the quality of its writing claims our trust as it moves towards its indeterminate conclusion where the verbal man and the non-verbal man, the man who proposes and the man who resists, face one another like two aspects of the one person, and their words fall into final silence. It is a silence in which our sense of the author – still present in his absence, and empowered not by his personal ideas but by the impersonal springs of nature within him – remains to challenge us with his desire for 'a proper world' ritually united in 'a common purpose and a common sympathy'.

Notes

1 See Witter Bynner, *Journey with Genius: Recollections and Reflections concerning the D.H. Lawrences* (Peter Nevill, 1953), p. 166, for the complete text of the poem.

2 Bynner used the phrase as title of chapter XLI of his book.

3 Nehls, i. 353. See John Worthen, *D.H. Lawrence and the Idea of the Novel* (Macmillan, 1979), pp. 106–7, for a discussion of *The Lost Girl* as a would-be 'popular' novel.

4 John Keats, 'Why did I laugh to-night?' *The Complete Poems*, ed. Miriam Allott (Longman, 1970), p. 488, ll. 1–4.

5 Ibid., p. 489, l. 13.

6 *Aaron's Rod*, ed. Mara Kalnins (Cambridge: Cambridge University Press, 1988), 33:33–40. Subsequent references to this edition appear in the text in the form (*AR* 33:33–40).

7 Quoted in Knud Merrild, *With D.H. Lawrence in New Mexico* (Routledge & Kegan Paul, 1964), p. 12.

8 This phrase is the title of chapter VII of Elaine Showalter, *The Female Malady: Women, Madness and English Culture, 1830–1980* (Virago Press, 1987), a chapter studying the vicissitudes of the concept of hysteria in England at the time of the First World War.

9 *Fantasia of the Unconscious* (Harmondsworth: Penguin Books, 1971), p. 18.

10 'On Human Destiny' in *Reflections on the Death of a Porcupine and Other Essays*, ed. Michael Herbert (Cambridge: Cambridge University Press, 1988), 205:1–5.

11 T.S. Eliot, 'Little Gidding', *The Complete Poems and Plays* (Faber and Faber, 1969), p. 194.

12 *Le Rire: essai sur la signification du comique* in *Œuvres* (Presses Universitaires de France, 1959), p. 389; the translation here comes from *Laughter: An Essay on the Meaning of the Comic*, by Cloudesley Brereton and Fred Rothwell (Macmillan, 1911), p. 5.

13 *Jude the Obscure* (Macmillan, 1906), p. 372.

14 Henrik Ibsen, *Emperor and Galilean* (1873), I.

15 See *A Propos of "Lady Chatterley's Lover"*, in *Lady Chatterley's Lover*, ed. Michael Squires (Cambridge: Cambridge University Press, 1993), 307:15–16.

16 *Lady Chatterley's Lover*, ed. Squires, 101:20.

17 See my essay 'Purity and Danger in D.H. Lawrence's *The Virgin and the Gipsy*' in *D.H. Lawrence: Centenary Essays*, ed. Mara Kalnins (Bristol: Bristol Classical Press, 1986), especially pp. 151–6, for a discussion of this point.

18 'Pan in America', in *Phoenix: The Posthumous Papers of D.H. Lawrence*, ed. Edward D. McDonald (New York: Viking, 1936), p. 22.

19 George Grove, *Beethoven and his Nine Symphonies* (Oxford: Oxford University Press, 1896), p. 244. For the original German see *Gesammelten Schriften und Dichtungen* (Leipzig, 1872), iii, 113.

20 Mikhail Bakhtin, *The Dialogic Imagination: Four Essays*, ed. Michael Holquist, trans. Caryl Emerson and Michael Holquist (Austin: University of Texas Press, 1981), p. 7.

21 'Pan in America', *Phoenix*, ed. McDonald, p. 29.

22 DHL is describing the fitful progress of *Aaron's Rod*, and his uncertainty about its future direction.

23 *The Freud Journal*, trans. Stanley A. Leavy (Quartet Books, 1987), p. 123.

~ 4

D.H. Lawrence and his 'gentle reader': The furious comedy of *Mr Noon*

Lydia Blanchard

I

When the shadow of F.R. Leavis's great tradition passed across the work of D.H. Lawrence, it fixed, for a generation, Lawrence's reputation as a 'religious, earnest, suffering man', to quote Lawrence's own description of himself to Edward Garnett (ii. 165). That emphasis on moral earnestness was central to the creation of the canon of what most critics agree are Lawrence's greatest novels – *Sons and Lovers, The Rainbow* and *Women in Love*. Even critics who disagreed with Leavis's evaluation of Lawrence accepted his understanding that Lawrence's reputation rests on a moral vision, however much they might, like many feminist critics, have disagreed with Leavis's belief in the moral centrality of that vision.

For most readers, the establishment of the canon of three great novels inevitably diminished the work after *Women in Love*. Leavis himself diagnosed a problem with Lawrence's development, suggesting that Lawrence 'wrote his later books far too hurriedly'.[1] Among those critics who consider the later novels, few admire *The Lost Girl, Aaron's Rod, Kangaroo, The Boy in the Bush, The Plumed Serpent*. Critics who choose to study the later novels are most often critical or apologetic, arguing – like Judith Ruderman – that these works 'it is hoped, will never be considered Lawrence's finest'.[2] If readers have seen Lawrence as a novelist whose reputation is based primarily on his moral vision, then they have also judged his long fiction after *Women in Love*, with the problematic exception of *Lady Chatterley's Lover*, as not only undistinguished but – in its political and moral positions – preposterous. Most readers outside of Lawrence's most devoted followers have simply ignored his later work.

The publication in 1984 of a fuller version of Lawrence's *Mr Noon* has helped change that perspective, for this unfinished novel shows Lawrence entering into what Robert Alter has called 'The Other Great Tradition': the tradition of the playful, self-conscious, richly comic novel of writers such as Fielding, Sterne and Joyce. Lawrence's later fiction may well be best thought of as answering questions different from those addressed to his earlier work. *Mr Noon* is, among other things, Lawrence's analysis of the fictionality of his own fiction, a prolegomenon to the novel George Levine has called 'importantly about novel writing,' *Lady Chatterley's Lover*. Alter defined the self-conscious novel as one that 'systematically flaunts its own condition of artifice, . . . [probing] into the problematic relationship between real-seeming artifice and reality'.[3] *Mr Noon*, in its two parts, is just such a flaunting. In this novel Lawrence battles with his reader who will, in turn, battle back, and thus prepares the way for the parody of his own fiction that will come in *Lady Chatterley*.

Some of Lawrence's readers have sensed the potential for this development existing in his previous fiction. For example, Alter suggested that the open forms of *The Rainbow* and *Women in Love* realise Miguel de Unamuno's understanding that art must embody randomness; and Alan Friedman believed that *Women in Love* is elaborately self-conscious about its conclusions, embedding 'an explicit essay on the theory of fiction within the very text of [the] novel, almost in the manner of Fielding and Gide'.[4] But these studies addressed only the potential for Lawrence's full-scale consideration of the fictionality of his art: without *Mr Noon*, the pattern of development after *Women in Love* was less than clear. In *Mr Noon*, however, Lawrence began to approach his materials in a significantly different way.

If Lawrence continued to view himself as a prophet and sage, he nevertheless also realised he could not save the world through the verisimilitude of fictional realism, through the representation of individuals acting out their solutions to moral dilemmas in a social context. The more passionately Lawrence felt about his mission, the more he was rejected – through censorship and poor sales. If he were to succeed, he would have to create a new reader. Indeed, by January 1917, he had realised that: 'It is necessary now for me to address a new public' (iii. 73). He worked toward that goal through the last decade of his life. *Mr Noon* was the first important step.

II

In retrospect we may see Lawrence as a writer whose ideas have shaped the twentieth century, but Lawrence was far less sanguine about the possibility of significant influence. Certainly he wanted his work to change the lives of his readers – how else could the novel be the one bright book of life? – but Lawrence saw himself in battle with an audience that paid scant attention. What value the message of *The Rainbow* and *Women in Love* if it reached no one, or if it reached only readers who misread? In May 1917, Lawrence wrote to Sallie Hopkin, 'As for the people, nowhere do I find them wanting anything good. They want to go on from bad to worse' (iii. 123), and in July he told Waldo Frank that 'I think there ought to be some system of private publication and private circulation. I disbelieve *utterly* in the public, in humanity, in the mass' (iii. 143). As late as March 1921, he told S.S. Koteliansky, 'I get bored with people altogether of any sort' (iii. 676).

But Lydia Lawrence's son was, finally, no defeatist. At the same time that he was – apparently – seriously considering giving up writing fiction, in 1917, Lawrence was bringing *Women in Love* into the shape in which we now know it; and in 1921 he was also considering how he might create a new reader, one who would better understand, and thus accept, his ideas. The Foreword to *Women in Love*, which he wrote in 1919 for the novel's much-delayed publication the following year, shows him offering instructions on how to read the novel, on how to discern that – without mentioning war – the book is about the effects of war; on how to distinguish between pornography and writing that is concerned with the sensual passions and mysteries; on how to understand the novel as process, as a struggle for verbal consciousness, a '*passionate struggle into conscious being*'; on how to see the relation between that struggle and the fiction's 'continual, slightly modified repetition'.[5]

The Foreword reveals Lawrence coming to a new understanding of his readers, a new appreciation of their problems with his work. At about the same time, however, he commented (negatively) that Herman Melville, one of the American writers most important to him, was 'a real American in that he always felt his audience in front of him'.[6] In arguing that Melville was a better writer when he forgot that audience, Lawrence at last came close to the realisation that informs *Mr Noon*: the importance of *creating* the readers he wanted by guiding them through the process of fictionalising themselves. Such an understanding was by no means new. Father Walter J. Ong has considered the various techniques that writers from Chaucer on have used to help readers accomplish this very task.[7] Thus, the author *makes* his reader as much as he must create his work's characters (as Wayne Booth has also pointed out, following Henry James[8]), but nowhere in Lawrence is this so obvious – or is Lawrence so aware of its importance – as in *Mr Noon*. Booth has argued that he has trouble being Lawrence's 'mock reader'. *Mr Noon* shows how Lawrence anticipated exactly such a criticism and tried to show his readers how to fictionalise themselves, to become participants in the creation and realisation of his work.

By itself, Part I of *Mr Noon*, written 1920–1, may not seem especially innovative, however, and when it first appeared in 1934, it was certainly not seen as leading to any major formal breakthrough. The opening chapter in particular is reminiscent of the opening pages of *Sons and Lovers*, with many of the same narrative devices. The tone and style of the opening sentence – 'Her very stillness, as she sat bent upon her book, gradually made him uncomfortable'[9] – suggest a Lawrence not significantly different from that of the earlier major work. There is an overt narrator who appears in the fourth sentence, introducing a standard of acuteness – 'He kept glancing at his wife, whose intensified stillness would have told a 'cuter man that she knew he was fidgetting' (*MN* 3:7–8) – but this voice is not obtrusive.

In the second chapter, however, Lawrence introduces a far more obvious narrator. Six pages into that chapter, a dissertation on the fine art of spooning, he invites his reader to join him in the text ('Since the spoon is one of the essential mysteries of modern love, particularly English modern love, let us clasp our hands before its grail-like effulgence') and goes on to suggest, ironically, both the fictionality of his work and the importance of style over substance: 'Dear reader, have we not all left off believing in positive evil? And therefore it is not true that the seducer, invaluable to fiction, is dead? . . . It doesn't matter what you do only how you do it.—Isn't that the sincerest of modern maxims!' (*MN* 20:5–7, 12–13, 24–5).

Such a self-consciousness in the narration is not altogether typical of Part I of the novel, however: there are only four direct addresses to the reader (all as 'dear reader') in chapter II, three more in chapter III (one to 'gentle reader') a 'gentle reader' in chapter XI and two 'dear reader's and one 'gentle reader' in chapter XII. And in these early instances, the narrator mostly suggests a kind of sarcastic bond with his reader – 'Don't you agree, dear reader?' (*MN* 26:37) – by suggesting a common ground in their values: 'Emmie was now taking the right turning, such as you have taken, gentle reader' (*MN* 86:37–8). He also shows concern for what his reader might be learning from the text (in applying art to life, for example, he warns 'Beware . . . !' – *MN* 27:20). The affirmation of his reader's middle-class values is clearly ironic of course, but the narrator is nevertheless genuinely sympathetic with Patty Goddard's need for her husband at the end of chapter IV and light-heartedly attuned to the Bostocks' 'sound British sense' – both at one with his readers and their self-satisfaction, and poking fun at certain domestic values (*MN* 69:5). He never directly confronts these values, however, and in fact reminds his readers that he is not entirely in control of the text, as, for example, when Emmie's forgetfulness about her own engagement causes similar forgetfulness in the narrator.

This somewhat uncertain relationship between narrator and narratee in most of Part I is similar to the narrator's ambivalent relation to the tradition of fictional realism. By the beginning of the third chapter, for example, the narrator had identified himself with Stendhal – 'Let none complain that I pry indecently into the privacies of the spoon. A spoon is an open mirror, necessarily a public concern. I do but walk down the public road. . . .' (*MN* 25:3–5 and note) – a connection again strengthened by Lawrence's revision of the original sentences in the manuscript. Lawrence also establishes distance from Stendhal's metaphor, however, for the mirror turns into a camera. What the narrator records is not simply what has been selected but what has been framed 'through the aperture in the big doors' (*MN* 25:6–7); in the second chapter, Noon had seen 'a framed picture of wet pavements and passers-by' (*MN* 24:26–7), strengthening the idea that the novel, while it may mirror a real world, is also like a camera, selecting and framing that world through a conscious creative act.

In such a created world, the narrator maintains some control over the text; it is he who chooses what to include. But at the same time, he also recognises an independent existence for his characters. The narrator understands his characters as types: of Mrs Britten he writes, 'We've all known her. Such conscientious people don't let themselves remain unknown' (*MN* 52:34–5). But they are also types who can construct their own narrative (Emmie 'plotted for settling down in life,' deliberately constructing a drama in which she acts, with Walter as an audience, opening 'the last long chapter of a woman's life, headed Marriage' – *MN* 69:29, 11) and who, like Mrs Britten, either function as or are at the mercy of a Dea (or Deus) ex machina (*MN* 52:22; 92:28, 34).

The literary metaphors are appropriate. At the same time as the narrator appears to give his characters at least some control, he also recognises the fictionality of his creation. The narrator uses literary allusions[10] not only to connect Noon to the tradition of fiction, but also to undercut, through exaggeration and contrast, his characters and thus their tradition. For example, a comment like 'We little know the far-reaching results of our smallest actions' (*MN* 76:4–5) refers to no significant act, only to the odour of baked onion that whets the appetite of young schoolchildren. Walter is Emmie's Childe Roland to the dark tower come, a Childe Roland who falls on his face, however, when the mat on which he is 'so springily poised' slides back (*MN* 85:22). The narrator is aware not only of the power of the literary tradition, but also of the power of language ('We only wish there might be a few more *ands*, to prolong the scene indefinitely' – *MN* 84:31–2); and at one point the inserted interruption for commentary is so long that the narrator must reorient us ('with this word the story gets on its feet again' – *MN* 69:24), an awareness that challenges the sense of historical realism of Lawrence's earlier work.

Such references in Part I of *Mr Noon* are not extensive, however, and part of the initial reaction in 1934 to this first segment, when it appeared in the posthumous collection *A Modern Lover*, came understandably from puzzlement about the narrative voice. The *Times* reviewer, for example, complained about the passages of direct address to the reader, calling them examples of the story's 'odd button-holing, interjectory style' (*MN* xxxvi); the reviewer for the *New York Herald Tribune Books*, judging *Mr Noon* as bad, said Lawrence provided 'his own Greek chorus of what is meant for sardonic comment,' but called that comment 'rather vulgar and unamusing carping' (*MN* xxxvi).

These objections to the narrator – and to what *The Times Literary Supplement* called the work's 'grotesque exposition of lower-middle-class vulgarity' (*MN* xxxvii) – need however to be modified in the light of what happens in Part II, first published in 1984. In this section, Lawrence rewrites Part I, moving *Mr Noon* up-scale and forcing his readers into battle. In this process, Lawrence creates what Linda Hutcheon has called a narcissistic text, one in which '*the reader, like the writer, becomes the critic*.'[11] And he moves from the kind of ironical declaration of a standpoint shared with the reader (implicit in the usual affirmation 'dear reader') to a mocking, antagonistic relationship (implicit in the far more common address 'gentle reader'). We can see that change occurring in the last two pages of Part I, as Lawrence apparently resumed work on his previously written section and took it in a wholly new direction, around 12 December 1920.

III

In Part II Lawrence moves to a climactic confrontation with his implied reader, deliberately challenging the assumption of such critics as Wayne Booth that the most successful reading is one in which the created author and reader 'can find complete agreement'.[12] In chapter xviii, appropriately titled 'The First Round,' the narrator actually reconstructs his reader: 'why the devil should I always *gentle-reader* you. You've been *gentle reader* for this last two hundred years' (*MN* 204:39–40). The *OED*'s first reference actually dates from the 1540s: having originally been 'Used in polite or ingratiating address', by the 1890s it had become '*Obs*. exc. as a playful archaism'. Wordsworth had used it ironically: Thackeray had used it playfully.[13] The narrator of *Mr Noon*, however, continues the attack on his own particular construction of readers who believe themselves to be, in the first place, genteel and superior: 'what reader *doesn't* belong to the upper classes', he asks sardonically (*MN* 20:8). And, having made the insulting assumption that all readers pretend to gentility and superior standards (which of course account for their shock when they are confronted by actual experience), he further assumes that (whatever their actual gender) his readers are also of the 'gentler sex'. So, after two hundred pages, it is time they were reconstructed: 'Time you too had a change. Time you became rampageous reader, ferocious reader, surly, rabid reader, hell-cat of a reader, a tartar, a termagant, a tanger' (*MN* 205:1–3).

In the novel's second section, Lawrence creates a conflict between the narrator and narratee similar to Noon's conflict with Johanna, as well as Lawrence's conflicts with Frieda; and in the narrator's comments to the reader, there is a duplication of the movement of the novel in which the reader, like Johanna and Noon, must decide whether to continue or not. In Part I the narrator had argued that life should imitate art, that we could all learn to spoon from Noon and Emmie. Now, on a far more serious level, in the battle with his readers, Lawrence asks for a different relationship. As he found his woman for a lifetime in his battles with Frieda, and as Noon found his 'meet adversary' in Johanna (*MN* 185:35) so Lawrence consciously creates a reader adversary, 'The magnificence of opposites' (*MN* 186:24), who will join issues with him in the creation of life *and art*.

While the narrator of Part II appears at first to continue an accommodation with the reader – he identifies the reader with the British Isles, the 'Islands of the Blest' (*MN* 97:16) – such efforts to meet the narratee's expectations continue to be ironic, now without any mitigating sympathy for the reader's values. Basically the narrator and narratee are at odds from the start of Part II, the narrator making clear he will not fulfil reader expectations. For example, he will not go into the bedroom with Gilbert and Johanna, and he tells the reader not to interrupt him: 'Am *I* writing this book, or are you?' (*MN* 137:24–5). Refusing to accommodate reader preferences, the narrator insists he will not be intimidated by his reader and even refuses (at times) to play the conventional explanatory role of the omniscient narrator: 'How Gilbert came to be living in his flat I shan't tell you. I am sick of these explanations' (MN 100:16–17). Compared with his ambiguous stance in Part I, the narrator of Part II insists that he controls the creation of the text. He labours alone 'up the steep incline' of his pages, refusing to include a shoemaker's 'tale of woe' because 'there is not space' (MN 97:24; 240–45).

The narrator does attempt, however, to draw his reader into agreement about the quality of his heroines, agreement that would bind the narrator and narratee against critics who had complained that Lawrence's heroines 'show no spark of nobility' (MN 140:28–9). Perhaps the strongest effort to create this bond occurs in chapter XVI, 'Detsch', when the narrator identifies his reader not only as British and upper class, but also as a woman. In opposition to critics – normally of the 'sterner sex' – the gentle reader is also 'gentille lecteuse' and 'gentilissima lettrice' (MN 141:6, 14). In this effort to divide his reader from his critics the narrator comments, 'No one really takes more trouble soothing and patting his critics on the back than I do. But alas, all my critics are troubled with wind' (MN 142:3–4).

The text not only addresses itself directly to two critics at the start of chapter XIV – critics whose reviews of the recently published novel *The Lost Girl* had just arrived in Sicily, where Lawrence was writing his new novel – but from that point on, apostrophes to the reader and attacks on the critics become a significant portion of the text in Part II. In chapter XVIII, for example, the narrator self-consciously realises that the narratee may shy at the words 'gentle reader', and urges 'If you don't want to read, turn the page ' (sentence unfinished, Shandy-like, without page number or full stop – MN 185:8). For those who do not turn on, the narrator lets the 'cat out of the bag' so that the reader, like it or not will know exactly what is coming: 'nobody shall think it's a chaste unicorn or a pair of doves in a cage' (MN 185:9, 40). Here, within the space of two pages, the narrator addresses the gentle reader fourteen times to prepare for two ensuing crises: the first between Johanna and Noon, precipitated by Johanna's husband and resulting in her uneasy rejection of middle-class values; the second between the narrator and narratee, precipitated presumably by the exasperation Lawrence feels for this gentle reader who, like Johanna's husband, avoids conflict and values conformity.

This attack on the reader – and on the critic – must have been focused very precisely at the start of the writing of Part II of the novel by the various problems brought about by the recent publication of *The Lost Girl* and the imminent publication, in England, of *Women in Love*. Back in October 1920, the English lending libraries had demanded cuts and changes in *The Lost Girl*, with which Lawrence – at his English publisher's Secker's earnest entreaty – had complied, gently cautioning Secker 'Put not your trust in the British public' (iii. 621). Lawrence had simultaneously been correcting proofs of *Women in Love*, and as a result had started to wonder whether it would not be best 'not to send out review copies *at all*, but just to publish ... I do so hate the critics, they are such poisonous worms' (iii. 625). And just when that idea might have been about to drop, Secker had sent Lawrence chapter vii of *Women in Love* back again, asking him to make changes because enemies might fasten on it; Lawrence sent back the chapter, having 'altered it a bit: enough, I think. If enemies want to fasten, they'll fasten anywhere' (iii. 628). And then, finally, came the reviews of *The Lost Girl*, two of which Lawrence had seen by 12 December 'and snap my fingers at them: the drivel of the impotent' (iii. 638). His opinion of his critics and of his readers – especially their supposed sensitiveness to sexual matters – could hardly have been lower. And these factors influenced Part II of *Mr Noon* a good deal. As he noted of his reader at the start of chapter xiv, 'I call you gentle, as a child says "Nice doggie" because it is so scared of the beast' (*MN* 118:5–7).

By the time Lawrence finally explodes at his reader, in chapter xviii, there is a certain relief. If nothing else, the exhortations have become wearisome, the reader trapped and enmeshed in irony. When the narrator now refuses to use 'gentle' reader and instead challenges his 'sniffing mongrel bitch of a reader', the battle between narrator and narratee has become, explicitly, as important as the battle between Noon and Johanna. Indeed, the two battles are joined, as Lawrence encourages us to 'Make a ring then, readers, round Gilbert and

Johanna' (*MN* 205:22, 37–8). As Noon's love for Johanna creates a new Noon, through a 'bloody and horrid and gruesome' rebirth (*MN* 291:13–14), so the old, gentle reader must undergo a similar rebirth. In the final paragraphs of the novel's manuscript, Lawrence makes that connection explicit:

> Do not imagine, ungentle reader, that by just chasing women you will ever get anywhere. Gilbert might have had a thousand Emmies, and even a thousand really nice women, and yet never cracked the womb. It needed the incalculable fight such as he fought, unconscious and willy-nilly, with his German Johanna: and such as I fight you, oh gentle but rather cowardly and imbecile reader...
>
> (*MN* 291:38–292:4)[14]

Emmie, in rejecting Noon for Whiffen at the end of Part I, knows that she is choosing cabbages, middle-class respectability, rather than roses, the life of a free spirit. When Noon accepts Johanna's tearing up his postcard to Emmie, he makes a final break with those same respectable middle-class values, forcing himself to accept (albeit reluctantly) that Johanna will continue as free spirit, taking lovers when the spirit moves her. The creative result of the battle makes such a relationship worthwhile, however: 'What was the good of anything that wasn't a fight,' Noon asks (*MN* 173:35), and later the narrator exhorts the reader, 'let us pray for our shattering' (*MN* 227:13). The fight with the reader, and on behalf of the reader, is not one that the novel ever really gives up. Like Wordsworth, Lawrence knows that he has to create the taste by which he is to be enjoyed: and he is terribly afraid that, left to their own devices, his readers will simply hold up their hands in horror. They must therefore be *made* to attend.

In a number of ways then, Part II rejects art in favour of life, specifically the lessons Lawrence had learned from life. In chapter XIV, the narrator responds to the *Observer* criticism that Lawrence was on the quest of 'some blotched lily of beauty' by saying that he is 'really quite fond of truth' (*MN* 118:10, 16–17); and he later comments – through Noon – that he did not want to be a 'picked blossom', 'stuck in a nice aesthetic jar' (*MN* 174:20, 21). As Noon insists Johanna write the truth to her husband, so Lawrence wants the truth for his reader to confront and be confronted by, and the narrator insists that if he had to choose between truth of art and the truth of life, life is the winner: he tosses his books 'on to the winds of time. The static, written-down eternity is nothing to me' (*MN*190:9–10). Placing his immortality 'in the dark sap of life', he rejects the *apriority* of language: 'In the beginning was *not* the Word . . . let the Logos look after itself' (*MN*194:1–2, 4–5).

IV

However, for a novelist the Logos can hardly look after itself, and to so insist is the ultimate paradox. Thus the narrator does admit that he may be more like Beardsley than Swift, and Part II draws even more heavily and ironically than Part I on the literary tradition, opening, for example, with a heavy parody of the Bible as comment on Noon's reincarnation: 'For behold, the snow is melting, and is piled in heaps in the thawing streets. Behold, the sun is shining, and the time of the singing of the birds has almost come. Behold, the long, watchful line of the ice-pale Alps stands like a row of angels with flaming swords in the distance . . .' (*MN* 97:7–11). Anticipating the playfulness of a novel such as John Fowles's *The French Lieutenant's Woman*, the narrator of Part II is a major actor in the text, addressing Emmie (Mrs Whiffen) and apostrophising desire to give Noon time alone with Johanna, without the reader: also insisting that, having been too close to the borders of novelistic sexual explicitness before (perhaps thinking of *The Rainbow*), he has been taken advantage of by the reader:

> No, gentle reader, please don't interrupt, I am *not* going to open the door of Johanna's room, not until Mr Noon opens it himself. I've been caught that way before. I have opened the door for you, and the moment you gave your first squeal in rushed the private detective you had kept in the background. (*MN*137:16–20)

While the narrator tells his critic that he is writing the book himself – 'nobody is chirping it out to me like a piece of dictation' (*MN*137:30–1) – the reader does nevertheless enter into the construction of the text. As

Noon must deal with what for him is the horrible realisation of dependence on another – 'It is a terrible thing to realise that our soul's sanity and integrity depends upon the adjustment of another individual to ourself' (MN 231:31–3) so the narrator must deal with his dependence on the reader: 'why must I be the whale to swim back to the right shore with you, gentle reader' (MN 226:23–5). Such an anger with dependence on the reader leads to avoidance, and to the narrator's eventual profession of apology, 'I hope you're not sulking, and on the brink of closing this friendly book for ever' (MN 256:27–9): itself, of course, a new challenge rather than an apology. As Noon chooses Johanna with the clear knowledge of ensuing battles, so the narrator explicitly chooses a reader who will continue to battle with him. Their conflict is essential to the creation of the text: and the narrator's eventual assertion that the reader is 'gentle but rather cowardly and imbecile . . . for such, really, I find you' (MN 292:3–4) cannot have helped the novel reach its hoped-for conclusion; indeed, it came to a final halt within twenty lines of that statement.

More self-conscious about the process than in any of his earlier works, Lawrence, through the narrator of Mr Noon, considers not only how a writer's life determines the shape of his fiction, but also how art shapes his life. As Lawrence reshaped the battle between himself and Frieda through the story of Noon and Johanna, reflecting on the advantages of their conflict for his art, so he used the story to comment on his protracted battle with critics and readers. Conflict was good not only for Lawrence and Frieda, Noon and Johanna, but for the narrator and his reader as well. Lawrence's reader, created so consciously in Mr Noon, becomes the narratee to whom Lawrence would address the fiction of the last decade of his life, battling to crack the womb, to break out of the 'dry integument' that enclosed them both (MN 291:11).

V

Lawrence's battle with his reader was at first a destructive one. After the disappointment of The Rainbow and Women in Love he wanted The Lost Girl serialised as a safeguard against prosecution, and his work during the first part of the decade of the 1920s shows a continuing distrust of the reading public (*MN* xxxii). Trying in *The Lost Girl* to write for commercial publication because he had given up on finding a serious reader, Lawrence prostituted the vision of his earlier work. In the world of *The Lost Girl*, James Houghton's experiences are a reflection of Lawrence's: a man of imagination, taste and originality is forced to limit his inspiration more and more to accommodate the middle-class tastes of his customers. Houghton's daughter calls his audience 'stupid'.[15]

And yet, as David Gordon has pointed out, Lawrence, like Yeats, yearned 'for an age in which the artist was one with his audience'.[16] Lawrence knew that his work was created in collaboration with his reader, that reaction to *The Lost Girl* depended on 'what centre of oneself one reads it from' (iii. 550). Anticipating the importance of *Konkretisation*, Lawrence thus uses *Mr Noon* to force his readers to consider the way in which readers themselves realise the text, to understand the dialectical structure of reading. This dialectical structure may sometimes be destructive. As Marshall Alcorn and Mark Bracher have pointed out, in a somewhat different context, 'Literature may sometimes have the negative effects of a traumatic experience, evoking destructive processes that result in disease and fragmentation rather than health or wholeness.'[17] Like Alcorn and Bracher, however, Lawrence stresses the positive effects of such disintegration. As Alcorn and Bracher put it: 'If, as Kohut, Meissner, and others suggest, the self has an inherent teleology for growth and cohesion, then literature can have an important and profound positive effect as well, functioning as a kind of bountiful, nourishing matrix for a healthy developing psyche': and for Lawrence, the only way to be at one with his reader was to be in creative conflict.[18] In the heteroglossia of the novel, Lawrence includes the reader's voice.

In *Mr Noon* Lawrence finds that this voice of the reader, earlier the cause of such frustration and despair, can – when accepted in dialogue – be as freeing as his battle with Frieda. Rather than searching for a reader who agrees with him, or giving up because he faces only readers who do not share his values, the narrator discovers the advantages of the incalculable fight.[19] His fictionalised reader remains, in continually modified forms, the narratee of Lawrence's last decade, responsible for many of the most puzzling aspects of Lawrence's later fiction. The controversial doctrines about male-female relationships, the extreme political positions of *Aaron's Rod*, *Kangaroo* and *The Plumed Serpent* are thus deliberately provocative, calculated to bring the ungentle reader into battle again.

For Lawrence, that battle was never over: like the narrator of *Mr Noon*, declaring of Gilbert 'Rooted in battle he was', he too would continue to fight: 'So be it. Thank God the battle is never quite won. It always has a new phase tomorrow' (*MN* 174:36–7). The narrator comments, too, in the final pages of *Mr Noon*, 'the painted ceiling of the old ideal doesn't fall all in one smash. It first gives a little crack, yielding to pressure.' Having once seen the crack, however, as the reader has seen it in *Mr Noon*, 'one will come to the crack again, and madly fight to get a further glimpse, madly and frenziedly struggle with the dear old infinite. And thus rip just a little wider gap in it, just a little wider: after tearing oneself considerably' (*MN* 291:28–9, 33–7). Such a mad tearing is the only way to realise the 'wonderful, unbreathed firmament' (*MN* 291:22–3), a conflict necessary for both author and reader to be reborn, a conflict never finally resolved.

In the first chapter of *Mr Noon*, Noon had argued that, only art being perfect, life does not matter. Patty Goddard had predicted, however, that 'You'll find that life matters before you've done' (*MN* 12:23). While Noon moves with Johanna to a new understanding of the relationship between art and life, Lawrence also moves to a new fusion of art and life. He may not want to be an aesthetic blossom, but his work is a creation, a creation of the narratee as well as the narrator, the reader as well as the writer. The gentle reader of the tradition of the novel must become the ungentle reader of *Mr Noon*, fighting to free himself from the text. As Noon learns he cannot control Johanna, so Lawrence, like the narrator of *Mr Noon*, learns he cannot – should not – imagine that his reader can ever, finally, be controlled. And there are advantages. By the time Lawrence comes to *Lady Chatterley's Lover*, he is able to perform the extraordinarily difficult artistic feat of simultaneously parodying his own canon and reaffirming his belief in life and growth, trusting his reader to understand the complex play that underlies his final novel.

VI

Lawrence has too often been declared to be both humourless and mono-maniac in pursuit of his peculiar certainties. Even Katherine Mansfield suggested to Ottoline Morrell, at the end of the war, that Lawrence's trouble was his lack of any 'real sense of humour. He takes himself dread-fully seriously nowadays: I mean he sees himself as symbolic figure – a prophet – the voice in the wilderness crying "woe".[20] However true that may (or may not) have been of Lawrence in private life – and there are many other observers who saw things very differently – there can be no doubt that, as a writer, such tendencies were kept in check, in particular, by the deliberate comedy of his work: he embraced the comic form of the novel with particular eagerness. In comedy, he could express a sense of multi-voicedness that corresponded closely to his own conviction that good writing always argued the opposite of his own profoundest convic-tions. Thus Ursula, attacking Birkin, offered not only a useful counter-balance to Birkin's ideas – setting him right when he was foolish, so to speak – but also made those very ideas more vital: exactly as *his* convic-tions vivified her opposition. The dynamics of such fiction were one of Lawrence's abiding concerns. Writing to Carlo Linati in 1925, he offered a version of his fiction and his audience which fits the battles between nar-rator and reader in *Mr Noon* with particular appositeness:

> I hate the actor and audience business. An author should be in among the crowd, kicking their shins or cheering them on to some mischief or merriment – That rather cheap seat in the gods where one sits with fellows like Anatole France and benignly looks down on the foibles, follies and frenzies of so-called fellow-men, just annoys me . . . whoever reads me will be in the thick of the scrimmage, and if he doesn't like it – if he wants a safe seat in the audience – let him read somebody else. (v. 201)

Mr Noon was perhaps the first text in which Lawrence took such an atti-tude with real seriousness, and made it not peripheral but the real centre of the work; so that one is not only reading a novel in which serious ideas are taken seriously, but also one in which those same ideas are subjected to a kind of furious comedy, in the battle between the narrator and that great body of received opinions and conventional attitudes which are constantly being ascribed to the reader.

VII

Mr Noon concludes in mid-sentence. Johanna has received a hatbox of clothes from her sister Lotte. The final contents that the narrator lists are 'a voluminous dressing-gown wrap of thin silk and endless lace; a chemise of more lace than linen; two pairs of high laced shoes, of greeny grey thin kid with black patent golosh:' (*MN* 292:17–20) – Lawrence wrote no more. Presumably that final colon was intended to introduce yet another glorious item of clothing. But to the extent that the final colon, as a mark of punctuation, is used to introduce an idea that repeats in different form the idea of the preceding material, the ending of *Mr Noon*, as it stands, is a peculiarly appropriate conclusion. Lawrence's work in the final decade of his life would repeat, in different form, the insight which he had achieved in *Mr Noon*.

Notes

1 *The Great Tradition* (Chatto & Windus, 1948), p. 26.
2 *D.H. Lawrence and the Devouring Mother: The Search for a Patriarchal Ideal of Leadership* (Durham, NC: Duke University Press, 1984), p. 21.
3 Robert Alter, *Partial Magic: The Novel as a Self-Conscious Genre* (Berkeley: University of California Press, 1975), pp. ix–x; George Levine, *The Realistic Imagination: English Fiction from Frankenstein to Lady Chatterley* (Chicago: University of Chicago Press, 1981). Levine argues: 'In *Lady Chatterley's Lover*, [Lawrence] creates a work that resonates parodically with the now dead traditions of realism ... It stands in parodic relation to the tradition of moral-aesthetic realism, while itself (good parody that it is) belonging to that tradition' (pp. 232–4). In a related argument, Evelyn J. Hinz writes: 'Lawrence's own criticisms of various types of fictional practices and attitudes in the final version of the work and in "A Propos of *Lady Chatterley's Lover*" are as much directed against his own practice in the first two versions as they are

against any other examples' ('Pornography, Novel, Myth Narrative: The Three Versions of *Lady Chatterley's Lover*,' *Modernist Studies*, iii, 1979, 36). David Lodge calls attention to the 'parodic, travestying, tongue-in-cheek writing' in *Mr Noon* as part of 'the metafictional strain in the text', making *Mr Noon* carnivalesque and particularly appropriate for the theoretical framework of M. M. Bakhtin ('Lawrence, Dostoevsky, Bakhtin: D. H. Lawrence and Dialogic Fiction', *Renaissance and Modern Studies*, xxix, 1985, 31).

4 Alan Friedman, *The Turn of the Novel* (New York: Oxford University Press, 1966), p. 153.

5 *Women in Love*, ed. David Farmer, Lindeth Vasey and John Worthen (Cambridge: Cambridge University Press, 1987), 486:6, 13–14.

6 *Studies in Classic American Literature* (New York: Seltzer, 1923), p. 216.

7 'The Writer's Audience Is Always a Fiction', *PLMA*, xc (1975), 9–21.

8 *The Rhetoric of Fiction* (Chicago: Chicago Press, 1970), pp. 49, 138.

9 *Mr Noon*, ed. Lindeth Vasey (Cambridge: Cambridge University Press, 1984), 3:3–4. Subsequent references to this edition appear in the text in the form (*MN* 3:3–4). See too Lindeth Vasey and John Worthen, '*Mr Noon* / Mr Noon', *D. H. Lawrence Review*, xx (1988), 179–89.

10 Many of these allusions, but not all, are identified by Lindeth Vasey in the Cambridge Edition. The best study of DHL's allusions has been done by Dennis Jackson, who describes the allusions in *Lady Chatterley's Lover* as a 'primary means by which [Lawrence] defines character and themes and creates dramatic irony . . . In the novel's thematic structure the use of allusion helps create a philosophic subject that awakens the reader to the larger implications of the lovers' sexual and psychic regeneration' ('Literary Allusions in *Lady Chatterley's Lover*', in *D.H. Lawrence's 'Lady': A New Look at 'Lady Chatterley's Lover'*, ed. Michael Squires and Dennis Jackson, Athens: University of Georgia Press, 1985, p. 170).

11 *Narcissistic Narrative: The Metafictional Paradox* (Ontario, Canada: Wilfred Laurier University Press, 1980), p. 144.

12 See Christine Brooke-Rose, *A Rhetoric of the Unreal: Studies in Narrative and Structure, Especially of the Fantastic* (Cambridge: Cambridge University Press, 1981), p. 30, for a discussion of this position, held by many critics besides Booth. Walker Gibson argues, for example, that 'a bad book . . . is a book in whose mock reader we discover a person we refuse to become' ('Authors, Speakers, and Mock

Readers', *College English*, xi, February 1950, 265–9; reprinted *Reader-Response Criticism: From Formalism to Post-Structuralism*, ed. Jane P. Tompkins, Baltimore: Johns Hopkins University Press, 1980). See Don Bialostosky ('Booth's Rhetoric, Bakhtin's Dialogics and the Future of Novel Criticism', *Novel*, xviii, 1985, 209–16) for a discussion of the inadequacy of Booth's monologic focus for a writer like DHL. Booth memorably recanted his earlier position in 'Confessions of a Lukewarm Lawrentian' in *The Challenge of D.H. Lawrence*, ed. Michael Squires and Keith Cushman (Madison: University of Wisconsin Press, 1990), pp. 9–27. In a related argument, Lodge argues that DHL's development from *Sons and Lovers* to *Women in Love* was towards what Bakhtin calls the polyphonic novel, one that 'generates and sustains a continuous struggle between competing interests and ideas' ('Lawrence, Dostoevsky, Bakhtin: D. H. Lawrence and Dialogic Fiction', p. 20). Bakhtin's typology of fictional discourse, which considers doubly-oriented or doubly-voiced speech, is particularly useful to an analysis of DHL, as Lodge points out. The approach taken by Bakhtin, with its emphasis on dialogics, dramatises the inadequacy of most other critical theories of the novel for discussing DHL; see, in particular, *The Dialogic Imagination: Four Essays*, ed. Michael Holquist, trans. Caryl Emerson and Michael Holquist (Austin: University of Texas Press, 1981), pp. xxvi–xxvii.

13 *OED2* 3b; see 'Simon Lee', *Lyrical Ballads* (1798), 1. 67, and *The Newcomes* (1853), chapter VIII.

14 In *The Reader's Construction of Narrative* (Routledge & Kegan Paul, 1981), Horst Ruthrof argues that 'offending the audience' can be a 'paradostic device of revitalizing literary conventions' (p. 153).

15 *The Lost Girl*, ed. John Worthen (Cambridge: Cambridge University Press, 1981), 137:28.

16 *D.H. Lawrence as a Literary Critic* (New Haven: Yale University Press, 1966), p. 99.

17 Marshall W. Alcorn, Jr., and Mark Bracher, 'Literature, Psychoanalysis, and the Re-Formation of the Self: A New Direction for Reader-Response Theory', *PMLA*, c (1985), 352.

18 Ibid. As Wolfgang Iser has written: '[The reader] must actively participate in bringing out the meaning [of the text] and this participation is an essential precondition for communication between the author and the reader' (*The Implied Reader: Patterns of Communication in Prose*

Fiction from Bunyan to Beckett, Baltimore, MD: Johns Hopkins University Press, 1974, p. 30). Thus, as Hutcheon points out, the reader must face responsibility for the novelistic world he/she is helping to create (*Naracissitic Narrative*, p. 27). Many of Iser's observations about *Tom Jones* (particularly about Fielding's contrast of social class, conscious effort to help his reader realise the text and awareness of conflict with the reader), as well as Hutcheon's observations, might be applied to *Mr Noon*. DHL differs from Fielding primarily in his stress on the importance of the *battle* between the reader and narrator in constructing a text.

19   In a related argument, L. D. Clark contends that the marriage of DHL and Frieda 'resembled their wanderings: the course of it was as full of abruptness and reversal as the course of the travels' (*The Minoan Distance: The Symbolism of Travel in D.H. Lawrence*, Tucson: University of Arizona Press, 1980, p. 4). Clark points out that DHL accepted the Heraclitean tenet 'that the strife of opposites is the basis of all things' (p. 157).

20   Quoted in Paul Delany, *D.H. Lawrence's Nightmare: The Writer and his Circle in the Years of the Great War* (New York: Basic Books, 1978), p. 386.

'Homunculus stirs': Masculinity and the mock-heroic in *Birds, Beasts and Flowers*

Holly Laird

I

Sometime after the war ended and Lawrence had exiled himself from England, he began to write poetry with a sharp, comic edge and a distinctly new style. So different are the poems in *Birds, Beasts and Flowers* from the anti-lyrical love poems, dialect verse and elegies that preceded them that they mark as clear a break from the past as did Lawrence's physical exit from England. Sympathetic readers of Lawrence have tended to praise this verse for attentive observation of non-human creatures and have argued that Lawrence turned away in them from direct autobiographical love poems to a more effectively distanced mythopoesis. But what is most striking about the change in aesthetic stance is not a new impersonality; as some readers have also recognised, these poems are as self referring as any that preceded them.[1] The new art of the poetry is an art of parody and, above all, of self-parody.

In the language of Lawrence's 1928 Note to the *Collected Poems*, he let not merely the 'demon say his say', but also the faintly ridiculous 'young man' and even the silly 'young lady'.[2] Lawrence split himself into two figures, enlarging one and dwarfing the other, but instead of eliminating the second, he left it standing as a mockery of the first. While mocking himself, Lawrence nonetheless magnified himself, producing alongside the image of his humbly dwarfed self, a heroic one – the 'real demon'. These self-reflections confront each other nowhere more vividly perhaps than in his well-known poem 'Snake', where the 'I in pyjamas' with the 'voice of my education' encounters a 'guest', a golden snake emerged 'from the burning bowels of the earth' (*CP* 349–50). The double-edged sword of such poems – comic miniaturisation and comic exaggeration – not only cuts between the Lawrentian speaker and one of his creatures, but also splits each figure: in the heroic antics of the tiny tortoise or, later the homunculus of 'Virgin Youth'. Even the lordly snake is momentarily brought low, its royalty undermined, when the Lawrentian persona throws a 'clumsy log' at it, and the 'part of him that was left behind convulsed in undignified haste'. But then it 'Writhed like lightning', leaving the speaker alone with his own 'paltry' act, a parodic figure (*CP*351).

Birds, Beasts and Flowers as a whole enacts, as previous defenders have said, an Orphic descent into the underworld – a claim that secures Lawrence a place within the Blakean heritage of revisionary myth[3] – but this mythos transpires through the mode of the mock-epic: mock-epic struggle with the contemporary world. The poems of *Birds, Beasts and Flowers* set the stage for all the verse that followed, which variously attempts to balance the serious with the comic, the mythic and the satiric: in the 1928 revisions of poems like 'Virgin Youth' for *Collected Poems*, in the satiric *pensées* of *Pansies* and *Nettles*, and in the diminutive 'ship of death' of *Last Poems*. These poems also play an important role in the development of new methods in the prose fiction focused on male leadership. Lawrence's achievements in mock-heroic poetry suggest that he be compared not only with Romantics like Wordsworth and Keats, Blake and Whitman, but also with twentieth-century modernist and postmodern texts with a focus on anti-heroic folly: *The Waste Land* and *Ulysses*, *Pricksongs & Descants* and *Lolita*.

'Achievement' must in this context be a muted, ironic one: for the mock-heroism of many of these texts, and certainly of Lawrence's poems, involves an extended, disillusioned assault on, and retreat from, the world of his contemporaries. To acknowledge the mock-heroism of Lawrence's *Birds, Beasts, and Flowers* – and to recognise its power – does not mean that we will uniformly applaud its satiric aims. On the contrary, recognition of these aims brings us close to some of the most controversial themes of Lawrence's unfolding philosophies. Most obviously perhaps, the mock-heroic was a mode in which Lawrence could investigate his own crises of manhood and, to some extent, correlatively for Lawrence, the 'viciousness' of modern women ('Pomegranate', CP278).

But the poems remain fascinating for the way in which they surround the Lawrence persona in a ludic hall of mirrors. These are mostly not poems that wound, whether directed against their subjects or their readers; their points frequently become lost in comic scuffles. The Lawrentian persona itself is undone – and outdone – by the antic skirmishes in which it is enmeshed. In seeking to determine the 'natures' of his quixotic creatures, the speaker reaffirms their, and his, contradictory multitudinousness. Nothing has been more obvious than this to readers or has drawn more admiration. But where others attribute these qualities selectively to the poems, often seeking to separate poems which, they claim, succeed in reaffirmation of the creatures' otherness from poems in which Lawrence uncongenially cauterises his antagonists, I would insist on the poems' linkage of comedy and myth, self-mockery and self-assertion.[4] While they certainly range in tone, from the serious to the comic, from a delight in mystery to irritation with the mundane and from mockery to assertion, these are shifting emphases in poems that are themselves linked, first, in nine sections of 'fruits', 'birds' and 'beasts', and, second, in a single ambitious sequence. This is not a miscellany of self-mocking nature poems; it is a mock-heroic verse book.

II

My focus in re-examining the mock-heroic character of these poems will be on the final published sequence rather than on the chronological sequence of their composition, not only because dates of composition have not been established for all the poems but because Lawrence organised them to reflect his own journey around the world, his self-mocking quest for a new world. Yet it is illuminating first to look at what are generally considered the earliest poems composed in Birds, Beasts and Flowers for what they indicate about Lawrence's new methods and aims. Keith Sagar takes 'The Mosquito' as one of the earliest (possibly the first) composed for *Birds, Beasts and Flowers* since it was located by Lawrence in 'Syracusa' where he stayed one night in May 1920 at the Grand Hotel: Lawrence called this 'rather a dreary hotel—and many bloodstains of squashed mosquitos on the bedroom walls. Ah, vile mosquitos!'[5] This mosquito-stained bedroom became the occasion for a poem in which the speaker attempts to outwit a 'queer' bug, a mock-heroic figure which is so 'frail' as to seem 'a nothingness' yet at the same time is utterly exultant in its 'devilry' (*CP* 332). Split between its 'accursed hairy frailty' and 'Winged Victory' (*CP* 334), the mosquito appears to the speaker alternatively too shifty – using the 'filthy magic' of 'invisibility' – and too brazen – 'It is your hateful little trump, . . . / Which shakes my sudden blood to hatred of you' – to be tolerated (*CP* 332, 333). And it is all too close for comfort, absorbing Lawrence's identity with his blood: 'enspasmed in oblivion, / Obscenely ecstasied / Sucking live blood, / My blood', in an 'obscenity of trespass' (*CP* 333–4). But Lawrence refuses to be outdone by a mosquito and squashes it. We are left with the speaker wondering at his own big stain next to the tiny corpse of the mosquito: 'Queer, what a big stain my sucked blood makes / Beside the infinitesimal faint smear of you! / Queer, what a dim dark smudge you have disappeared into' (*CP* 334).

Various critics have admired this poem for its close attention to a mosquito: Sandra Gilbert counts the mosquito, as represented in this poem, one of several 'pure examples of living otherness'. Philip Hobsbaum says more simply that 'this creature, which anybody else might dismiss as a nuisance, Lawrence contemplates with wry interest'. Marjorie Perloff sees the poem as presenting 'precise, scientific knowledge of what a mosquito is and does'.[6] But the primary aim of Perloff's essay is to trace the performative rhetoric of the poetry, and so she goes on to describe this poem as 'a delicately satirical treatment of man's need to triumph over the very smallest and most paltry creatures of the insect world . . . the poem foregrounds the rhetorical situation, the relation of "I" to "you", of manly poet to foppish "Monsieur Mosquito"'. The 'manly' speaker is satirically exposed and unmanned in his imbalanced battle with a puny mosquito. Further, Perloff acutely finds in the poem a mocking account of Lawrence's failed quest for blood brotherhood and for power among men. Noting the parallels between this poem and the prose fiction of the

(*CP* 297). Parodying late Victorian Darwinian cliche, Lawrence reappropriates both visual and verbal stereotypes, amusingly undercutting not only the Leonardos of the western canon, but the latinate roots of modern English to produce a semi-satiric, semi-mythic eulogy of the laughing Etruscans:

> Dusky, slim marrow-thought of slender, flickering men of Etruria,
> Whom Rome called vicious.
>
> Vicious, dark cypresses:
> Vicious, you supple, brooding, softly-swaying pillars of dark flame.
>
> . . .
>
> Were they then vicious, the slender, tender-footed
> Long-nosed men of Etruria?
> Or was their way only evasive and different, dark, like cypress-trees in
>   a wind?
>
> . . .
>
> What would I not give
> To bring back the rare and orchid-like
> Evil-yclept Etruscan?
> For as to the evil
> We have only Roman word for it,
> Which I, being a little weary of Roman virtue,
> Don't hang much weight on.   (*CP* 297)

This coy, conversational speaker with his parodic phrases, polemical taunting repetitions and re-mythologisation of the Etruscan produces just the kind of 'oral, dialectical parodic, and polyglot manner' that Fleishman praises in *St. Mawr* and that readers of the poetry herald as 'the mature Lawrence, in complete control of his medium, or completely controlled by his demon'.[14]

IV

Critics have generally valued the poems most, of course, when they appear to 'say' least, to be least didactic: when they objectively attend to an ordinary, yet mysterious beast or when they move so rapidly among

period, Perloff concludes, 'Here is a man absurdly contemplating his male rival, absurdly needing to "win in this sly game of bluff", to "out-mosquito you" . . . the poem allows Lawrence to handle lightly and humorously what is, in *Women in Love* or *Aaron's Rod*, a deadly contest between male rivals.'[7]

The mockery, and self-mockery, of 'The Mosquito' soften its 'deadly' sting, so readers don't take this rivalry seriously and instead consider the poem a lesson about the 'otherness' of mosquitos or the follies of mice and men. This poem became the first, however, of a long series of poems in which Lawrence seeks suitable comrades, a suitable battleground and appropriate opponents, and so its mockery – its mock rivalry – should, as I will argue, be taken more seriously. Sagar indicates that, soon after the encounter recorded in 'The Mosquito', Lawrence wrote 'Tropic', 'Peace' and 'Southern Night',[8] none of which attends to beasts or flowers (and all of which, in the final arrangement of poems, are placed outside the nine sections of birds, beasts and flowers); these three poems unmockingly utter the speaker's yearning for revolutionary change. In 'Tropic', he asks us to 'Behold my hair twisting and going black . . . / Negroid', as he joins 'Columns' of 'Sunblack men . . . / As frictional, as perilous, explosive as brimstone' (*CP* 301). From these new comrades may come revolution. In 'Peace', he denies any peacefulness in the spectacle of black lava cooled long ago: 'My heart will know no peace / Till the hill bursts' (*CP* 293). Most interestingly, in 'Southern Night', he is bothered again by mosquitos, biting like 'northern memories', and he invokes the blood-red moonrise to explode these memories, to 'Burst the night's membrane of tranquil stars / Finally' (*CP* 302). Here the rivalry between man and mosquito is overlaid with an earnest cosmic war between moonlight and starlight, or (in thinly veiled allegory) between Lawrence's dark primeval life of the blood and the white mentalised world of European civilisation which he abhors. In subsequent poems, Lawrence advanced into the mock-heroic mode in full battle regalia with various flora, fauna and beasts as his antagonists – this would become the primary mode of the finished book of poems.[9] And he investigates his creatures as mirrors of his own heroic possibilities and obstacles.

III

In *Desperate Storytelling*, Roger Salomon argues that

> Writers of mock-heroic tend to be those whose lives have straddled major cultural 'breaks', themselves divided like their culture into a youth of high emotional and ideological commitments and a maturity of scepticism, dislocation, and the failure of hope – writers in their own 'displaced persons' or 'exiles' like their protagonists . . . At the very least, writers of mock-heroic are among those who have been heavily subjected during the course of their (usually early) experience to a compelling version of the heroic life and who then, by tempera- ment or situation or both, must spend a significant part of their literary careers coming to terms with it in an explicit and self-conscious way.[10]

Among modernists whom he includes in his discussion of the mock- heroic – Joyce, Williams and Stevens – Salomon does not mention Lawrence, perhaps because Lawrence continues to be thought of and read as a novelist, to the exclusion of his poetry. But the paradigm Salomon draws fits Lawrence even more exactly than his modernists of choice, driven as Lawrence was by intensely held ideals as a youth, severely disillusioned and exhausted in his ambition during the war.

Thus Lawrence wrote of himself in October 1915:

> how shall one submit to such ultimate wrong as this which we commit, now, England – and the other nations. If thine eye offend thee, pluck it out. And I am English, and my Englishness is my very vision. But now I must go away, if my soul is sightless for ever. Let it then be blind, rather than commit the vast wickedness of acquies-
> cence.   (ii. 414)

The war 'was the spear through the side of all sorrows and hopes', he wrote still earlier, in January 1915 (ii. 268), and this was just the beginning of the most frustrating, desolate period in his life. Yet he remained throughout the war preoccupied by a sense of messianic mission: by his roles both as a prospective leader of Rananim – his name for the utopian community he envisaged at that time – and as a potentially prophetic writer for cultural change.

Despite repeated defeats to his dream of Rananim, when he resurfaced in Italy, he clung as tenaciously as ever to the heroic vision for himself at which he had hinted in the autobiographical figures of Paul Morel and Rupert Birkin. Avrom Fleishman and others describe the 1920s, however, as a 'plateau' in his prose fiction, as he set aside his previous accomplishments in the novel and began to explore other modes of writing.[11] Fleishman sees Lawrence's heroic 'campaign' as a specifically literary one, a writer's 'campaign to engender a new language' and 'to answer the question, how shall mankind speak when all the languages have been debased?' Fleishman locates the 1922 Verga translations and the 1921 travel book *Sea and Sardinia* as genres in which Lawrence tried his hand more effectively than in the post-war 'leadership' novels at a narrational heteroglossia comparable to the logomachies of *Gargantua and Pantagruel, Don Quixote* and *Ulysses*. Lawrence's experimentation, which Fleishman believes bore fruit in *St. Mawr*, joins these other texts in 'participat[ing] in and dramatiz[ing] acute cultural-historical transi- tions'. But many of the strategies that Fleishman attributes to a successful narrational heteroglossia appeared first in the poetry of 1920: 'double- voicing', parody, hidden polemic, hidden dialogue and even 'parodic skaz' where, as Bakhtin defines it, 'one speaker very often repeats literally an assertion made by another speaker, investing it with a new intention and enunciating it in his own way'.[12] It is unfortunate that Fleishman missed the role of *Birds, Beasts and Flowers* in this development, for it is here that, in Salomon's words, 'a complete and sophisticated confronta- tion' both with worldwide crisis and with personal disillusionment is most obvious and most successful, and these combine in the poems with the quest for a new language.[13]

For Lawrence, the search for a new language was one and the same as the search for a new world with new heroes in it. Thus in 'Cypresses', the best known of the poems for its enunciation of a linguistic quest, Lawrence seeks the camaraderie of 'a dead race and a dead speech' and imagines a resurgence of both: 'They say the fit survive, / But I invoke the spirits of the lost. / . . . To bring their meaning back into life again' (*CP* 296, 298). It is not the fittest who survive longest, but 'He laughs longest who laughs last; / Nay, Leonardo only bungled the pure Etruscan smile'

different interpretations of a creature that the reader is distracted from a single 'message' and awakened to the fluidity or 'vitality' of the creature. But poems can be multivalent *and* polemical; they can be powerfully engaging and display attitudes we may or may not wish to emulate. Among the rapid changes of the speaker's thoughts in these poems are ongoing polemics against the social movements of Lawrence's day (whether capitalist, socialist or feminist), and these occasionally 'hidden polemics' (occasionally unhidden) constitute a primary source of vigour as well as point in these poems – all of which is to be expected of a mock-epic.

It is odd to see even Perloff, who is probably more concerned than any other critic to uncover the wit in this poetry and its performance of paro-distic repartee, seemingly contradict herself and retreat from the 'lead-ership' struggles suggested by the poems to their objectivism. She claims that the pomegranates in the first poem of *Birds, Beasts and Flowers* are 'aggressively masculine ("barbed, barbed with a crown"...)' and that Lawrence believes that 'only out of intense struggle (the willingness to engage the Greek women whose viciousness almost prevents the growth of the flowering tree...) can the heart be broken and made new'. Lawrence reanimates the pomegranate with the Dionysos myth, 'the transformation of the blood of the dying god into the scarlet flower', and 'finds in himself both aspects of pomegranatehood, the crowns ... and the fissure'. But she adds to this reading these somewhat contradictory assertions: that Lawrence has 'made it impossible for us to allegorize the object ["the fissure"], to relate it to Woman', and 'much has been written about Lawrence the Orphean Seer, uncovering the secrets of nature ... But this is to ignore the other, more "hard-boiled" or practical side of Lawrence, his stubborn insistence that a flower or animal or bird should be taken for what it is.'[15]

The not-so-hidden polemic of 'Pomegranate' is indeed a gendered battle in which in the second stanza he opposes the 'rock left bare by the viciousness of Greek women' (*CP* 278) to his own more fruitful vision of pomegranates and then appropriates for male 'Kingly'ness the obvi-ously female 'fissure'. The fact that the 'fissure' may be read as both male and female does not cancel the possibility of an 'allegorical' or polemical reading of this poem; it only means that 'the delicate self-parody of the narrator's rhythms, the comic bullying of his tone', as Perloff says, are more likely 'to bring the reader round to the poet's point of view, to adopt his stance toward the successive version of the pomegranate'.[16]

Similarly, 'The Mosquito' has been read unquestioningly as 'he' because Lawrence refers to it in the second line as 'Monsieur' (otherwise it is addressed as 'you'), but in the fourth stanza, Lawrence again co-opts a prior feminine imagery for an assertively masculine one. The mosquito itself mocks a woman's interpretation of mosquitoes as female by responding with a satirical, male sexual gesture: 'I heard a woman call you the Winged Victory . . . / You turn your head towards your tail, and smile' (CP 332). Lawrence then builds upon this portrait of the mosquito as a (male) demon and re-genders the 'Winged Victory' as male: with 'so much devilry', 'streaky sorcerer', 'Ghoul on wings / Winged Victory' (CP 332), with 'your hateful little trump, / You pointed fiend', 'your small, high, hateful bugle in my ear' (CP 333), 'Are you one too many for me, / Winged Victory?' (CP 334). Through repetition he transforms the 'Winged Victory' into a thoroughly male combatant. Yet since the double-edged language of 'Winged Victory' retains the female innuendo, this bedroom battle may be read as re-enacting not only the 'male rivalry' Perloff notices, but also a gender war in which woman is devilish yet may, if necessary, be outmatched by man. It is, after all, only the female mosquito that bites.

As Lawrence moves us through the sequence of poems, he frequently focuses more directly than this on the sexual struggles between men and women, in 'Figs', 'Purple Anemones', the 'Tortoises' and the 'Ass' and 'Goat' poems, for example. In these, the woman would seem to outmatch man in size and in her greater indifference to sex. Yet, as in 'Pomegranate' and 'The Mosquito', these female achievements of indifference act primarily as a foil for Lawrence to investigate the problems of masculinity and to suggest that the 'woman problem' would be solved by resolution of the man problem: 'Forget the female herd for a bit', he tells the He-Goat, 'And fight to be boss of the world' (CP 383). Men must regain their own 'demonish' otherness and their power.

This is not to say, then, that the poems should be read only 'allegorically' – in the narrow sense of that term – in only one way, or that their investigation of gender differences lacks complexity; rather, it is to argue for wariness about what meanings we exclude as we focus on others.[17] The 'demon' itself and its cognates, like 'devil', become such privileged terms in this book's Orphic descent as to suggest that rather than 'mock-heroic' the poems might be better termed 'mock-devilish', but devil and demon are themselves mock-heroic figures: figures that refuse or fail to be fixed in one state, neither stably grand nor suitably humble, but whimsically oscillating between the silly and the serious. Such complexity does not prevent polemical emphases from emerging, and it works to enhance Lawrence's powers of persuasion. As a poet, he was fully capable of admiring the quiddity of a mosquito and acknowledging the instabilities of its identity, even while invoking the mosquito as the devilish harbinger of another world, engaging the mosquito as if it were a manly rival *and* waving his taunting tail at women.

V

From 'Pomegranate' and 'Peach' where Lawrence throws down his gage, laughingly teasing readers – women and men – to pick it up and either fight or join him in his vision of a 'new day' ('Would you like to throw a stone at me? / Here, take all that's left of my peach', *CP* 279), to the last poem of the volume, 'The American Eagle', where Lawrence teases the eagle to choose once and for all whether to command 'myriads' and shed 'a little blood' (*CP* 414) or to fall laughably short of his heroic possibilities (so that he remains a silly democratising pelican nurturing other little states around the world or a democratic hen nursing its own little golden eggs), Lawrence conducts a polemical quest and satiric struggle for a new, non-democratic heroic age. It is this mock-epic struggle that I now wish to trace and, while pursuing Lawrence's developing polemic, to consider the accompanying changes in kinds of mockery that Lawrence deploys, as he shifts from Quixote-like vision to Swiftian satire, from comic invocation to bitter irony, and back again.[18] In 'Fruits', after announcing himself humorously battle-ready in 'Pomegranate' and 'Peach', Lawrence semi-mockingly, semi-mythically expresses his love for 'delicious rottenness' and his eagerness to leave behind the 'pussyfoot West', to join in fruity solidarity with the 'morbid' 'Medlars and Sorb-Apples', with their 'strange retorts' (*CP* 280–1). Then in the satiric allegory of 'over-ripe' women in 'Figs', he mocks self-assertive women – or rather, as he sees it, they make a mockery of themselves, doomed to 'burst' like rotten figs (*CP* 283–4). 'Grapes', the last poem of this first section, counterposes the 'Rose of all the world' which 'simper[s] supreme' (much like the fig) with the 'invisible rose' of the vine, the godly grape of Bacchus (much like the medlar and sorb-apple), invoking a 'lost, fern-scented world' (*CP* 285–7). In these three 'Fruits', Lawrence directs his parody against others rather than himself and, alternatively, conjures up a mythic 'other-world', yet such conjurings always spring from, and remain rooted in, a mock-turtle world of diminutive heroic birds, beasts and flowers such as Lewis Carroll might have imagined.

Together with the 'Cypresses', where Lawrence took up his concomitant search for a lost language and Etruscan race, the second section 'Trees' presents mock-heroic figures of masculine culture. 'Bare Fig-Trees' plays upon the term 'Demos' and its verbal kinship with 'Demon' to recapture the fruitfully devilish side of the otherwise silly, ultimately self-defeating 'equality puzzle': every new male-citizen twig ironically 'over-equal[s]' and 'over-reach[es]' the last as it 'issue[s]' from the 'thigh of his predecessor' in masculine self-propagation (*CP* 299–300). In 'Bare Almond-Trees' Lawrence wonders aloud about the stark male spectacle of the stubborn wet almond-trees 'like iron sticking grimly out of earth'. But in spite of their apparent immobility, these trees, 'brandishing and stooping over earth's wintry fledge, climbing the slopes', serve as Lawrence's darkly comic advance troops (*CP* 300–1).

Progress through *Birds, Beasts and Flowers* is episodic, the continuities produced through Almond-Tree-like association as in the picaresque and mock-heroic modes generally rather than through structures of logical or narrational development. But, logically enough in this case, from the seeds of 'Fruits' come first 'Trees', then 'Flowers', and the third section of 'Flowers' begins explicitly where 'Trees' left off: in

'Almond Blossom', 'Even iron can put forth' (*CP* 304), much like the tree of Demos. This elaborate demon-birth poem ends, however, not with a heroic vision, but with a reminder of the deep disillusionment at the heart of these mocking poems: the trees 'given, and perfect; / And red at the core with the last sore-heartedness, / Sore-hearted-looking' (*CP* 307). Two of the remaining three 'flowers' of this section are well known for their satires: Lawrence's rewriting of the Persephone myth in 'Purple Anemones' which re-genders springtime 'pomp' as male teasing, the superior mockery of her husband Pluto (*CP* 309), and Lawrence's satiric allegorisation of the 'socialist' equality puzzle in 'Hibiscus and Salvia Flowers'. Between these, in 'Sicilian Cyclamens', the mood shifts back to the dreamy and mythic, as Lawrence allows female flowers a form of devilry – their own 'witchery'. But these females are located 'at his toes': at the toes of an Adamic Mediterranean 'savage' (who stands with his Eve) are bunches of 'greyhound bitches' (the cyclamens' 'whispering witchcraft' (*CP* 310–11). 'Hibiscus and Salvia Flowers' ends this section, however, again with a sore heart, a sense of defeat, reminding the reader that while the mockery in these poems is, in part, a satiric device honed to criticise and attack what Lawrence disapproves of and, in part, a mode of complication aimed at enlarging possibilities for man and beast, it is also a means of simple self-defence: 'I cannot bear it / That they [socialists] take' the aristocratic 'hibiscus and . . . salvia flower' (*CP* 318).

'The Evangelistic Beasts' of the fourth section are, as Lawrence says from the start, 'not all beasts'; one is a man, 'St Matthew' (*CP* 320). Playful as this poem is, it could also be taken as the central doctrine in this book about the nature of 'man' – what he is and should be: neither entirely angel, nor entirely beast, occasionally as grand as a god and as puny as a bat, but mostly both, 'travell[ing]' in both directions: 'I will be lifted up, Saviour, / But put me down again in time, Master, / Before my heart stops beating, and I become what I am not' (*CP* 323, 321). Paradoxically, if one doesn't embrace the mock-heroic (refusing the 'travelling' instinct), one becomes merely a mockery. Beasts too simply make fools of themselves when they try to confine themselves to one form, especially when they try to be angelic lambs. The lion of 'St Mark' is winged, but once he loved to think lustfully 'of voluptuousness / Even of blood'; now he's become 'a curly sheep-dog', the domesticated patriarch of 'a well-to-do family' who is 'going blind at last' (*CP* 324–5). Even the 'bull of the proletariat', 'St Luke', was once as mighty as the lion king: in the past his breast was 'a fortress wall, and the weight of a vast battery', yet he now confines all his fire to 'the narrow sluice of procreation', 'such narrow loins, too narrow' (*CP*326–7). Finally, 'St John' was an 'honourable bird', 'high over the mild effulgence of the dove', but Jesus 'put salt' on the tail of 'The sly bird of John', and it gave birth to the 'word'. The eagle will have to give itself to the fire, phoenix-like, so that from the ashes, 'a new conception of the beginning and end / Can rise' (*CP* 328–9). The 'word' will, in a Lawrentian transformation, be transubstantiated into manly flesh. These deliberately emblematic 'beasts' seem more nakedly allegorical than some of the other creatures in this book, as if – despite the paradoxicality with which this section begins – Lawrence were indeed embracing a single 'nature' for each creature. At the cost of imagining all that they (or we) might be, Lawrence's dancing, variable mockery is directed nonetheless effectively at parodic images of these beasts' various forms of entrapment.

Among the first small beasts of the next section of 'Creatures', Lawrence's mock-heroism – his jousting with the world's myriad windmills – becomes more focused: from the generalised encounters of the 'I' with an unnamed 'you' or with representations of various modern European social types, the book now turns to particularised dramas of the 'I' battling with 'alien' creatures, with the mosquito, with a fish and with a bat. These, and the following section of 'Reptiles', are among the most admired poems for their ecological exploration of the 'living otherness' of non-human creatures. Yet these creatures also allegorize much that Lawrence wishes for in a newly heroic age of men as well as much that he abhors in his own era. In 'The Mosquito', 'Fish', 'Bat' and 'Man and Bat', the creatures turn out to be greater demons than himself, despite self-mocking assertions like the bats in 'Man and Bat': '*But I am greater than he . . . / I escaped him*' (*CP* 347). The Lawrentian persona itself thus becomes a personification of impulses he disdains – as he puts it in the first poem of the next section, 'Snake', he becomes the agent of 'pettiness' (*CP*351). The speaker of these poems knocks his head against the opposition of creatures who will not permit him – or not for long – to dictate their movements or absorb their identities (unless he murders them, and in that case he is left with nothing). Still, these battles get his blood up and alert him not only to his shortcomings as a 'paltry' man, but also to what the demon might look like in himself.

The larger problem for man, as Lawrence explores it in 'Reptiles', is that he is not 'one', not self-sufficient. Whatever women and beasts might be – they seem to the speaker, by turns, falsely 'unnatural', inedibly 'over-ripe' and admirably impregnable in their sardonic otherness (even when they can be physically penetrated) – men feel incomplete without female mates. This pivotal section of 'Reptiles', including 'Snake', with its widely discussed re-enactment of Lawrence's pyjama-clad encounter with the lordly, penile snake, seeks clues to men's littleness, their insufficiency and especially their sexual uneasiness. In the first three poems of 'Tortoises', the most tightly woven mini-sequence of the book, though the tortoise starts out as a child like a 'little Ulysses' (*CP* 353), enviable in his insouciant independence, he is 'crucified' in adolescence (*CP* 361), driven by sexual desire; he turns into a 'little' man, pathetically enchained to the tail of the greater female (*CP* 363). The female meanwhile mimics what man would like to be, with her enormous size, her indifference and her self-containment, and she drives man mad with desire to master her. Why, the speaker asks repeatedly, is this necessary?

Yet comedy in these poems about manhood – targeting a 'mere' tortoise – has its familiar Shakespearean, conservational function, productive not of bitter, angry or ironic satire about the tortoise, but of affable, sympathetic respect, and this mood paves the way for the tortoise's heroic transformation. When he is at his most pathetic, stretched punily over the female, the tortoise orgasmically 'shouts', and in shouting re-remembers every other primal utterance he had ever heard or imagined: including not only the cry of birth and the mating call, but the death scream and war cry (*CP* 364). All these, Lawrence decides, take place at moments of extremity, when the 'I' is stretched beyond itself. In the 'cross' of 'sex', the 'I' is immersed not just in 'you', but in 'it', in 'they', in all that is other: 'That which is whole, torn asunder, / That which is in part, finding its whole again throughout the universe' (*CP* 367). Crucial (literally) to the attainment of one's own inviolable, demonish 'other-ness' is the Osiris moment of self-undoing: of overreaching, being belittled, and torn apart, 'burst' in one's own shell. A primal language, a new man, the new world can occur, again paradoxically, only through an excruciatingly simultaneous diminishment and enlargement of the self. This 'tortoise shout' would seem funny, or satirical, only to a hostile reader; the mock-heroic now simply *is* the heroic. For the engaged reader, the residue of comic effect – as we watch a tortoise turn into Osiris – intensifies rather than diminishes the poignancy of this discovery of a newly primal language, as if spiking its immensity with a remnant sense of the littleness of the tortoise and hence of man.

The end of 'Tortoises' leaves the Lawrentian quester more sure of his way. In the next section of 'Birds', he conjures up two aboriginal creatures, 'Turkey-Cock' and 'Humming-Bird', who in their diminished modern forms mirror back to him the lost majesty he seeks. In neither of these do we encounter the self-torturing questions or witness the self-mocking spectacles of the previous sections of beast poems. But the poet still wonders at these two relics of a primeval 'other-world' and tries to pinpoint where the turkey-cock stands in the turning cycles of the ages: 'Do [the Amerindians] stand under the dawn, half-godly, half-demon, awaiting the cry of the turkey-cock? / Or must you go through the fire once more, till you're smelted pure' (*CP* 371–2). In the third poem of this section, 'Eagle in New Mexico', Lawrence assaults his chosen beast, but this time the beast is not an accidental nuisance or unequal opponent; rather it is a potential antagonist and an appropriate opponent: 'Sun-breaster ... / The god-thrust entering you steadily from below' (*CP* 373). Lawrence is wrestling now, not with a diminutive creature and possibly not even with a living one, but with a kingly bird of prey and a dying symbol. He stands up to the eagle: 'I don't yield to you ... / ... nor your blood-thirsty sun ... / And you, great bird, sun-starer, heavy black beak / Can be put out of office as sacrifice bringer' (*CP* 374). This poem, the first of the sequence to be located in America, does not attract much praise from critics, who tend to see the American poems as a descent into heckling or 'thinning' of style,[19] but its rhetorical and imagistic strategies and its claims are not inconsistent with what precedes it: what is different here is the speaker's greater self-assurance – he has seized the heroic stance for himself, let fly the 'real demon'.

'The Blue Jay', another American poem (and the last one in this group), is routinely overlooked, though this beast is allowed to laugh at Lawrence: 'It's the blue jay laughing at us' and 'Turning his back on us all' (*CP* 375). This poem becomes a metatextual comment on Lawrence's own rhetoric: the bird, 'acid-blue metallic' like the Almond-Trees of the early part of the book, speaks with a '*voice of the Lord*', which is, according to Lawrence, the same sound as 'the scrape of ridicule'. Lawrence questions the bird, 'Whose boss are you?' But he does not question its 'jeering' or mosquito-like offered tail; the blue jay enunciates Lawrence's own heroic mockery.

In 'Animals', which contains more poems than any other section of the book, Lawrence begins by reviewing some previous territory, then moves around the globe in quest of a place to stand. He replays the helpless desire of his tortoise in 'The Ass' and the 'He-Goat', which he contrasts with the defiant solidness of the female ass and goat. These males, though technically large and, originally, fighting beasts, are nonetheless more ridiculous and more thoroughly degraded than the tortoise in their 'fall' into 'the rut of love' (*CP* 378). By the end of 'The Ass', however, the male ass is able to announce, in obvious parody of Nietzsche, that '*All mares are dead!*' (*CP* 380). The remaining poems in this section retrace Lawrence's actual journey 'backwards' southeast to Kandy, to Australia and finally to America. He satirises the Prince of Wales who fails to speak with the voice of command, '*Dient Ihr*', which the elephants and servants crave; the poet longs to speak for, and as, the prince – to herald himself: '*A prince . . . come back to you*' (*CP* 392). Female beasts, similarly, compel both pity and ridicule: he notes pityingly the kangaroo's wistful patience and her gravitation downward into the earth, as she yearns 'for a new signal from life' (*CP* 394); while he jeers at the craven little dog Bibbles – who fawns over people and flees other dogs – for 'lov[ing] . . . indiscriminat[ely], a 'democratic' pup (*CP* 399). 'Learn loyalty rather than loving', he says, and then 'I'll protect you' (*CP* 400).

There is a more heroic role than this, however, awaiting him in this section, and a more serious tone increasingly takes hold, as he turns from disillusionment and satire to two direct confrontations, first, with the destruction of the great beasts of prey in America, in 'Mountain Lion', and then with a proud Indian in 'The Red Wolf'. In 'Mountain Lion' he recognises 'men' as the only creatures to fear in the wilderness; mourning men's killing of a mountain lion, he says wistfully, there 'was room' enough for 'me and a mountain lion' (*CP* 402). More sinisterly, he also says 'we' wouldn't miss 'a million or two of humans' (*CP* 402) as we miss a mountain lion. Moving on from this holocaustal 'joke' about discardable people, he enters directly, once again, into its opposite, the visionary mood. The next poem presents his mutually combative, mutually respectful dialogue with an Indian who calls himself both by ethereal and earthly names, 'Star-Road' and 'red wolf'; the Lawrentian persona had at first claimed for himself, as a new chief, the title of 'red wolf', but is compelled eventually to come up with a new name, a hybrid: 'red-dawn-wolf' (*CP* 405). Commentators frequently single this poem out for praise, for the 'I' at last takes on a fully dramatised role as an animal-man in dialogue with an equal; one commentator even argues that the book should have ended here.[20] If it had, one of two consequences might have occurred for the reader, who (if the reader were persuaded by its vision) would then have perceived the book as ending outside the mock-epic or (if unpersuaded – and a writer such as Lawrence would naturally anticipate this) would have seen this last poem as merely a joke – an impossible, unbelievable ending. A mood of near-certainty and attained heroism has almost entirely taken over from the querying, querulous movement of the mock-heroic, and few readers would suspend disbelief for this particular vision. There is something dreamily Quixote-like about the idea of Lawrence remaining on respectful terms with 'Star-Road', and the slight comic effect of this poem points to New-Red-Dog's lingering desire to succeed or supplant 'Star-Road' (his keenness to be top dog) as well as to the unlikeliness of their encounter. Yet it is a more serious poem than most others in this book, and it succeeds in seeming visionary for some readers, I would argue, precisely because it occurs as yet another residually humorous event in a picaresque quest that has no clear ending, no final sense of closure.

The book goes on to a last section of 'Ghosts' and a closing poem (standing outside the last section), 'The American Eagle'. In 'Ghosts', the now-bardic speaker faces an odd, mildly funny world of sleepers. He confronts first the 'Men in New Mexico', but not only the men: he sees the grand mountains, Indians, whites, all asleep and unable to wake up. In 'Autumn at Taos', he wonders, with some irony, at a landscape made up of the unmoving skins of wild animals who (in their sleep) let him trot along at ease on his pony. Then, in 'Spirits Summoned West', a fantasy about women parallel in both theme and spirit to his previous dream of male bonding in 'The Red Wolf', he turns from musing on a slumbering landscape to summoning the spirits of all the dead and deliberately buried women of the past. Disinterring the term 'virgin', he conjures them to return, not as devouring mothers or wives, but (in contrast to the over-ripe 'Figs') as women still yearning for a home in a man: 'It was only I who saw the virgin you / That had no home', 'Come... / Now [that] the divided yearning' between husband and child 'is over' (CP 411). This flock of virgins may, as Kate eventually does in his subsequent novel The Plumed Serpent, join the red wolves of America in a new race of men and women. But such an end is yet to come. In the last poem, 'The American Eagle', he stops short with the mock-heroic. Speaking once more with a voice half-satiric, half-conjuring, he prods the unheroic male beast, telling the eagle (like 'St Mark') to choose what he will be: one who will shed 'a little blood', 'commanding a teeming obedience', or one who will misplace his powers (and his sex) in mothering others (CP 414).

To summarise a mock-heroic work in this way, particularly a mock-heroic book of poems, is necessarily to reduce it, to 'mock' – in my turn – its complex means and ends. It is not my desire to make the poems seem simpler than they are. But it is necessarily difficult to disassociate mockery from heroism in reading 'little' epics like this one: the more earnestly heroic parts (as in 'Spirits Summoned West') can seem absurd, while the more light-heartedly mocking parts (as in 'Pomegranate') may, paradoxically, seem brave and even visionary; then again, a single poem may produce wildly divergent reactions on the part of different commentators (as with 'Snake').[21] At the same time, the varying moods reinforce the sense of movement, of journeying, in this book, as both the 'mock' and the 'heroic' are pressed into service in a single epic quest and as mockery gradually gives way to heroism. Lawrence explores his Aesopian creatures in order to mirror not only his own divided image back to himself, but the diverse imagery also of women against men, of men against men, of man's effeminacy against his manliness and of contemporary society against an imagined past and future. The result is, I think, a manifoldly amusing, compelling and irritating set of poems: prolific as it is in representing the multitudinous creature-world, it is also a fragmented and polemical – divided *and* divisive – text.

Notes

1 See, for example, *D.H. Lawrence: Selected Poetry and Non-fictional Prose*, ed. John Lucas (Routledge, 1990), p. 18.

2 *The Complete Poems*, ed. Vivian de Sola Pinto and Warren Roberts (Harmondsworth: Penguin Books, 1971), pp. 27–8. Subsequent citations to the poetry appear in the text in the form (*CP* 27–8).

3 For previous readings of the mythic narratives in *Birds, Beasts and Flowers*, see Sandra Gilbert, *Acts of Attention: The Poems of D.H. Lawrence*, 2nd edn (Carbondale: Southern Illinois Press, 1990), pp. 131–89 and 'Hell on Earth: *Birds, Beasts and Flowers* as Subversive Narrative', *D.H. Lawrence Review*, xii (1979), 256–74. See also Harold Bloom, 'Lawrence, Eliot, Blackmur, and the Tortoise' in *A D.H. Lawrence Miscellany*, ed. Harry T. Moore (Carbondale: Southern Illinois University Press, 1959), pp. 360–9; M.J. Lockwood, *A Study of the Poems of D.H. Lawrence: Thinking in Poetry* (New York: St Martin's Press, 1987), pp. 102–42; and Gail Porter Mandell, *The Phoenix Paradox: A Study of Renewal Through Change in the Collected Poems and Last Poems of D.H. Lawrence* (Carbondale: Southern Illinois University Press, 1984), pp. 96–119.

4 See, for example, Gilbert, *Acts of Attention*, p. 142 and Lockwood, *A Study of the Poems*, p. 139.

5 Keith Sagar, *D.H. Lawrence: A Calendar of His Works* (Austin: University of Texas Press, 1979), p. 101; Introduction to Maurice Magnus's *Memoirs of the Foreign Legion, Phoenix II: Uncollected, Unpublished and Other Prose Works by D.H. Lawrence* ed. Warren Roberts and Harry T. Moore (Heinemann, 1968), p. 343. Sagar lists 'The Mosquito' as the 'earliest' poem in *The Art of D.H. Lawrence*

(Cambridge: Cambridge University Press, 1966), p. 118, but investigates uncertainties in its dating in *D.H. Lawrence: Life into Art* (Athens: The University of Georgia Press, 1985), p. 216.

6 Gilbert, *Acts of Attention*, p. 164; Philip Hobsbaum, *A Reader's Guide to D.H. Lawrence* (Thames and Hudson, 1981), p. 132; Marjoric Perloff, 'Lawrence's Lyric Theater: *Birds, Beasts and Flowers*' in *D.H. Lawrence: A Centenary Consideration*, ed. Peter Balbert and Philip L. Marcus (Ithaca: Cornell University Press, 1985), p. 121.

7 Perloff, 'Lawrence's Lyric Theater', pp. 121–2, 122.

8 Sagar, *The Art of D.H. Lawrence*, p. 118 and *Life into Art*, pp. 208, 216.

9 Only two other poems like 'Tropic' and 'Southern Night' eventually made their way into *Birds, Beasts and Flowers*, yet their positioning is significant. Together with 'Peace', 'The Revolutionary' (in which 'I' imagines himself a Samson pulling down the pillars of European civilisation) and 'The Evening Land' (in which he toys with the possibility of 'demonish' America as the ultimate goal of his picaresque journey – which indeed it became in this book) are placed following the first section of nature poems, where they announce the larger epic aims of the book (*CP* 287, 293). 'Tropic' and 'Southern Night' appear following the second section, where they target the geographical direction 'south' of these early sections (all placed in southern Europe) as a likely site for revolutionary upheaval.

10 *Desperate Storytelling: Post-Romantic Elaborations of the Mock-Heroic Mode* (Athens: The University of Georgia Press, 1987), p. 4.

11 Fleishman, 'He Do the Polis in Different Voices: Lawrence's Later Style', in *D.H. Lawrence: A Centenary Consideration*, ed. Balbert and Marcus, p. 162.

12 Ibid., pp. 169, 167–8.

13 I am not the first to point to the poetry as an important link in DHL's narrational development. Gilbert stresses its role in the shift from the earlier novels 'of society' to the mythic revisionism and romances of the later prose ('Hell on Earth', p. 258); and most critics of the poetry point to the thematic connections between these poems and the later prose.

14 Fleishman, 'He Do the Polis', p. 169. *D.H. Lawrence: Selected Poems*, ed. Kenneth Rexroth (New York: Viking Press, 1959), p. 14.

15 Perloff, 'Lawrence's Lyric Theater', pp. 118–20.

16 Ibid., p. 118.

17 In 'West by East: The Psycho-Geography of *Birds, Beasts and Flowers*', *D.H. Lawrence Review*, xii (1979), 241–55, George Y. Trail has been almost alone in examining DHL's anxiety about his masculinity in these poems, and though he neglects the witty contradictoriness both of DHL's creatures and his polemics, Trail's reading is not as 'limited a view' as Mandell suggests (*The Phoenix Paradox*, p. 98); he dwells both on the psychological dimensions of this anxiety and on its linkage to DHL's mythologisation of himself at the end of a cycle of civilisation. My own previous reading of this book neglects the gender theme almost entirely, instead stressing the multiple structures that organise the book – its disorderly order – and the generic character of the poems as 'fables' or little (Aesopian) epics, in *Self and Sequence: The Poetry of D.H. Lawrence* (Charlottesville: University Press of Virginia, 1988), pp. 126–47.

18 In *A Theory of Parody: The Teachings of Twentieth-Century Art Forms* (New York and London: Methuen, 1985), Linda Hutcheon makes a trenchant distinction between 'parody' and 'satire' in her delineation of 'parody' as a primary mode of modern, and postmodern, writing; parodistic modern writing is not, as she rightly points out, intrinsically satiric. She argues additionally that a text may be parodic without necessarily being funny. But the parodistic mock-heroism of DHL's poems frequently does include satire, and it is often funny (in satiric as well as non-satiric moments); and it is illuminating to consider the shifts and combinations in such attitudes as this book develops because they manifest DHL's divergent, yet compatible, aims: to cauterise contemporary social ills, to jog readers into accepting change, to fend off despair, to explore alternatives and to acknowledge the humble as well as the heroic in himself and other creatures.

19 Lockwood, *A Study of the Poems*, pp. 138–9; Sagar, *Life into Art*, p. 245.

20 Lockwood, *A Study of the Poems*, pp. 140–1; see also Mandell, *The Phoenix Paradox*, pp. 116–17 and Gilbert, *Acts of Attention*, pp. 332, 342, 347.

21 Consider, for example, the contrast between the unstinting praise of 'Snake' by Hobsbaum, *A Reader's Guide*, pp. 132–3, and the criticism by Lockwood, *A Study of the Poems*, pp. 126–7.

～ 6

Comedy and provisionality: Lawrence's address to his audience and material in his Australian novels

Paul Eggert

I

Applying a new and at first sight unlikely focus to Lawrence's writings – the presence and workings of comedy in them – has, I believe, the power to help clear a now-historical log-jam in Lawrence criticism. His post-Second World War critics inevitably constructed their image of him according to the needs of their age, and those needs have changed: the seductions of the saviour-Lawrence or normative-Lawrence of the 1950s to 1970s are rapidly losing their allure. I am not offering in this essay to contextualise historically the rise and dissemination of this Lawrence: the priest of love, the anti-mechanisation vitalist, the morally intelligent prophet of Life, the exposer of the distorting effects involved in the tyranny of mind over body. Yet, it seems to me, a historiography of Lawrence criticism badly needs to be done. It would, I envisage, relate the normative-Lawrence to the increasing numbers of departments of English after 1945 (and especially in the 1960s); and it would examine the rise of New Criticism and Leavisism as their intellectual vehicles in a period when commitment to older forms of historicism (requiring large research libraries) was gradually falling away.[1] The account would discuss that sense of post-war cultural crisis which the Lawrence of the period was, at some level I suspect, felt to be addressing: industrial and atomic age anxieties; the de-politicised cultural navel-gazing caused by the deadly melodrama of Cold War politics – or, putting the emphasis differently, the fear of a politicising style of literary criticism in a McCarthyite era. And it would speak of Lawrence's recruitment, as the author of *Lady Chatterley*, to the doctrines of sexual permissiveness of

131

the 1960s. This Lawrence could, I suspect, then be seen as a construction of the period, a Lawrence who has, inevitably, been speaking to fewer and fewer people.

What I would like to see emerge is a new approach which permits emphasis on aspects of the man's life and writings which the older construction found inconvenient, and ignored, or sought to explain away. For instance, Kingsley Widmer's study of Lawrence's fiction published in 1962, *The Art of Perversity*, predictably (one sees in retrospect) did not find much favour. When, as a postgraduate student, I came across it in the late 1970s, I breathed a sigh of relief to find someone saying the unsayable, breaking the taboo, even though I could find no after-echoes of his voice. Widmer, without realising it apparently, had developed an argument which John Heywood Thomas had memorably inaugurated in an article published by T.S. Eliot in the *Criterion* in 1930: 'The Perversity of D.H. Lawrence'.[2] In a commentary, in 1955, on the posthumous disputes about Lawrence's status as a novelist and worth as a man, F.R. Leavis would refer to it dismissively on the basis of its title.[3]

Heywood Thomas had seized on what the post-war critics would not wish to notice or at least to stress. As an essayist of the 1930s and later a professor of French, Heywood Thomas was in a good position to register his (and in many ways, his educated class and period's) unease with Lawrence's mode of thinking. His essay (and it is an *essay*) is a distillation and exploration of the kind of objection which gentleman-critics had been mounting in reviews of Lawrence's works throughout the 1920s. Thinking probably of *Women in Love* and certainly of *Twilight in Italy*, Heywood Thomas nominated as perverse the way in which Lawrence

> deprives things and persons of their identity and submerges them in the flux of an abstract principle . . . This prejudice of Lawrence's gives one a curious and unpleasant feeling of unreality. It deprives persons and things of their opaqueness; there remains nothing beyond them. And that is so stifling . . . Uninterpreted, facts seem to enjoy a certain freedom and independence; they give one a feeling of spaciousness. Lawrence robs them of this independence by showing them up as the products of a close, inner necessity.[4]

Heywood Thomas was objecting to the way in which Lawrence's polari-
ties relentlessly draw into their opposite interpretative orbits his render-
ings of landscape, peoples, character types, events. The polarising clarity
comes at a cost – which Widmer put his finger on. Lawrence, he wrote,
could deal with creative marriage in essence but not (after 1915) with its
existence over time; Lawrence was interested in vital sexuality but not in
procreation and its responsibilities. A stagnating marriage or family relations, on the other hand, characteristically uncover a morally cowed
society whose vital energies are trammelled and subdued (e.g. Mr and
Mrs Crich in *Women in Love*, the Lindleys in 'Daughters of the Vicar', the
Saywells in *The Virgin and the Gipsy*). The plight is seen as general; the
offered solution is correspondingly drastic, even repugnant. So Banford
(in 'The Fox') must be killed, various demon-lovers (such as Count
Psanek in 'The Ladybird') honoured and obeyed. As a reader of
Lawrence's prose, one is frequently encouraged, especially when intense
emotions are being treated of, to participate in the production of meaning
via a predominantly co-ordinative syntax with frequent use of incanta-
tory repetition, and with occasional sentence elements that are syn-
tactically ambiguous and which one needs to resolve. Lawrence does not
allow us to occupy a distanced position from an already resolved meaning.[5] Deliberately stepping back from the seductions and identifications-
with-the-experience such prose offers the reader, Widmer underlined the
morally questionable outcomes of Lawrence's developing extremist positions: his vilifications of the power of the mind over the body, of the
repression of feelings, of female possessiveness and of industrialisation.

Widmer was literally right about the extremism. Recent and younger
readers of Lawrence sense it straight away; the tactic of explaining away
the outcomes because of the essentially health-giving emphases of
Lawrence's thought does not, in my experience, wash any longer. I, personally, never accepted it – except in a half-comprehending, wishful way
as an undergraduate in the early 1970s. 'My' Lawrence has had to be
described in other terms, ones that acknowledged the extremism not as
a problem but as an aspect of their *modus vivendi*. I have tried to understand the process or dynamic of his writing, to identify the sources of its
reach and compellingness, not in terms of its 'metaphysic' but of its

process.[6] Although there are exclusions and vilifications, there can be also clarifications in tracking extreme states of feeling and thinking, and liberation in the process of reaching them. From 1913, the distance and detachment that Heywood Thomas so desired is denied us in Lawrence's participatory prose: Lawrence knew how to take the reader intensely or exhilaratingly with him. He was just as interested in plumbing extremes of degradation and vengefulness as he was in understanding the emotional and creative vocabulary of marriage. His reading of Dostoevsky had not been in vain. In a letter of 1916, he honoured Mark Gertler for the depraved, mechanised spirit he could, in his paintings, create so thoroughly (ii. 660–1); and equally he honoured the apparently despicable Maurice Magnus, in 1921, for being the courageous wizard rat who could tunnel through sewers of spiritual degradation and corruption.[7]

Lawrence's interests were only sometimes on the side of the angels. To defend his personal integrity and purity of motive, and to demonstrate his psychological undividedness as Catherine Carswell in the 1930s and, especially, Leavis from the 1950s sought vigorously to do was understandable, but is surely now beside the point.[8] Insistence on his human centrality can only sound pious or nostalgic nowadays. And it misses the way Lawrence could throw himself into his characters' states of mind with an amoral changeability and willingness to experiment. His philosophy did not come from a single speaking position. Yet this has been the working assumption of much Lawrence criticism – whether in defence of him or in attack. To attack, one objects to the extremist outcomes (Lawrence as male chauvinist, fascist, etc.) This is to convert such outcomes into a series of nasty propositions, a specifiable, more-or-less systematic philosophy, a monologic. Or one goes further and constructs the method and mind which lies behind them (Heywood Thomas). One defends in essentially the same way. By showing an array of counter-indications, one constructs from his writings a health-giving philosophy of body and mind which assigns his extremist conclusions to a subsidiary place. Critics have time and again been embarrassingly beholden to his vocabulary when engaged in this expository task.[9] But Lawrence in his writing, it seems to me, was more chameleon, mercurial, even at times slippery, than has been recognised: not casuistical in regard to what he espoused, but changeable in his address to it – and thus changeable about the very basis of 'espousal'.

To recognise this is to wish to alter the tenor of prevailing accounts of his achievement. And it is to recognise the function of comedy in his writing. This is where the present volume on comedy should be of benefit. Other chapters in this volume describe Lawrence's 'comedy' as emerging from his habit of employing two voices: one, let us say of the Birkin kind, which allows Lawrence to philosophise, speculate, even rant; the other, of Ursula's sarcastic or affectionately ironic kind, which pricks the ballooning implications of Birkin's extremist intellectual positions.[10] Bakhtin's notion of dialogism, of polyvocality, has recently been called on by Lawrence critics to theorise this approach, potentially turning attention from unified theme or philosophy (imagined as stemming from a 'monologic' voice) to a less readily reassuring emphasis on techniques of divided expression.[11]

Thus Wayne Booth confessed in 1985 that

> much of my initial distress in reading *The Rainbow* and *Women in Love* came from my failure to recognize just how often Lawrence attempts double-voiced narration . . . I fell into the very trap that I've spent a lifetime warning my students against – assuming that a character's words and judgments belong to the implied author. Lawrence was experimenting radically with what it means for a novelist to lose his own distinct voice in the voices of his characters, especially in their inner voices . . . This is not simply the traditional problem produced by subtle but stable irony . . . Again and again Lawrence simply surrenders the telling of the story to another mind, a mind neither clearly approved nor clearly repudiated yet presented in a tone that demands judgment. I don't know of any novelist, not even Dostoyevsky, who takes free indirect style further in the direction of a sustained surrender to a passionate mimicry that gives us two or more voices at once: the author's and the independent character's. The result inevitably blurs our picture of just where the implied author stands.[12]

An essay by David Lodge on Lawrence and Bakhtin also appeared in 1985. In it, as well as making a similar point to the one Booth makes, he drew comparisons between *Women in Love* and a comment of Bakhtin's about Dostoevsky. Bakhtin wrote:

> Everything in this novel [*Crime and Punishment*] – the fates of people, their experience and ideas – is pushed to its boundaries, everything is prepared, as it were, to pass over into its opposite . . . everything is taken to extremes, to its uttermost limit. There is nothing in the novel that could become stabilised, nothing that could relax within itself, enter the ordinary flow of biographical time and develop within it . . . everything requires change and rebirth.[13]

In a fine, independent-minded essay of 1978, Richard Drain had developed a similar case about *Women in Love*, about the instabilities, the sudden psychological irruptions, the absence of cause-and-effect explanations, the physical surprises, the continuous intellectual tension and strain which characterise it.[14] In a number of articles from 1979 I have tried to portray the push toward extremes as an intrinsic part of the processes of Lawrence's polarised imagining and thinking – as well as to date their development in and from his revisions of *The Prussian Officer* stories in July 1914. What Bakhtin calls the social-psychological novel with its 'already available and stable positions – family, social, biographical'[15] and its reliance in its plotting on a law of cause and effect were increasingly left behind after *Sons and Lovers* – as a comparison of the stories of Arnold Bennett's Anna Tellwright (from *Anna of the Five Towns*, 1902) with Lawrence's Anna Brangwen, or the 1912–13 versions of Lawrence's travel essays with their 1915–16 developments in *Twilight in Italy*, will, I have argued elsewhere, readily show.[16] Although I did not know the word in the early 1980s, I was arguing in essence that a 'monologic' account of Lawrence's metaphysic would be simply misleading unless one paid attention to the motor forces which drove it. The coming of Bakhtin's ideas on to the Lawrence scene since the mid 1980s tempts me to insist that an understanding of Lawrence's processes of polarised thinking, his attitude to them and to his audience, ought, at least *pro tem*, to occupy centre stage. The biographical and textual scholarship of the last ten or fifteen years has been providing the evidence – the textual and intertextual traces of those processes – from which to work and to begin to generalise with confidence.

Bakhtin's emphasis on contrary voices within the texture of novelistic prose (dialogism) is a powerful concept.[17] Because language is always in a process of becoming, he argues, and is embedded in social and historical contexts, stratified 'languages' usually act in the novel as carriers of contrary ideologies, or world views. A novelist can activate this potential for internal dialogue in many ways; a comic playing with different characters' 'languages' is an obvious form of it. Bakhtin also maintains that the author's conscious manipulation of dialogism through characters' disagreements in dialogue is only a surface form of 'a more fundamental speech diversity' which allows those oppositions to be voiced.[18] Although Bakhtin's approach recognises the role of authorial intention and of the listener (and 'his apperceptive background'[19]) in discourse, his emphasis falls on the structural importance of dialogism in language. This emphasis widens the concepts of parody and comedy and so opens up the novel form to untraditional kinds of commentary, based on the flexibilities of voice. I wish to particularise this theme, hoping to demonstrate the rewards of listening for Lawrence's encounters, in the moment of writing, with his material and his audience.

Behind the often earnest and passionate engagement with ideas and intense emotions – which, for so many people, is the Lawrentian trademark – lurks a form of comedy. It is to be found in the self-distancing implied by the encounters, especially in the early 1920s when his earlier aspiration of writing for his civilisation[20] had been replaced, under the strains of the suppression of *The Rainbow* in 1915 and of the war, with a wary alienation from his audience. The publication in 1984 of *Mr Noon* (written 1920–1) drew attention to a canniness that had been little remarked on.[21]

The tensions generated by Lawrence's feeling obliged to set Part I of the novel in the provinces are evident. He had not been able to get *Women in Love* published until 1920. He had just based on Eastwood the first section of *The Lost Girl* as part of his declared effort to make some money from his writing. And for the previous two or three years he had been consciously trying to satisfy the demand of magazine editors for relatively undemanding love stories set in familiar territory.[22] Using his home-town material yet again in *Mr Noon* was an explosive recipe. Only too aware of the artificialities of a realist tradition, Lawrence turns mocking ironies, even abuse, on the contractual partner in his writing – his readers – and on their expectations. Deep tonal fissures open up between his inward and apparently sympathetic accounts of Emmie's and Noon's awakening passions, and Lawrence's skirmishes with the middle class 'rather cowardly and imbecile' audience he constructs. Nevertheless, the satirical mode allows him to puncture some balloons delightfully: 'Emmie, we had forgotten to say, was engaged to Walter George all the time she was carrying-on with Mr Noon. The fact so easily slipped her memory that it slipped ours.'[23] In the appreciation of this kind of thing, another audience is implied; but there remains a brittle-ness in the comedy.

The writing of Part II obviously released some of the pressures. An unfinished manuscript, it retains a first-draft freshness. The ironies become affectionate as the immediate concerns and pressures of 1921 give place to a lightly fictionalised, travelogue-type recall of his early months in Germany and Austria with Frieda in 1912. He found it possible to voice a fuller-bodied, ambitious but (as compared with Part I's combativeness) more vulnerable narrative response to landscape; and readers of Part II feel far less badgered and buttonholed – as they are apt to feel in Part I. Although Lawrence revised Part I after having written Part II and, with various touches, heightened the element of witty display in the former's verbal comedy, no peace treaty with his audience was entered into.

II

Lawrence's comic-contemptuous attitude to his audience and its expectations in *Mr Noon* is tied up with his attitude to his home-town material. In *Kangaroo* (written in 1922) however, his material is at least ostensibly Australian; but again his attitude to his material is deeply equivocal. Summaries of the novel's 'concerns' usually refer to the alternation of Somers's loyalties between isolate manhood and collabo-rative social action, and demonstrate how they form part of a continuing

1920s' discourse in Lawrence's prose on male leadership. In looking to establish the philosophical or political reach of the novel, such accounts are apt to find curious or lamentable the narrator's admissions of having run out of inspiration and his deliberate undermining of the pretence of his fiction-making. Yet those passages reveal more about the basis of Lawrence's art than the more satisfyingly dramatised sections: they bring to the surface the many-voicedness, experimentality and risk-taking that monological accounts of Lawrence's philosophy tend to cast to the margins of his achievement.

Lawrence's material consisted largely of his and Frieda's thin vein of encounters with Australian people and his richer vein of encounters with towns and landscapes during May–August 1922 in Western Australia and New South Wales, some reading of newspapers and magazines while at Thirroul (NSW) and, possibly, some information from someone he met about an Australian secret army of returned soldiers.[24] Lawrence does not maintain a constant distance from this material nor from the character it is filtered through – Somers. Sometimes, Lawrence's relations with him seem straightforwardly autobiographical (e.g. the self-justificatory tone of Somers's run-in with the taxi-driver in chapter 1); at other times, satirical (Somers as reserved and stubborn Englishman), or imbued with the kind of impersonality which comes from intense personal involvement in recording or exploring-on-the-page a disorienting experience (as in Somers's fear in the West Australian bush at night). Correspondingly, Lawrence's relations with his audience waver or swing through varying distances and intensities.

Comedy inheres in this instability which is intrinsic to his art. While all critics of the novel point to Harriett's mocking and deriding voice, it is not the only source of dialogic:

> Man is a thought-adventurer. Man is more, he is a life-adventurer. Which means he is a thought-adventurer, an emotion-adventurer, and a discoverer of himself and of the outer universe. A discoverer.
>
> "I am a fool," said Richard Lovatt [Somers], which was the most frequent discovery he made. It came, moreover, every time with a new shock of surprise and chagrin...

> Now a novel is supposed to be a mere record of emotion-adventurers, flounderings in feelings. We insist that a novel is, or should be, also a thought-adventure, if it is to be anything at all complete.[25]

The mock-solemnity of the professorial 'We' (and the audience it teasingly constructs) is followed by an article of faith, it would seem. But it is no sooner stated than found wanting: what then follows is a (failed) attempt to wring some thought-value for understanding Somers's conflicting impulses for isolation and social involvement out of variations on the metaphor of the fly in the ointment. Lawrence takes his inspiration as he finds it; this is the end of it: 'I am sorry to have to stand, a sorry sight, preening my wings on the brink of the ointment-pot, thought Richard. But from this vantage ground let me preach to myself.—He preached, and the record was taken down for this gramophone of a novel' (K 280:15–18). Lawrence's attempts elsewhere to weave meaning out of the miscellaneity of Somers's meetings and excogitations do not always share the comic wryness of this attempt; and indeed the earnestness of the attempts elsewhere gives an edge to the comic element here, preventing it from becoming free and easy. But the difference throughout is one of tonal address rather than of kind. 'Chapter follows chapter, and nothing doing' (K 284:3), laments the narrator at the beginning of the next chapter. Lawrence dares his reader to give up – or to give up cherishing novelistic expectations.

The 'novel' is a rag-bag of a category, accommodating multifarious forms of prose and defensible as a generic term probably only in terms of its bulging convenience. Even so, in *Kangaroo* Lawrence gives its boundaries an extra stretch. Much of it is a series of meditations, or meditative sorties; and, as the above quotations whimsically indicate, it is aware of its own proceedings. Lawrence gives his own different moods, perspectives and temptations their own voices by having the characters argue them out idiomatically and in action, dramatically. So Jack Callcott and Jaz, and later Kangaroo and Willie Struthers, tempt Somers into the kind of political and manly action for which one part of Lawrence must have yearned. Somers becomes also a voice for Lawrence the landscape-writer in his effort, throughout the novel, to articulate the antipodean foreignness: 'You feel you can't *see* – as if your eyes hadn't the vision in them to correspond with the outside landscape' (*K* 77:3–5). The ready capacity for ethno-geography by which Lawrence had been able to interpret Austrian and Italian peasants as expressions of their European landscape in the essays in *Twilight in Italy* (1916) and in the mountain chapters in *The Lost Girl* deserts him in Australia:

> "It always seems to me," said Somers, "that somebody will have to water Australia with their blood before it's a real man's country. The soil, the very plants, seem to be waiting for it."
>
> "You've got a lurid imagination, my dear man," said Jack.
>
> "Yes he has," said Harriett. "He's always so extreme." (*K* 78:14–18)

The bower-bird in Lawrence is at work here in Somers: someone in Western Australia had probably put the idea into his head (it recurs in *The Boy in the Bush*, probably courtesy of Mollie Skinner's 'The House of Ellis').[26] Lawrence has the narrative method to entertain the idea earnestly as well as mock it, but without finalising an attitude to his material and without establishing a pact – reliable common ground for understanding it – with his reader.

Occasions like this stress the provisionality of his art. It is there equally in the sections where we would not think of looking for it, as for instance in the account in chapter VI of Harriett and Somers's visit to Sydney to see Kangaroo. Annoyed at Harriett's disbelief, Kangaroo gives a vision-ary account of his principle of Love:

> "... But if I can let out the real fire of happiness from the heart and bowels of man that is born of woman and woman that is born of man—" Then suddenly he broke off: "And whether I can or not, I *love* them," he shouted, in a voice suddenly become loud and passionate. "I love them. I love *you*, you woman born of man, I do, and I defy you to prevent me. Fiery you are, and fiery am I, and fire should be friends with fire. And when you make me angry, with your jealousy and mis-trust like the ants, I remember, I remind myself: 'But see the beauty of the fire in her! And think how the ants have tortured her and filled her with fear and with horror!'" (*K* 121:33–122:2)

The sermonising can be annoying if one is looking to attach its sentiments to aspects of Australian political history or national character-
types. But Lawrence is master of the chant: the fervour, in setting aside
one's expectation, has its effect.

> "But the men that are born like ants, out of the cold interval, and are
> womanless, they are not sick of themselves. They are full of cold
> energy, and they seethe with cold fire in the ant-hill, making new cor-
> ridors, new chambers—they alone know what for. And they have cold,
> formic-acid females, as restless as themselves, and as active about the
> ant-hill, and as identical with the dried clay of the building ... This is
> the world, and the people of the world. And with their cold, active
> bodies the ant-men and the ant-women swarm over the face of the
> earth.   (K121:5–10,13–16)

The account is capped off by the horrible story of the Ceylonese puppies
found eaten alive by white ants. The tonal disjunctions offered by the
polarising metaphor (ant-coldness versus fire-warmth) support the
meditation on Love. Lawrence is pushing towards a polar principle, an
extreme, and Kangaroo is given a personality robust enough to localise,
if not fully to individualise, the meditation. But Lawrence rapidly
changes level, scaling down to the ironic and affectionate tones of an
exchange of letters between Kangaroo and Harriett on the mock-
question of ownership of Somers. Is this now the 'real' Lawrence, a
recognisably sane ironic controller of his tale's significations, one the
reader can identify with?[27] No, as we soon find, it is only a gesture toward
his duties as novelist – an acknowledgement of the need for scepticism,
humour, irony. If the meditation cannot withstand gentle undermining,
Lawrence must have felt, it does not deserve to stand: some undercutting
might even offer, serendipitously, opportunities for development or
variation of the basic terms. It is this sort of chameleon attitude to his
material to which I believe we need to attune ourselves as readers.

Disconcertingly, the meditative ambitiousness abruptly resumes with
Somers on the beach, contesting Kangaroo's terms:

> These days Somers too was filled with fury. As for loving mankind, or
> having a fire of love in his heart, it was all rot. He felt almost fierily

cold. He liked the sea, the pale sea of green glass that fell in such cold foam. Ice-fiery, fish-burning.—He went out on to the low flat rocks at low tide, skirting the deep rock-holes that were full of brilliantly clear water and delicately-coloured shells and tiny, crimson anemones Strangely sea-scooped sharp sea-bitter rock-floor, all wet and sea-savage. And standing at the edge looking at the waves rather terrifyingly rolling at him, where he stood low and exposed, far out from the sand-banks, and as he watched the gannets gleaming white, then falling with a splash like white sky-arrows into the waves, he wished as he had never wished before that he could be cold, as sea-things are cold, and murderously fierce. To have oneself exultantly ice-cold, not one spark of this wretched warm flesh left, and to have all the terrific, ice-energy of a fish.   (*K*125:7–21)

Thus Somers contests the principle of Love by re-imagining its negative pole (coldness) as a positive one. In terms of character, neither Somers (nor, behind him, his creator), keeps to a steady centre of self; no thick outline contains him. Rather, his moods are followed; they lead to surprising turns of fancy which are yet gripping in their urgency or violence. The common element with Kangaroo's meditation is the intensity; and Somers's half-admission of complicity in it here ('this wretched warm flesh') shows he will swing between the two poles throughout the novel. The Secret Army plot is only the occasion for this inner, meditative drama whose terms are pushed and extended till they touch and differentially enlighten modern marriage, male comradeship, left-wing revolt and benevolent autocracy.

'The Nightmare' chapter is a *tour de force*, as most readers agree; but for all its urgency it is also a piece of stylised prose – no less than the mock-serious account of modern relationships in chapter ix, 'Harriett and Lovatt at Sea in Marriage'. Only the tonal vehicle is different. 'The Nightmare' is an anger-*driven* recollection of Somers/Lawrence's wartime call-up for medical examination and of the events surrounding it. It seems to be written from the quick of a now-erupting resentment; there is a thronging plenitude of recollection. Yet, for all that, it is another verbally constructed voice unconstrained by a steady notion of Somers's 'character'; the voice is another participant in the polyphony of this novel. There is no attempt to disguise the personal basis of the case about the collapse of English society around 1916. The angle Lawrence takes only coheres in the resentment he expresses: significantly, one does not try to disconnect the case from the speaker. That relationship is its ambience, its life. Thus despite the reversion to a setting in wartime England, the chapter is not disjoint from the novel's procedure: Lawrence argues with and from different sides of himself throughout. The chapter also explains the genesis of Somers's belief in isolation. It was a needful defence against the psychological depredations of the military, and now it is a defence against the ideals of Kangaroo and Struthers.

The eruption of this voice may well have been a surprise to its author – 'why had it all come back on him? It had seemed so past, so gone' (K 260:11–12) – but his decision (as I imagine) in the act of writing to give it its head is another example of the risk-taking provisionality I have mentioned. A chapter of wound-licking follows, and then there is 'Bits' with its self-conscious construction of the novel from amusing snippets from Australian newspapers and the Sydney *Bulletin* magazine which Lawrence had happened upon. The reader finds reliable ground neither with the tale nor the teller. Lawrence's relationships with his material and audience are too slippery or unpredictable – too comic – for that.

III

Many readers of *The Boy in the Bush* have difficulty with Jack Grant's pretensions to an Abraham-like Patriarchy in the empty Australian North-West, with the portentousness of the aspiration, and with the excessiveness of his revulsions and hatreds. They find themselves suspicious of Lawrence's failure to 'see through' Jack, to put his devilishness in perspective. Instead he seems to be sympathetically endorsing Jack's violent feelings. Locally, this argument will often be hard to contest, and the dialogism Bakhtin describes will be difficult to detect if Lawrence is pouring himself into the main character, as Booth puts it. The temptation to read the novel for its biographical relevance then becomes strong. So the bigamous proposal Jack floats with Mary could be seen as a result of Lawrence's having been left in the lurch by Frieda when she returned

to Europe from New York in August 1923 and he went west to Los Angeles
and then to Mexico, writing *The Boy in the Bush* from Mollie Skinner's
'The House of Ellis' en route. Jack's intention to start a farm in the
North-West with his loyal retainers, Tom and Lennie, could be drawing
on Lawrence's inspection of farms in a little-inhabited part of Mexico
with Kai Götzsche while they were travelling from Los Angeles to
Guadalajara. And the last chapter, written after Lawrence's return to join
Frieda in London in December 1923, could be said to envisage a *ménage à
trois* for Lawrence later in New Mexico with Dorothy Brett (whom Hilda
Blessington is based on) and Frieda.[28]

However the constraints and opportunities of writing – which differ
from those of other kinds of activities and experiences in his life – have to
be taken into account. Lawrence cannot fail to have been aware that the
predictions and interpretations he made in his dealings with other
people were only too likely to be confounded. In his writing he had more
control – although even there he must inevitably be middleman between
his material and the expectations of his audience. Nevertheless he could
activate and explore his aspirations (such as Jack's relationship with a
sustaining personal god) or resentments (at social entanglements), and
see whither they led, partly because he knew it *was* writing. It is easy to
overlook the dark comedy involved in this awareness. Chapter alternation, the feeling of a fresh start, a having another go at a problem so difficult to define and to test in conversation, inner monologue and dramatic
action, is a significant aspect of Lawrence's art. It is very clear in *Women
in Love* (with its very pronounced chapter disjunctions) and in
Kangaroo. Lawrence must have known that if he resumed writing
tomorrow, he might well be writing out of a different mood, and that
yesterday's problem would be inflected differently. He might discover a
strong thematic direction or philosophical position in the process of
writing; revision-stage was only just around the corner and would prove
another opportunity; and even when the work was published its concerns would be only gradually resigned, mixing intertextually with the
next book review, poem, short story or novel.[29]

His addition of the last chapter of *The Boy in the Bush* in London a
couple of months after having, as he had thought, finished the novel

demonstrates this kind of provisionality sharply.[30] The prior chapter had ended with Jack's expression of a suppressed rage at Mary's refusal of his bigamous offer. The new last chapter begins with a linking sentence, acknowledging the mood of the previous chapter. Unlike his treatment of character in *Kangaroo*, Lawrence had decided to work much harder on a coherent psychological development for Jack (his visionary deliriums during illness and when lost in the bush are crucial in this endeavour), and to link that to a case about manly isolated independence versus the cowardices of social living. It is another version, but under different pressures, of the polarity of cold aloofness and warmth of Love in *Kangaroo*. Mollie Skinner's material had, as John Middleton Murry put it, relieved Lawrence of 'the burden of foundation',[31] providing him with the occasion – that story of a new chum accommodating himself to the unforgiving rigours of life in the outback – to spark off his meditative departures.

A different, more hopeful mood is soon apparent in the last chapter. Jack, in his inner monologue, is defensive, wounded; but, freshening with the morning and his feeling of oneness with his horse, he is able to reconcile himself to his rejection by Mary. The chapter ends hopefully for Jack after the arrival of Hilda Blessington with her promise to join him and Monica at Christmas. In typescript revision (a stage which probably came after the writing of the new last chapter), Hilda receives corresponding touches of vitality which she had lacked in the manuscript, and the portrait of Perth society hardens. Lawrence had become surer of the direction of the novel, surer where he stood in relation to Jack's rejection of civilised society. But his assurance only comes about through a revision, itself demonstrably the result of what he was reading and people he was seeing in London. Such revision is indeed re-vision, and there is no intrinsic reason why it should stop there, except that Lawrence lived by his pen, and looked to publication (in this case, to make money for himself and Mollie Skinner). Nevertheless the point stands: only the constraints of publishing schedules give an appearance of fixity to a process that was essentially ongoing.

Readers of *The Boy in the Bush* cannot fail to notice the extreme position Jack gradually reaches against the compromises involved in social

living. Its logic, as so often in Lawrence's writing, depends on a polarising pressure worked through, in image, language and the exploration of
psychological states, in the course of a series of meditative excursuses
emanating from each stage of Jack's story. The novel's theme itself is an
excursus and experimental; it is Jack's and occasional. With many of the
early reviewers, we can, if we wish, ridicule Jack's pretensions by iso-
lating them from the polarising imaginative process which produced
them; but to understand them as part of a process of creative thinking (as
Lawrence surely must have done) that was only temporarily committed
to its conclusions is what the novel implicitly asks of us. In June 1925
Lawrence would write in reply: 'if a character in a novel wants two
wives—or three—or thirty: well, that is true of that man, at that time, in
that circumstance ... But to infer that all men at all times want two, three,
or thirty wives; or that the novelist himself is advocating furious
polygamy; is just imbecility.'[32]

IV

I am arguing, then, that Lawrence could give himself up to the imagining
of a state of furious independence like Jack's, and also, at another level or
at another time, be aware of the provisionality of his effort. What he did
not do was reconcile the differing orientations within the one reliable
mode which his readers could come to recognise and upon which they
could depend. There is, I have suggested, a comedy in this – a dark one,
granted – that many readers fail to see. To look back at the early chapters
of *The Boy in the Bush* is to see much more clearly not only the comedy,
but the determination not to reconcile, and to see how, in this, we are
being readied as an audience for the disorienting experience that is to
follow later in Jack's story.

The first chapters are obviously comic. The novel begins thus:

> He stepped ashore, looking like a lamb. Far be it from me to say he was
> the lamb he looked. Else why should he have been sent out of
> England?—But a good-looking boy he was, with dark-blue eyes and
> the complexion of a girl and bearing just a little too lamb-like to be
> convincing.

He stepped ashore on the newest of new colonies, glancing quickly around, but preserving his lamb-like quietness. Down came his elegant kit ... He kept his eye on that also, the tail of his well-bred eye.

(*BinB* 7:4–11, 13–14)

Whether the as-yet-unnamed Jack deserves the narrator's irony we have little idea. To read the rest of the first page is to feel oneself being nudged into a position which, a little mysteriously, keeps shifting and whose justice one is not yet sure of. John Bayley talks of Lawrence's 'adversarial humour' and his 'one-upmanship' – that he seems to know something that we do not know. This would be an example.[33] Comedy is the point of return – a sort of resting point – at the end of each paragraph on the first page. But it is also a restless point: the narrator is elusive, relishing his ironies, yet slippery, resisting identification with his audience.

And then the prose opens out unexpectedly, drawing the reader along into a vista of physical and spiritual opportunity:

And Jack was not quite eighteen, so he ignored a great deal. He didn't pay much attention even to his surroundings. Yet from the end of the wharf he saw pure sky above, the pure, unknown, unsullied sea to westward; the ruffled, tumbled sand glistened like fine silver, the air was the air of a new world, unbreathed by man.   (*BinB* 7:32–8:2)

A turning point comes at the start of the third sentence. It is quite deliberately crafted. For the first two sentences, Lawrence's manuscript at first read 'Jack didn't pay much attention to landscape.' before he altered it to the present reading, thus eliminating the tendency of that over-familiar cultural category, 'landscape', to pre-encapsulate and, so, defuse Jack's experience. However his original typist ran the second and third sentences together, exchanging the full stop for a comma ('... surroundings, yet ...'), thus alerting us accidentally to the significance of the tonal shift. The new sentence, restored in the Cambridge Edition, gives us Jack's readjustment of mood and attention. The opposition of commercial surroundings to the unhumanised natural environment represents a first delicate intoning of the polarity that will come to dominate the novel. For the moment, all we see is that the ironies are not ones that offer to encompass, to know finally – to 'place' – the hero. The narrator is having to be cunning because there is some reserve capacity in Jack that the narrator's ironies do not touch.

Gradually a free indirect style of presentation begins to render Jack's consciousness sympathetically. The opening questioning of his lamb-like nature is resumed in his recollections of childhood accusations about his being a 'little sinner' (*BinB* 11:3). An uncertainty about the valency of the term is continued when the focus of narration shifts to Jack's mother and her 'jolly sensuousness' (*BinB* 11:28). In the narrator's lightly ironical pursuit of the term's meaning, he picks up points of view, a trifle maliciously, only to drop them: 'She was the despair of the true English wives, for you couldn't disapprove of her, she was the dearest thing imaginable, and yet she introduced a pleasant, semi-luxurious sense of – Of what? Why, almost of sin. Not positive sin' (*BinB* 11:37–12:1). This comic mode is gingerly balanced over what the reader senses is a hinted-at abyss of seriousness. The narrator is acknowledging the abyss only by pointedly stepping around it. This is comedy, but it is a serious game that is being played – and, as yet, we do not know the rules.

The narrator exposes his agenda in attributing to Mrs Grant distinctions, coming from her Australian background, between 'tame innocence and wild innocence, and tame devils and wild devils, and tame morality and wild morality. Let's camp in the bush and be good . . . it didn't matter *what* you did, so long as you were good inside yourself' (*BinB* 12:14–16, 20–1). Her preference for wildness is historically unlikely. True, she was living abroad and might tend to sentimentalise her birthplace, but the sentiment ignores the colonists' struggle for survival *against* the wild and the attempt to establish a version of Home – a struggle which is in fact rehearsed later in the chapter. Her Australian birth is not a sufficient explanation for her anti-Establishment inclination. But, then, did we expect anything else from this shifty narrator who is – we gradually realise – carefully planting thematic seeds?[34]

A sudden transition to dramatised conversation is made. We are jolted awake to what is going on around Jack, just as he is, leaving us with the uncomfortable feeling that the free indirect style has been something of an arbitrary enclosure:

The easy laugh that made his nurse say: "You little sinner!"

He knew he was a little sinner. It rather amused him.

Jack's mind jolted awake as he made a grab at his hat, nearly knocking it off, realising that he was being introduced to two men ...

(*BinB* 13:3–7)

A joke is then rather ponderously played out, and a history of the colonists is provided in dramatised fashion: a moderately funny verbal joust between Messrs Sparrow and Bell (who are thereafter forgotten about) and Mr George. The latter begins to emerge as a pseudo-Dickensian character. Again Jack is onlooker and listener; our feeling so far is that the narrator would have us be most involved in Jack's consciousness, but for the moment the narrator is busy staging the comic dialogue, having switched modes.

This chapter has been one where we have had to remain on our toes. But by our participating in it, it has acquired sufficient robustness (or even, strange to say, verisimilitude) to be the object of a droll joke:

> Mercifully, the train [which Jack had boarded near the wharf in Fremantle] jerked to a standstill beside a wooden platform that was separated from a shady space by a picket fence. A porter put his hand to his mouth and yelled "Perth," just for the look of the thing— because where else could it be? They all burst out of the train. The town stood up in the sand: wooden houses with wooden platforms blown over with sand.   (*BinB* 23:3–8)

The drier joke is the let-down of expectations: the principal town of the colony is half-covered with sand. There has been no continuity of realist illusion, nor any steady centre of authorising wisdom. The narrator has wound in and around his characters: putting them on stage, imitating them from within, identifying himself with Jack, feeling Jack's surprises and shocks, directing irony at them, laughing at the transpiring events on the wharf and at the station. This twisting, opportunistic narrator also takes his chances, striking serious notes, or valencies, in Mrs Grant's and Mr George's voices. Issues are afloat in an alert way that consorts with comedy.

The dinner and concert in chapter 11 are a trial to Jack who finds himself the centre of female attention. His personal space is repeatedly invaded, his name is changed to a nickname, his way of taking a cup of tea is compared to his father's and his evening dress is adjusted by the young women. While implicitly sympathising with Jack's dilemma, Lawrence is able to enjoy the comedy around that silent suffering. He can even provide stage directions: 'Entered the Good Plain Cook' (*BinB* 30:25), he writes at one stage. Later they attend

> a benefit concert in the Town Hall, with the episcopalian choir singing: "Angels Ever Bright And Fair," and a violinist from Germany playing violin solos, and a lady vocalist from Melbourne singing "home" solos, while local stars variously coruscated. Aunt Matilda filled up the end of the seat—like a massive book-end: and the others like slender volumes of romance were squeezed in between her and another stout book-end. Jack had the heaving warmth of Aunt Matilda on his right, the electric wriggle of Monica on his left, and he continued to breathe red-hot air.   (*BinB* 34:7–15)

Comedy, yes; but Lawrence will not leave it alone as an easy experience for the reader: the 'red-hot air' disturbs any comfortable irony we may have been enjoying. And he picks it up at end of the chapter as Jack, alone in his room, repossesses his physical space and regains contact with his body through exercise. A new note of respect for Jack is struck by extending the signification of his unease throughout the chapter. Lawrence has been busy reminding us that Jack is decidedly a young man, but here he points at a deeper quality: his energy of distaste for the self-suppression involved in 'civilised' living as represented by the formal dinner and the recital. How the narrator might jump in the next chapter is unknown. The reader–narrator–character relationship is, we are learning, temporary, always renegotiable, often necessarily re-negotiated.

Drollery and other forms of comedy continue a long way into the novel: for instance, Lennie's antics as a boy, the Jamboree chapter, the account of Joshua Jenkins the joiner-cum-undertaker in York, the funeral scene. Serious notes qualify their effect; and these notes, centring on Jack's dawning physical awareness of a life-quality of biblical proportions, are gradually evoked with the 'passionate mimicry' of which Booth speaks, especially in the last chapters. Can comic continuities from beginning to end be detected? – I think they can.

I have elsewhere given a detailed reading of the novel,[35] so it may be sufficient here to point to the tonal instability – the comic edges – in even the most seemingly doctrinal passages. When Jack strikes gold in the Northwest (chapter xxiii), Monica is already his drudge, sustained by and not questioning his aura. He is joined by Tom and Lennie who refer to him as the General. Wish-fulfilment? the situation is not so simply explained. Lawrence is following the trajectory of an extreme state of being and awareness of which we saw the first glimmerings in chapters i–ii: that of someone who has entirely rejected the social world. If following the trajectory meant that Lawrence's own inner divisions would be exposed by giving them voice, rather than reconciling them in an enlightened manner, then what Bertrand Russell once referred to as Lawrence's 'odd streaks of prudence'[36] kept him nevertheless returning to the common arena. Thus the details of Monica's refusal on the goldfields to sew Jack's clothes for him and his getting eczema just (only just) keep the late chapters of the novel from a ballooning pretentiousness. The disproportion between Jack's fiercely individualistic aspirations and the mundane details is not funny exactly; but it is tensely comic in a provisional way that Lawrence does not have under assured control – and similarly Jack's wound-licking plight after he fails to convince Mary to come and sleep with him in the barn (at the end of chapter xxiv). Although Jack's resentment at this point drives the prose (as in 'The Nightmare'), and although a sympathetic response is thereby invited, Mary's distress at his being deliberately oblivious to her feelings finally puts his fierceness, for us, in the parentheses of the novel's structural logic of polarisation. The asocial extreme has, for now, been reached; it is not stable; and chapter xxv (the last chapter in the manuscript version) shows Jack trying to make a stand on his now definitely isolated dignity. In that context the new last chapter, which I have already discussed, is a fresh start: it is another attempt to unlock the dilemma – to show that extremes are livable by Jack's establishing a colony in the

Northwest. But its actual achievement is, unsurprisingly, deferred beyond the end of the novel.

Taken as a collaboration, *The Boy in the Bush* must have involved an added dimension of conscious address on Lawrence's part to his material. Having 'The House of Ellis' to hand did not make the writing of this novel any faster than *Kangaroo* or *The Lost Girl*. So here we have the prospect of a writer – not driven by inspiration, but consciously out to write a novel – entertaining, and being entertained by, ideas, characters and situations that he finds in a badly prepared typescript which he is reading.[37] And then, on different paper, writing, with one (narrowing) eye on Mollie Skinner, a nurse in the Darlington hills outside Perth, 10,000 miles away; one (dilating) eye on Jack and the possibilities for situating him in a continuity of his, Lawrence's, own thinking in this period; and a third awareness of his audience, the marketplace and the need for a level of professionalism, organisation and comprehensibility which his collaborator had apparently not managed to achieve. He was having to remodel, reject, add, alter, re-position material of hers, and then physically rewrite with all the control over content, pacing and emphasis which that effort implies. Interestingly, a recent computer stylistics study of various literary collaborations shows Lawrence to have been an 'extraordinarily deep reviser' when 2,000-word sections of *The Boy in the Bush* are compared for word-frequency with sections from *Kangaroo* and Mollie Skinner's *Black Swans* (1925). Chapters I and II, with all their historical material which must have come from Mollie Skinner, align closely with the Lawrentian norm on the graph.[38]

The playful surface on the first two chapters shows a writerly self-consciousness. The very act of rewriting must surely have kept this awareness alive: impossible, then, to believe that Lawrence could not see beyond Jack's portentous aspirations later in the novel; impossible to believe that Lawrence's abandoning himself to the imagination of them was anything other than an act of *writing*, of seeing where it would lead, what it would enable him to say, what pay-off there would be from what we must see as the (at one level) deliberate polarisation of choices. In *The Boy in the Bush*, reading and writing were interlinked processes. If Lawrence wrote from his reading, we can, if we choose, read for his writing – read for that provisionality of address to his material and audience that I have been nominating as intimately related to the comic.

Notes

1 Witness e.g. the demise of courses in Research Methods and Bibliography in the 1970s.
2 'The Perversity of D.H. Lawrence', *Criterion*, 1 (1930), 5–22. The approach was, in some respects, continued in John Middleton Murry's *D.H. Lawrence: Son of Woman* (1931; Cape, 1936) as part of his psychobiographical case, and in William York Tindall's *D.H. Lawrence and Susan His Cow* (New York: Columbia University Press, 1939).
3 *D.H. Lawrence: Novelist* (Chatto & Windus, 1955), p. 11.
4 'The Perversity of D.H. Lawrence', pp. 10, 14.
5 See Paul Eggert, 'Lawrence Criticism: Where Next?', *Critical Review*, xxi (1979), 72–84 and 'Lawrence and the Futurists: The Breakthrough in His Art', *Meridian*, i (1982), 21–32.
6 DHL began to use the term for his philosophy when he encountered it in 1913 in Lascelles Abercrombie's *Thomas Hardy*: see (i. 544).
7 DHL's Introduction to Magnus's *Memoirs of the Foreign Legion, Phoenix II: Uncollected, Unpublished and Other Prose Works by D.H. Lawrence*, ed. Warren Roberts and Harry T. Moore (Heinemann, 1968). For a new discussion of the effect of Dostoevsky on Lawrence in 1915–16, see the Introduction to *Twilight in Italy and Other Essays*, ed. Paul Eggert (Cambridge: Cambridge University Press, 1994).
8 Carswell, *The Savage Pilgrimage: A Narrative of D.H. Lawrence* (Chatto & Windus, 1932); and Leavis, *D.H. Lawrence: Novelist* and *Thought, Words and Creativity* (Chatto & Windus, 1975). Of his numerous articles and reviews on DHL, see, in particular, his review of Edward Nehls's *A Composite Biography*: 'Romantic and Heretic', *Spectator*, ccii (1959), 196–7. Leavis had abandoned the significant reservations he had expressed in the 1930s about DHL's achievement: see e.g. his *For Continuity* (Cambridge: Minority Press, 1933).
9 Examples are cited and discussed in Eggert, 'Lawrence and the Futurists'.

10 Thus Howard Mills argues that the 'constant irruptions of disarming good humour' in the chapter 'Mino' in *Women in Love* qualify or mollify Birkin's domination of the intellectual space in his relationship with Ursula and his nomination of the terms in which their relationship will be defined and understood (p. 65, and cf. p. 199).

11 The work of Mikhail Bakhtin (1895–1975) began to appear in English from 1968, but the works with most obvious application to DHL came later (the book on Dostoevsky in 1973, and *The Dialogic Imagination* in 1981).

12 'Confessions of a Lukewarm Lawrentian' in *The Challenge of D.H. Lawrence*, ed. Michael Squires and Keith Cushman (Madison: University of Wisconsin Press, 1990), pp. 16–17.

13 Quoted in Lodge, 'Lawrence, Dostoevsky, Bakhtin: Lawrence and Dialogic Fiction', reprinted in *Rethinking Lawrence*, ed. Keith Brown (Milton Keynes: Open University Press, 1990), p. 96.

14 *'Women in Love'* in *D.H. Lawrence: A Critical Study*, ed. Andor Gomme (Brighton: Harvester, 1978), pp. 70–93.

15 Quoted in Lodge, 'Lawrence, Dostoevsky, Bakhtin', p. 97.

16 Eggert, 'Opening Up the Text: The Case of *Sons and Lovers*' in *Rethinking Lawrence*, ed. Brown, pp. 38–52 and 'D.H. Lawrence and the Crucifixes', *Bulletin of Research in the Humanities*, lxxxvi (1983), 67–85.

17 See Bakhtin, *The Dialogic Imagination*, ed. Michael Holquist (Austin: University of Texas Press, 1981), *passim*.

18 Ibid., p. 326.

19 Ibid., p. 346.

20 Cf. his letter to Gordon Campbell of *c.* 3 March 1915: 'You see we are no longer satisfied to be individual and lyrical – we are growing out of that stage. A man must now needs know himself as his whole people, he must live as the centre and heart of all humanity . . . each work of art that is true, now, must give expression to the great collective experience, not to the individual' (ii. 300–1).

21 *Mr Noon*, ed. Lindeth Vasey (Cambridge: Cambridge University Press, 1984). Cf. also the discussion of DHL's revision of Luis Quintanilla's essay as 'See Mexico After' in Eggert, 'D.H. Lawrence and Literary collaboration' in *D.H. Lawrence: Critical Assessments*, ed. David Ellis and Ornella De Zordo (Christopher Helm, 1992), iv 683–90.

22 See 'Introduction', *England, My England and Other Stories*, ed. Bruce Steele (Cambridge: Cambridge University Press, 1990).

23 *Mr Noon*, ed. Vasey, 292:3, 67:3–5.

24 This question has drawn heated debate in Australia: see Bruce Steele, '*Kangaroo*: Fiction and Fact', *Meridian*, x (1991), 19–34.

25 *Kangaroo*, ed. Bruce Steele (Cambridge: Cambridge University Press, 1994), 279:13–18, 21–30. Subsequent references will appear in the text in the form (*K* 279:13–18, 21–3).

26 It may be that someone *re*-activated it, as a related idea appears in 'Study of Thomas Hardy': see Explanatory note on 23:13 in the Cambridge Edition of *The Boy in the Bush*, ed. Paul Eggert (Cambridge: Cambridge University Press, 1990), p. 390.

27 Cf. R. P. Draper's criticism of a defence of DHL's account of Will's ecstatic response to Lincoln Cathedral in *The Rainbow*: 'The "irony" is the problem, since the language's impressionist identification seems, at least for the time being, to exclude the ironic tone' (*Times Higher Education Supplement*, 27 March 1992, p. 21). The absence of ironic control has long been a problem for readers of DHL: e.g. S. L. Goldberg, '*The Rainbow*: Fiddle Bow and Sand', *Essays in Criticism*, xi (1961), 418–34.

28 For a full account of the writing and revision of *The Boy in the Bush* and for other factual claims made in this section relating to the novel, see Introduction, *The Boy in the Bush*, ed. Eggert, pp. xxi–liii. Subsequent references will appear in the text in the form (*BinB* xxi–liii).

29 See Eggert, 'Opening Up the Text'.

30 It is otherwise difficult to distinguish reliably his stints of writing in the manuscript.

31 Murry, *Son of Woman*, p. 262.

32 'The Novel', *Study of Thomas Hardy, and Other Essays*, ed. Bruce Steele (Cambridge: Cambridge University Press, 1985), 185:19–23.

33 'Lawrence's Comedy and the War of Superiorities' in *Rethinking Lawrence*, ed. Brown, pp. 6, 8.

34 One can imagine that it could be an old woman's freedom so to incline: Mollie Skinner's mother, whom DHL visited in 1922, provided the palette for this portrait; in her late sixties, she had been the wife of a British Army Officer who had died in 1902.

35 See Eggert, 'Introduction', *The Boy in the Bush* (Penguin Books, 1996), pp. xiii–xxxii.

36 *The Autobiography of Bertrand Russell* (Allen and Unwin, 1968), ii. 21.
37 See Lawrence's 'Preface to *Black Swans*' (*BinB* 375–9).
38 Paper by John Burrows, given at the National Library of Australia Canberra to the 1991 conference of the Bibliographical Society of Australia and New Zealand.

7

Lawrence's satiric style: Language and voice in *St. Mawr*

Paul Poplawski

I

If we are to establish that Lawrence is a comic writer in more than just a handful of 'unusual' instances, and in a way that goes beyond the merely adventitious, then we need to demonstrate the existence in his work of deliberately designed and systematically sustained comic strategies that might together be seen to define a distinctive comic style.

Literary style is a notoriously difficult thing to delimit in any simple and clear-cut way, but it must at least have something to do with recurring patterns of linguistic choice, and with strategies of narration in such things as choice of narrator(s), control of perspectives and orchestration of voices. And it is with these two broad categories – of linguistic choice and narrative strategy – that I want to begin the task of defining the style of Lawrence's comedy as it functions in its satiric aspect within *St. Mawr*.

My essay has two immediate aims, therefore: to demonstrate that in *St. Mawr* Lawrence does indeed employ strategies of linguistic patterning and narrative method that are *systematically* designed for satiric purposes; and to analyse some of the detail of these strategies as a step towards defining Lawrence's satiric method. A concern to establish a critical view of Lawrence as not simply a comic writer, but an accomplished craftsman and stylist in comic art, defines a third, longer-term goal for the essay. It goes without saying that my whole approach here is informed by a conviction that \St. Mawr – especially when considered from a Bakhtinian point of view – stands as one of Lawrence's late comic masterpieces: if some of the broader carnivalesque humour of the novel remains in the background of my discussion, this is partly because I have discussed it elsewhere,[1] and partly because I have set myself a task of formal analysis which must inevitably dwell on the smaller procedural details of Lawrence's comedy rather than on its overall nature and impact. Nevertheless, I hope my close attention to detail will send the reader back to *St. Mawr* with a clearer understanding of its comic texture and with a desire to explore its potential for comedy further, particularly as the potential resides in Lawrence's dialogising mimicry and his carefully staged inter-animation of voices (what Bakhtin calls heteroglossia).

I shall concentrate on just one representative section of the text, and organise my analysis around two areas of its linguistic style – its lexis and its figurative language – bringing in questions of narrative voice, perspective and focalisation as and when appropriate. The episode I want to look at occurs at the beginning of the second phase of the story just as the scene shifts from London to Shropshire following Mrs Witt's removal to her 'cottage' in the village of Chomesbury. The episode can easily be overlooked as merely a link-scene, but it represents one of Lawrence's most polished pieces of social comedy, as well as one of his most theatrical, for he brings almost the whole of the novel's cast of characters on to the stage at once here, setting off a rich and variegated polyphony of voices through a range of comic interactions and repartee. My discussion unavoidably sacrifices some of the impact of this polyphonic comedy to the exigencies of detailed analysis, but after finishing this essay I would urge readers to test the truth of this assertion by rereading the passage in question, giving full weight to each distinct voice identified in the following pages.

Limitations of space prevent the reproduction of the whole episode here, and readers are requested to consult the full passage in the published text.[2] The following extract, however, will provide an overall outline and impression of the scene and can serve as an initial point of reference for my analysis (line numbers correspond to those in the Cambridge Edition).

42:21–4   Rico consented to spend the month in Shropshire, because for near neighbours Mrs Witt had the Manbys, at Corrabach Hall. The Manbys were rich Australians

returned to the old country and set up as Squires, all in full
blow.

42:26–32   . . . So down went Lou and Rico, Lewis, Poppy and St.
Mawr, to Shrewsbury, then out into the country. Mrs Witt's
"cottage" was a tall red-brick Georgian house looking
straight on to the churchyard, and the dark, looming, big
Church.

"I never knew what a comfort it would be," said Mrs Witt,
"to have grave-stones under my drawing-room windows,
and funerals for lunch."

42:33–6   She really did take a strange pleasure . . . watching the
Dean or one of the curates officiating at the graveside,
among a group of black country mourners with black-
bordered handkerchiefs luxuriantly in use. . . .

43:3–8   The Dean . . . was a gentleman, and a man of learning in
his own line. But he let Mrs Witt know that he looked down
on her just a trifle—as a parvenu American, a Yankee—
though she never was a Yankee: and at the same time he had
a sincere respect for her, as a rich woman. Yes, a sincere
respect for her, as a rich woman. . . .

43:11–23   The Dean was more *impressed* by Mrs Witt than by little
Lou. But to Lady Carrington he was charming: she was
almost "one of us," you know. And he was very gracious to
Rico: "your father's splendid colonial service."

Mrs Witt had now a new pantomime to amuse her: the
Georgian house, her own pew in Church . . . a village of
thatched cottages—some of them with corrugated iron
over the thatch: the cottage people, farm laborers and
their families, with a few, very few outsiders: the wicked
little group of cottagers down at Mile End, famous for ill-
living. The Mile-Enders were all Allisons and Jephsons,
and in-bred, the Dean said: result of working through the
centuries at the Quarry, and living isolated there at Mile
End. . . .

43:28–34   But there she had the whole thing staged complete for
her: English village life. Even miners breaking in to shatter
the rather stuffy, unwholesome harmony.—All the men

touched their caps to her, all the women did a bit of a reverence, the children stood aside for her, if she appeared in the Street.

They were all poor again: the laborers could no longer afford even a glass of beer in the evenings, since the Glorious war....

44:10–11   The upshot was, she decided to supply one large barrel of beer per week and the landlord was to sell it to the laborers at a penny a glass....

44:14–21   By the time Lou and Rico appeared, she was deep in. She actually interfered very little ... But she *did* know everybody by sight, already, and she *did* know everybody's circumstances. And she had attended one prayer-meeting, one mother's meeting... one Sunday School treat. She ignored the poky little Wesleyan and Baptist chapels, and was true-blue episcopalian.

44:22–4, 30–5   "How strange these picturesque old villages are, Louise! ... How *easy* it all seems, all on a definite pattern. And how false! And underneath, *how corrupt!*"

She gave that queer, triumphant leer from her grey eyes, and queer demonish wrinkles seemed to twitter on her face.

Lou shrank away. She was beginning to be afraid of her mother's insatiable curiosity, that always looked for the snake under the flowers. Or rather, for the maggots.

Always this same morbid interest in other people and their doings, their privacies, their dirty linen. Always this air of alertness for personal happenings, personalities, personalities, personalities. Always this subtle criticism and appraisal of other people, this analysis of other people's motives....

45:1–2   Mrs Witt was a pure psychologist, a fiendish psychologist. And Rico, in his way, was a psychologist too....

45:4–11   "Isn't the Dean a priceless old darling!" said Rico at breakfast.

And it had begun. Work had started in the psychic vivisection laboratory.

"Isn't he wonderful!" said Lou vaguely.

"So delightfully worldly!—*Some of us are not born to make money, dear boy. Luckily for us, we can marry it.*"—Rico made a priceless face.

45:10   "Is Mrs Vyner so rich?" asked Lou.

"She is, quite a wealthy woman—in coal," replied Mrs Witt. "But the Dean is surely worth his weight, even in gold. …"

45:27–35   Rico and Mrs Witt were deadly enemies, yet neither could keep clear of the other. It might have been they who were married to one another, their duel and their duet were so relentless.

But Rico immediately started the social round: first the Manbys: then motor twenty miles to luncheon at Lady Tewkesbury's: then young Mr Burns came flying down in his aeroplane from Chester: then they must motor to the sea, to Sir Edward Edwards' place, where there was a moonlight bathing party. Everything intensely thrilling, and so innerly wearisome, Lou felt.

II

There are five main butts of satire here: Mrs Witt, Rico, upper-class English society, Dean Vyner and English village life.

The figure of Mrs Witt dominates the piece, and it must be noted immediately that a degree of perspectual complexity arises from the fact that as well as being externally focalised, she acts as an internal focaliser too, thus serving simultaneously as both object and agent of satire. She is, for example, satirised for her cynicism, but at the same time her cynicism provides us with a necessary critical perspective on the hypocrisies and false enthusiasms of the other characters. One of the problems of the passage, then (and it extends to the entire story), revolves around the precise 'distance' we are asked to keep from Mrs Witt and her views.

Her cynicism is most obviously reflected by the macabre pleasure she takes in watching funerals, but it emerges from *all* the attitudes she displays here. Her obsessive prying into other people's affairs and the systematic single-mindedness with which she inserts and insinuates herself into the daily life of the local community are shown to be motivated, at base, by a misanthropic desire to find fault with everything and everyone. And the self-aggrandising conceit that seems to be a corollary of this attitude is well illustrated by her supercilious and officious, if free-handed, patronage of the local labourers in her buying of the beer. Her cynicism also generates arrogance in the way she looks frivolously down her 'well-bred' nose (*SM* 44:23) at the 'pantomime' of life and lives before her: as a rich tourist she does not have to take her host community seriously, and as a 'superior' person it can all too easily be dismissed as insignificant and '*corrupt*' anyway. Even her relentless drive to humiliate Rico can be seen satirically – as Lou seems to see it here – as a petty and niggling captiousness, a wilful and malicious exercise in 'psychic vivisection'.

Though, of course, we do not feel too much sympathy for Rico, who only represents the other side of the same coin as Mrs Witt, the other half of 'their duel and their duet'. Rico has already been satirised for his somewhat 'camp' manner of expression – 'Isn't the Dean a priceless old darling!' – and we have been made aware earlier of his 'arty' preciousness, so that Mrs Witt's jibes here (at his effeminacy, for example, (45:18–23) inevitably hit home. Moreover, the duplicity lurking beneath Rico's jaunty bonhomie is exposed by the reference to his 'formula', and by the more subtle satirisation of his motives for 'consent[ing]' to spend the month with Mrs Witt in Shropshire: his self-centred ambitions to become '*a famous and important Artist*' (*SM* 117:19–20) will of course be well served by fraternising with the 'Squires' of Corrabach Hall: and the 'girls' would make 'a great fuss of him' (*SM* 42:25). These hints at Rico's sycophantic tendency are consolidated by the business-like seriousness with which he seems to undertake his round of visits to the local squirearchy – the affected enjoyment of which is finely mocked in the final sentence of the passage.

The gilded society that Rico self-seekingly courts is satirised partly through simple association with him, and partly in its own right as a showy and shallow blemish on both cultural and, with its motorised playthings, physical landscapes. Its juxtapositioning beside the poverty of the labourers in the village accentuates its heartless frivolity and hedonism. If Mrs Witt is the rich tourist cynically observing how the 'natives' live, Rico and his rich friends are simply oblivious of them.

A religious variation on this satirical theme of moneyed hollowness comes with the depiction of Dean Vyner, none of whose values seem to have anything to do with Christianity. He seems to have married his wife only for her money, and his 'respect' for Mrs Witt is really only a respect for her wealth. Her comment that he must surely be worth his weight 'even in gold' is characteristically telling, especially in its ironic collocation with the 'coal' of Mrs Vyner on which his actual wealth depends, and its playful allusion to his physique – 'The Dean was a big, burly, fat man' (43:3) – which stands as a solid embodiment of the true worldliness of the 'big Church'.

The problem of assessing the correct 'distance' we are asked to keep from Mrs Witt becomes most acute with respect to her attitude towards the village community, for to some extent the narrator himself seems to sanction her comments about the falsity and corruption of parochial village-life. He certainly makes no attempt to portray the locals in a seriously sympathetic light, and narratorial comments such as 'the rather stuffy, unwholesome harmony' and 'the poky little Wesleyan and Baptist chapels', though these are partly stylisations of Mrs Witt's way of thinking, still can be seen to suggest rather a degree of sympathy with her point of view. Other comments in the novel to the effect that there is a *universal* wasting away of the nation's vitalities would seem to support this. We hear, for instance, that 'England was not real either, except poisonously', and that even on the countryside 'the dead hand of the war lay like a corpse decomposing' (*SM* 132:7, 70:9–10). Mrs Witt's critical comments can thus be seen to fall congruently into a broader pattern of culture-critique on the part of the narrator; as indeed can the suggested insularity and in-breeding of the local population (43:21–2) (though again these are also satirical stylisations of Dean Vyner's 'voice'), and as can, in a slightly different way, the ironic capitalisation in the reference to 'the Glorious war'. Perhaps, then, we are asked here not only to recognise the cynicism of Mrs Witt in her disdain for the 'pantomime' around her, but also to recognise the validity of her comments – and to recognise, therefore, a certain narratorial cynicism too.

III

(a) Lexis: Semantic fields, complexity, register

One of the most obviously systematic ways in which the satire of this episode is realised by its language is through its lexical organisation into three distinct but interacting semantic fields. First of all, we have the field of words associated with social observation, and associated in particular with social class, money and leisure activities. On the one hand, high social status, wealth and privileged leisure are evoked ('Corrabach Hall', 'rich Australians', 'Squires', 'Lady Carrington', 'gold', 'flying down in his aeroplane', 'moonlight bathing party'), while on the other hand we have words and phrases signifying low social status, poverty and hardship ('cottages . . . with corrugated iron over the thatch', 'stuffy, squalid' (*SM* 43:36), 'farm laborers', 'The Mile-Enders . . . working through the centuries at the Quarry', 'isolated', 'poor'). The lexical opposition accumulates systematically throughout the piece to expose the true nature of social class relations in the society of the period. The unheeding extravagance of the Manby set, the mercenary considerations of the Dean and Rico, and the patronage of Mrs Witt, are all put into their true perspectives by such a stark contrast with the enforced subordination, and the mean and cramped conditions of the working classes. One thread of the piece's subtextual meaning thus reads more clearly: Sir Edward Edwards only has the wherewithal to organise his moonlight bathing parties because the sons of (and daughters of) the country have laboured through the centuries to provide it, at places like the quarry of Mile End. That the real, if harsh, life and labours of past centuries is shown here being frittered away by the likes of Rico and the Manbys provides an ironic gloss on Lou's later comment that 'All these millions of ancestors have used all the life up. We're not really alive, in the sense that they were alive' (*SM* 74:8–9). Even the Church, as represented by the Dean, seems mercenary and corrupt: hence too the opposition between the 'true-blue' episcopalian Church and the 'poky little Wesleyan and Baptist chapels'.

Cutting across this more obvious class-based social comment, however, the extract also glances at the narrow parochialism of English village-life, both through Dean Vyner's pseudo-aristocratic snobbery towards Mrs Witt – 'a parvenu American, a Yankee' – and through a lexical pattern suggesting inwardness and tightness amongst the cottagers and labourers: 'a few, very few outsiders', 'the wicked little group of cottagers', 'in-bred', 'isolated', 'on a definite pattern'.

The second major semantic field represented in this extract involves words connoting dirt, death, decay and corruption: 'black', 'gravestones', 'funerals', 'ill-living', 'unwholesome', 'squalid', 'false', *corrupt*', 'demonish', 'snake', 'maggots', 'morbid', 'dirty', 'corpses', 'infernal stink' (*SM* 44:36, 39).

On the one hand this imagery clearly helps to underscore the hollowness and hypocrisy of the satirised characters. In particular the references to dirt and smelliness conjure up stock phrases relating to money such as 'filthy lucre', 'filthy rich' and 'stinking rich'. On the other hand, it sustains a direct link, through Lou's apocalyptic vision of evil, with the final pages of the New England wife's story, where we hear that 'every civilisation, when it loses its inward vision and its cleaner energy, falls into a new sort of sordidness…An Augean stables of metallic filth' (*SM* 151:12–15).

The third semantic field draws on the sciences of psychology and physiology and is concentrated in two highly rhetorical paragraphs (44:31–45:3). Here, we find a high degree of repetition of words such as 'personalities', 'psychologist', 'criticism', 'analysis', 'anatomy', 'vivisection', 'corpse' and 'laboratory'. The anti-scientific, anti-analytical mockery implicit in these words glances both backwards to Mrs Witt's 'vivisection' of the local community, and forwards to her and Rico's niggling attempts to outdo each other in their cynicism and worldly wit. In some ways, rather than being fully satirical in its own right, this rhetorical passage merely points the moral of the satire surrounding it. Though if we ascribe its motivation to Lou rather than to the external narrator it might also be seen as reflecting back satirically on her for her somewhat shrill and self-righteous 'vivisection' of her mother and husband. After all, what is she doing here if not psychologically analysing 'people's motives': she shows herself to be guilty of the very practice she is engaged in deprecating, so that the outwardly orientated focalisation is inevitably refracted back on to and into its source.

Moving away from overt patterns of lexical denotation and connotation, we can learn much about the narrative voice of this text by considering two further formal features of the extract's lexical disposition – word complexity and register. Without resorting to morphological statistics, I think it can be agreed from just a careful perusal of the extract that both semantically and structurally there is a clear predominance of relatively simple, familiar, Anglo-Saxon-based words over 'complex' Latinate or otherwise-derived words. In the first twenty sentences, for example, leaving aside proper names, there is a mere handful of base forms which have foreign roots and more than two syllables – 'funerals', 'officiating', 'luxuriantly', 'audible' (*SM* 43:1), 'parvenu', 'colonial', 'pantomime', 'families'; and of these only three or four could be seriously termed 'complex' in a semantic sense. What is important about this fact, however, is not just that relatively 'simple' language can therefore be taken to be something of a textual norm, but that it should make us responsive to the deviations from this norm. Indeed, the evidence would seem to suggest that such deviation is associated with satirical intensification. In the sentence describing the funeral, for instance (*SM* 42:35–6), both 'officiating' and 'luxuriantly' jar comically against our conventional expectations of an appropriately subdued manner of behaviour at a funeral; and 'parvenu' (43:5) is clearly a double-edged satirical shaft at both the snobbery of Dean Vyner and the financially-based 'superiority' of Mrs Witt.

In order to explore this aspect of the extract's language further, however, we need to differentiate clearly between the different 'voices' that are brought into play, and in particular the different voices assumed by the narrator in communicating shifts in satirical tone (which also often indicate a temporary shift of perspective). It is at this point that the issue of register arises, for not only are satiric effects contrived by a pointed alternation between the narrator's own straightforward language, and the various forms of linguistic conceit associated with the butts of his humour, they also derive from his complementary use of idiomatic and colloquial forms in counterpoint with a more formal and sometimes more affected type of diction that alludes to the speech styles of Mrs Witt, Dean Vyner and Rico – all of whose actual speech appears too, adding further nuances of satirical interplay between types of diction and register.

The narrator seems to have two base-forms to his lexical range in this respect. On the one hand, in his most purely 'narratorial' role his words are, as I have suggested, relatively simple and down-to-earth, and his register is similarly familiar and unaffected. This is the style typified by the first five sentences (42:21–32), and by idioms and colloquialisms such as 'all in full blow', 'in his own line', 'The upshot was', 'she was deep in'. In its most obvious manifestation, the satirical function of these forms is simply to deflate implied pretensions, as in the second sentence where 'all in full blow' almost onomatopoeically blows a raspberry at the Manby's pompous ambitions to 'set up' as 'Squires'. More subtly, these demotic forms keep us firmly in touch with the fundamentals of everyday living and provide a solid subtextual foil to the 'melting magic-lantern show' which is so flickeringly represented at the satirical surface of the fiction.

On the other hand, when the narrator 'shares' the focalisation of events with Lou, much more sententious linguistic forms are engaged. This is most evident in the 'psychology' section mentioned earlier, where we have a marked increase in the use of longer, more learned, more specialised and more abstract words and phrases. While the register here may at first still seem to be conversational and familiar, this is clearly a function of the rhetorical nature of the sentences rather than of their deceptive idiomatic colouring, for they are not so much in a conversational and familiar style as in the 'spoken' and pseudo-familiar style common to rhetorical discourse, and the overall tone is that of a formal speech or sermon rather than that of a casual confiding conversation. To what extent the rhetorical style and moralistic tone are to be ascribed to Lou or to the narrator is a moot point; however, having provisionally suggested a 'pure' version of the narrator's voice which is different from this, and given that the only variable factor would seem to be Lou herself, I suggest that it is a property of *her* consciousness which makes the difference here, and that we are being presented with her indirect thought in a 'free' way. If this be accepted, then even though these are clearly the narrator's words, their tone reflects more upon Lou than upon him, and there is a possibility, as I suggested earlier, that the tone is partly intended to reflect satirically on her own psychologising self-righteousness. If this is correct then it serves as another example of how Lawrence's technique invites us to laugh at more than one satirical target at a time. Lou presents a narratorially sanctioned criticism, but exposes herself to the same in doing so.

In between the narrator's two base-voices are a variety of semi-imitative styles where the narrator blends his language with that of his characters according to the degree of satirical emphasis he wishes to convey. To effect this blending he incorporates within his own utterances more or less pointed references to his characters' words by means of speech allusion, paraphrase and direct quotation, either separately or in combination. For example, in the lines 43:11–14, all these techniques are employed in order to satirise Dean Vyner. The phrases 'charming' and 'very gracious' are a subtle form of speech allusion mocking Dean Vyner's ingratiating effusiveness on being introduced to the Witt household; and the material after the colon in both sentences skilfully combines ironic paraphrase and carefully edited direct quotation. The satirical counterpoint between the narrator's plain base-style and his Dean-Vyner-modulated style stands out in the sentence 'He was a gentleman, and a man of learning in his own line' (SM 43:3–4), where one can imagine that the source of the description in the first part is the Dean himself, while that of the idiomatic qualification 'in his own line' is the narrator. In the following sentence, the narrator employs a slightly more genteel register of idiom to mimic and mock the Dean, with 'just a trifle' and 'parvenu'; and the Dean is finally summed up by a very adroit modulation of voices across this and the next sentence, where the first 'he had a sincere respect for her, as a rich woman' initially appears to be only a mildly ironic narratorial observation before being recast unequivocally in the light of heavy sarcasm by the speech-allusive quality of the second, accentuated, utterance of the same statement (43:6–8). Another masterly interplay of voices is achieved in the lines 45:4–9, where Rico, while mimicking Dean Vyner, is himself mimicked both by the narrator and, to a less obvious extent, by Lou. Immediately after Rico's somewhat theatrical flourish in the phrase 'a priceless old darling', the narrator brings us to earth with an unadorned thud in the plain-spoken 'And it had begun', before edging us into Lou's consciousness once more through the sardonically repeated reference to a 'psychic vivisection laboratory'. Lou's spoken response to Rico is also sardonic in echoing, through 'wonderful', his and his circle's characteristic resort to vacuous superlatives – the narrator's 'vaguely' helping to underpin the sardonic note. As Rico begins again in the same exclamatory mode, he inadvertently mocks his own use of the word 'darling' a few lines before in drawing attention to the Dean's phrase '*dear boy*', before having his idiolect more directly mocked by the narrator in the pointedly repeated use of the word 'priceless' (45:9). Looking beneath the surface of the text's satire in this way shows just how much it relies upon a purposeful patterning of particular word-groups, as well as upon the tones and registers which these groups help to create.

In addition to adopting an imitative linguistic register to mimic specific characters in the episode, the narrator also sometimes adopts a form of – in Bakhtinian terms – parodic skaz or oral style, a 'gossiping' register which, by its trivialising effect, is designed mainly to disparage the particular subject in question, but which may also be seen to be mildly mocking of the parochial spirit of the whole local community. This is the register signalled at 43:15–23 by the chatty 'asides', 'it went with the old house' (*SM* 43:16) 'result of working through the centuries at the Quarry', and by the colloquial feel of constructions such as 'the wicked little group' and 'The Mile-Enders were all Allisons and Jephsons'. In the two sentences at 44:15–19, it emerges from the 'well-I-never' emphasis produced by the listing construction and by the two 'dids' in the first sentence and the initial 'And' of the second. A listing construction is used to the same end in the sentence beginning at 45:30, though here the 'gossip' has a more cynical and more clearly judgmental ring to it that pushes it closer to Lou than to a generalised 'gossip-narrator'.

(b) Lexis: Nouns and verbs

Nouns represent by far the largest major class of words in the extract. With 358 nouns out of a total of 1360 words they account for 26% of the text. Out of this number, 231 are common, and 127 are proper nouns. The vast majority of the common nouns are 'concrete', and if we discount those abstract nouns which relate to time and to common states, qualities or activities, we are left with only a very small handful of words which are abstract in the sense of being conceptually difficult to grasp – and, as I have already indicated, these are almost all concentrated in the 'psychology' section (44:31–45:3). This observation supports the idea of a plain-spoken narratorial norm in the extract, and it can perhaps also be taken to account in part for the sense of 'concrete' realism in the scene, particularly in relation to the daily life of the village community.

What is perhaps more important to note here, though, is the use made of proper nouns. On average, there is the equivalent of at least one proper noun per sentence throughout the extract, and this would seem to represent quite a high level of investment in proper names. Of course, by itself the quantitative fact need not be significant at all, but it strikes me that a stress on proper nouns is in fact a notable characteristic of the novel as a whole, and that in this particular extract it contributes qualitatively to the satirical timbre of the piece.

The peculiar insistence on names in the broader narrative is particularly noticeable in Lou's constant reiteration of the vocative 'mother' in talking to Mrs Witt, and, reciprocally, in Mrs Witt's reiteration of 'Louise' in talking to Lou; but it is also quite evident in the narrator's general presentational style. It is often the case, for example, that where, on stylistic grounds, we might reasonably expect the narrator to avoid repeating a name, he seems almost to go out of his way to repeat it as if to draw attention to some thematic purpose beyond the exigencies of merely getting the story told. And the purpose, I would suggest, is to place ironic stress on surface 'personae' in contradistinction to the pre-linguistic 'other egos' of the characters – on their nominal social image as opposed to their inevitably nameless 'essence' as individuals. Thus a pattern of opposition emerges between 'the sound of titles' (*SM* 27:29) – Lou, Louise, Loulina, Lou Witt, Lady Carrington, Lady Louise Carrington, Lady Henry Carrington, your Ladyship – and 'the successive inner sanctuaries' of the self (*SM* 139:21–2).

Moreover, the cumulative effect of the repetition of names is to create something of the comic mood of a melodrama or fairy tale, where characters are allegorically reduced to nothing but names, or named *figures*, and to what these are shown to stand for. Apart from simple repetition, the effect is augmented by the satiric use of subtle grammatic allusions to the conventions of address in melodrama and fairy tale. Specifically, we have, first of all, a mock-honorific use of the definite article in its aggrandising aspect in 'The Manbys' and 'The Dean', along with its fairy tale typologising effect both here and in references to 'the cottage people', 'The Mile-Enders', and 'the laborers'; and, secondly, we have the use of the stock (and mock-) sentimental epithet 'little' (as in 'little Nell') in 'little Lou', 'the wicked little group of cottagers down at Mile End' and 'the poky little ... chapels', as well as other pseudo-'fixed' epithets such as 'rich Australians', 'the old country', 'of good family' (*SM* 42:24–5), 'a rich woman', 'picturesque cottages' (*SM* 43:36), 'these poor laborers' (*SM* 44:6) 'poor Lou' and 'young Mr Burns'. In this sort of lexical 'environment' then, the effect of constantly repeating a name, far from establishing the name's holder more firmly as a verisimilar person-age, is actually to diminish the sense of a realistic, unique presence behind it and thus to diminish the putative personality to a 'flatter' fairy-tale figure. This figure can then be more easily satirised. This is fairly obvious in the case of the Dean, who in any case comes across as some-thing of a caricature in the episode; but once we start to read the extract as a whole in this vein, with a mock-naïve nursery rhyme lilt in our 'voices', then the full power of the satire against Mrs Witt and Rico is also made obvious – though instead of talking about nursery rhyme, fairy tale and melodrama, perhaps we should use Lawrence's own more ven-erable term for what is going on here and recognise that, for the duration of this episode at least, Mrs Witt and the others are simply engaged, themselves, in 'a new pantomime'.

Ironically, the verbs in the extract do not on the whole communicate action so much as inaction and impotence, a death-in-life prefigured perfectly in the image of 'funerals for lunch'. Indeed, transposing grammatical language into critical language, we can characterise this episode, from the evidence of its verbal style, in the following way: its mood is negative and conditional, its aspect is iterative and general-ising, and its voice is passive. Together, these verbal facets of the extract interact to produce an overwhelming sense of devitalisation and stasis in the fictional world, and to draw us, subtextually, into a discourse on states of consciousness, away from the dissolving actions and events at the surface of the text.

Let us consider the issue of voice first of all, the issue of how the action of the episode is 'spoken' by its verbs. Although in a strictly grammatical sense most of the verbs in the passage are in the active voice, a combination of grammatical and contextual features operate quite forcefully to negate the potentially 'dynamic' effect of this and to show almost all 'action', in a semantic sense at least, in a passive light. First and foremost, apart from about six or seven, almost all the verbs in the extract are stative verbs, so that very little dynamic action is actually predicated anyway, whether in the active or passive voice: the single most frequent verb is the copulative 'to be', which is intransitive and therefore without a passive voice, and the second most frequent, if we disregard speech-reporting verbs, is the possessive 'to have', which can hardly be said to denote any clear sense of 'doing', and which, again, though transitive, cannot easily be used in a passive sense. Second, with regard to transitivity, there is a predominance of intransitive verb-usage in the extract which produces a sense of 'blocked' action or of action turned in on itself, and which thus underscores the ideas of corruption, impotence and in-breeding in the passage. Of the transitive verb-usages, moreover, most are similar to the possessive 'to have' in expressing a highly abstract, notional sense of 'acting on' some object (e.g. 'to spend the month', 'anatomy pre-supposes a corpse' (*SM* 44:35), 'to make money'), and do not dispel the extract's overall impression of paralysis and stasis. Third, and closely allied to the previous point, the elliptical connection between transitive verbs and their objects is paralleled in the opposite direction by an equally elliptical connection between subjects and their 'actions', both transitive and intransitive. This distancing is effected both structurally and semantically. For instance, in the second sentence, after 'Australians' there is a form of rhythmic and grammatical caesura caused by the use of the nonfinite 'returned' instead of the more 'correct' finite structure 'who had returned'. The Manbys seem therefore to be distanced from their own agency as subjects of the action of returning (this also applies to 'set up' in the same sentence). In the fourth sentence, we are told that Lou and the others 'went down to' Shropshire (one of the few dynamic verbs in the extract), but the inversion of 'down' and 'went', and their separation from 'to' all contributes once again to a distancing of the characters from their own action – as though everything had happened without their active volition. Perhaps the best example of this dislocating effect, though, comes at 42:35–6, where the group of mourners do not actively *use* their handkerchiefs: their handkerchiefs are passively 'in use', and 'luxuriantly', to boot. This points to another way in which the sense of human action becomes muted in the episode. Just as here the subject-agency is taken away from the human subjects and passed on to inanimate objects, so in several other sentences stress falls on inanimate rather than animate 'activity'. Mrs Witt's house 'look[s]' on to the churchyard, as Lou's room 'look[s]' over the garden (*SM* 42:38); the shadow of the church 'mak[es] itself heard insistently' (*SM* 43:1–2); 'anatomy pre-supposes a corpse' and Mrs Witt's one public act 'is' the barrel of beer (*SM* 44:15). Along with this type of sentence we have several 'existential' constructions where the subject is neutral or anonymous: 'there was the *boom! boom!* of the passing-bell' (*SM* 42:39–40), 'the whole thing staged complete for her', 'How *easy* it all seems', 'it had begun', 'Work had started'. Finally, on this point, the static, and stative, nature of the piece is clearly accentuated by the fact that several sentences in the extract use only a very minimal verbal element (see, for example, 44:17–21 and the final sentence), while twelve sentences have no verb at all (i.e., the sentences beginning on 43:7, 24; 44:24, 24; 44:30, 31, 32, 33, 40; 45:8; 45:16; 45:18).

This whole sense of actionlessness is enhanced by a complementary sense of timelessness, and indeed 'personlessness', in the prominence of nonfinite verbal constructions. If we simply count the occurrence of infinitives, '-ing' and '-ed' participles and add these to the verbless and near-verbless sentences mentioned above then at least a third of all verb phrases in the extract can be interpreted as nonfinite. In addition to this, much of the extract is concerned with summarising a period of time and certain habitual states and actions, so that there is a sense of non-specificity and fluidity about exactly when, where and in what manner

the events and conversations of the episode take place. This is accentuated in verbal terms by a frequent use of the habitual past, as at 43:30–2,
the state present, as at 43:9–10, and (most frequently) the non-committal
simple past with copular verbs such as 'to be' and 'to seem'. There is in fact
only a clear sense of a story present at the beginning of the extract, and
briefly at one or two other places. If we add to all this the significant use of
past anterior and subjunctive constructions in the extract (e.g. 'had
known' (*SM* 42:24), 'if she appeared' (43:32), 'if they wish' (43:40), 'had
attended' (44:17), then it seems clear that the temporal aspect of verbal
elements in the passage is quite systematically designed to blur and
obscure the immediacy and specificity of actions and events – indeed, as
if their very reality were being thrown into question, despite their apparent 'concreteness'.

This brings us conveniently to the matter of mood, for there is in fact a
pervasive sense of unreality or 'conditionality' in the passage that is
partly established by the 'nonfactual' and negative mood of many of its
verb phrases. On the one hand, as I have just pointed out, there is a frequent use of nonfactual subjunctive constructions, and these are either
straightforwardly conditional or nonfactual in some less direct way, as in
constructions like 'I never knew what a comfort it would be', 'Then they
must have it—' (*SM* 44:9) and 'You can't imagine his wife ...' (*SM* 45:17).
On the other hand, there are nineteen sentences in the extract which
contain verb phrases in the negative, not to mention verbs which already
have a negative denotation, like 'shrank away' and 'ignored', or negative
connotations, like 'to shatter' or 'smell' (*SM* 44:39). Even if we were to
ignore all the other contextually-determined negatives and subjunctives
in the extract, then we would still have a quarter of all the sentences con-
veying a negative meaning, with at least another tenth of the sentences
communicating a 'conditional' meaning.

Analysing the verbs of this extract, then, takes us to the very founda-
tions of its satirical critique. For the word-picture we are presented
with, of an impotent, stagnant and disintegrating society, is perfectly
enunciated for us by the passive voice, the abstract-iterative aspect and
the conditional mood of the extract's verbal lexis. And while this lexis
precisely communicates its funereal theme, skilfully encapsulating the

self-stifling cynicism of Mrs Witt and the mechanical wasting motions of the rich, its very precision makes clear that what *is* vitally active and alive here is the language and 'consciousness' of the satirical discourse itself.

(c) Figurative language: Tropes

If we ignore the idiomatic usages we have already dealt with, then the most notable thing about the extract's figurative imagery is its sparsity. As though to highlight the prosaic barrenness of the world it is presenting, the passage engages only the merest handful of tropes, and even then they are tropes which signify only shallowness and death. There are essentially eight metaphoric figures in the extract, five of which more or less directly connote death and three of which refer to forms of hollowness or pretence.

Mrs Witt's semi-playful reference to having 'funerals for lunch' first announces the death trope. It is then developed through her being associated with fiends and devils ('queer demonish wrinkles', 'a fiendish psychologist' (*SM* 44:26–7, 45:1)), through the extended metaphor of 'the psychic vivisection laboratory', and through the co-reference to 'maggots' and 'the snake under the flowers', whereby Mrs Witt is associated explicitly with both death and devil (44:29, 30). Throughout the passage, Rico too is gradually implicated in the metaphorical censure, and the fifth figure in this group appropriately unites Rico and Mrs Witt in a sort of verbal dance of death, as we see the 'cut and thrust' of their 'deadly' 'duel and duet'.

The most prominent trope of illusion is perhaps the description of the local community as Mrs Witt's 'new pantomime', and the suggestion that life here has no real substance beneath the 'staged' 'unwholesome harmony' (*SM* 43:30) that is so '*easy*' and 'on a definite pattern'. There are possibly echoes of theatrical artifice and illusion in Rico's 'social round' too, with its show of mechanical energy and its 'moonlight bathing party'. A third metaphor of this sort comes as we are told that the shadow of the church is 'A very audible shadow, making itself heard insistently' (*SM* 43:1–2). The metaphor of the 'audible shadow' operates in a doubly ironic way. On the one hand it satirically collocates the noisy insistence and exhortations of the Church with an imputed spiritual shallowness. On the other hand, it simultaneously heralds the appearance, in the next line, of the embodiment of both these negative qualities in the signally non-shadowy form of Dean Vyner. His robust worldliness ironically accentuates the emptiness of his words, both here and later when he advocates the putting down of St. Mawr. Moreover, his linguistic vacuity aligns him with the insistently 'audible', but consistently cynical, Mrs Witt, whose shallow linguistic exhibitionism receives perfect expression in the image of an 'audible shadow'.

(d) Figurative language: Schemes

Much of the tone of the extract derives from the parallelistic patterning of its language, and in particular from its use of triadic or tripartite parallel structures. These contribute significantly to our sense of both its satirical and its rhetorical inflexions. On the one hand, they produce a degree of matter-of-fact patness and curtness in the rhythmic structure of the passage, and this provides both for an intoned aloofness in what is said, and for the crucial sardonic silences between clauses where the scorn of what is not said is conveyed – where, as it were, we receive the critical nods and winks from the narrator. On the other hand, the regular balancing of paralleled elements gives the passage a rhetorical confidence, and indeed, at times, an air of almost syllogistic surety.

The first paragraph provides a perfect example. It contains three sentences; each of these has almost exactly the same number of words (20–19–20), and can be clearly divided into three distinct tone groups (though sentence 2 is a little more ambiguous than the other two in this respect). Sentences 1 and 2 have almost exactly the same structure of information and intonation, with two long units presenting fairly straightforward objective information followed by a short appended unit apparently providing additional information of the same sort, but actually trailing a distinctly stressed note of either mock-respect or just plain mockery. Sentence 3 then changes the pattern and briskly rounds off the paragraph with three evenly balanced clauses, so that it functions rhythmically somewhat like the synthesising conclusion of a syllogism.

It reflects this sort of logical structure internally too, though this is precisely where *its* satirical value lies, for its concluding clause clearly clashes with the business-like expectations raised by the preceding clauses: it is not just another circumstantial fact that we finish with, but an ironic comment on Rico's self-centredness. This sentence demonstrates just how intimately connected are the rhetorical structure and the satirical tone of the paragraph.

This first paragraph sets the schematic pattern for the whole of the passage, and almost everywhere we look we find parallelism and triadic structures. In the fifth sentence (*SM* 43:27–9), there are three clauses and a parallel between two adjectival phrases of three elements each. The sentences at 43:11–14 form another group of three, organised partly according to the pseudo-logical rhythm of rhetorical stress ('The Dean ... But ... And ...'), and involving structural and satirical parallelism around the two colons in the latter two sentences. The paragraph at 43:28–32, too, forms a triadic unit similar to the first paragraph, with a three-step presentation rounded-off in the final sentence by a three-part summary statement.

As we might expect, the 'psychology' section (44:31–45:3) provides a veritable plethora of rhetorical schemes, and there is, too, a high concentration of triadic groupings. Immediately preceding it, Mrs Witt declaims 'How *easy* it all seems ... And how false! And underneath, *how corrupt*!' And then the section begins with an almost perfect parallel structure on a tripartite pattern, with three near-identical sentence constructions each containing a pronounced threefold stress ('their doings, their privacies, their dirty linen'; 'personalities, personalities, personalities'; 'criticism ... appraisal ... analysis').

The repeated use of triadic structures throughout the extract (and indeed throughout the tale) derives in large part from the time-honoured rhetorical device for achieving emphasis in speech. And this is a convenient point to finish on, not only because it indicates Lawrence's rhetorical purpose in the extract, nor only because it reveals the rhetorical style of his satire more generally, but also because it stresses the extent to which we need always to be alive to Lawrence's language as to a *spoken* voice – or rather spoken voices.

Notes

1 'Bakhtin, Rabelais, and the Laughing Voices of Lawrence's Later Fiction: The Example of St. Mawr, in D.H. Lawrence: New Directions, ed. Keith Cushman and Peter Preston, forthcoming.

2 St. Mawr and Other Stories, ed. Brian Finney (Cambridge University Press: Cambridge, 1983), 42:21–45:35; St. Mawr (Harmondsworth: Penguin Books, 1950), pp. 35–9. Subsequent references to the Cambridge Edition will appear in the text in the form (SM 44:23).

8

Humour in the letters of D.H. Lawrence

Mark Kinkead-Weekes

Here, as Frieda would say, is a letter – or part of one – to Esther Andrews, written from Cornwall in August 1917.

> The Starrs are at Treveal … Last night they gave a concert in St. Ives: the Starrs: in St. Ives' Pavilion. It was called a Concert Play 'East & West' – composed by Starr. I went down with the Hockings: Wm. Hy, Mary, Mabel, Stanley. It was *too* dreadful. There was a violin solo: then Meredith intoned a dreadful poem of his own concoction: "Oh East is East & West is West & *ever* the twain shall meet," fearful. He wore a long night-gown of dark green cotton with a white mark in it: & the violin moaned faintly from behind a curtain, pained. Starr has no ear, and was [illegible]. Then he was to have had an 'original' character, Old Rowe, the old man who looks after the mines at Treveal – who scared Gray and Heseltine, & gave Starr a bottle of rum, you remember. At the eleventh hour, old Rowe said he was buggered if he was going, one fool was enough, no need to make it two. The resourceful Meredith, however, in the afternoon came upon an elderly weed singing in the streets of St. Ives, gave him sixpence and his tea, and wherever, on the programme, it said "Daddy White, an Original Song, composed [sic] by Himself" – appeared this piece of street refuse, in Lady Mary's cotton kimono, and yowled a street song, putting up his hand occasionally, automatically, as if someone had given him a penny. The audience, many of whom had paid 3/3 for a seat: seats 1/2, 2/2, 3/3, were merely pained: Lady Hain, patroness of this affair, and Lady Hain's musical daughter exceedingly so. Then Lady Mary sang 'The Rosary' rather faintly and blankly. Then Starr recited 'The Bells' – giving a brief fore-speech 'This magnificent poem by Edgar Allan Poe is one of

the most wonderful in the English language. Edgar Allan Poe was a master of transcendental music, *far* greater than Shakespeare – etc.' – Then he recited the poem. It went awfully flat. People giggled a little at the winkle-winkle tinkle-tinkle business, then Meredith started to hop, he stamped at the 'Bells bells bells —' and jumped 'Bells!' and leaped into the air 'Bells!!!' It was most astounding. Unfortunately the Cornish *couldn't* laugh: they were too pained.

Then came 'Scene I. Leila & Majnoun – the Persian Romeo and Juliet (a) Dawn (b) Dusk.' – Leila lay on a couch, hair bushed out, orange butter-muslin frock, while Starr recited – intoned – read from a little book, another poem of his 'The red of dawn approacheth, The night doeth sound retreat——' ending each verse 'the love of your lily-white feet.' After a long poem, Lady Mary awkwardly awoke and gauchely got up & he kissed her – exit left. – re-enter Right: Starr lies down to sleep, she invokes him; he awakes (he wears a crimson satin coatee and a pale blue turban) – kisses her – exit left – Song by Daddy White 'Peek-a-bo' – Violin Solo. – 'Scene II, James O'Reilly Adventurer, & bride, Spanish Gipsy – Lady Mary and Meredith Starr.' – She in one of Frieda's frocks & the black silk shawl, sat very uncomfortably on the camp-bed (on which was our Ott. bed-cover) and very gawkily tried to fan herself with a big paper fan. Meredith, shirt & trousers & sash, read-intoned recited from a little book a long long poem about himself, every verse ending 'The Admiral's daughter Lulu.' Pained wonder on the part of everybody. So ended Scene II – Song Daddy White. 'Scene III. Queen Sheba The Angel of Destiny.' Lady Mary, with her hands drooping & shoulder shrugging recites a short poem by Meredith, of how she loves & does not love: Meredith's occult form looms behind the curtain 'Thou shalt etc –' Lady Mary sinks on the couch, Meredith bursts forth from the curtain, in his blue bed-gown with spots 'I am the Angel of Destiny, I govern you by fear.' – recites his own grandeur – exeunt omnes. – Violin Solo by Trevor White. – (a) African Dance: Starr, in a table cloth, stamps and stares (b) Indian Serpent dance – Starr in a towel, prances and undulates his arms. (c) Greek Flute dance – Starr, with his hands to his mouth, in trousers & sash, capers like figures on a Greek Vase. (d) Short Violin Solo.

After that, I, and, and [sic] most of the audience, left. – William Henry was almost in tears. We ate chip-potatoes in a side street, and drove home, black darkness, and howling storm of rain, rain like waves of the sea: William Henry shouting at the horse 'Rose – co-o-me up' then continuing in a heart-broken voice 'How! And have we come out of a night like this, and all——'

– I had to give you this in full, as it is the greatest event in Zennor for some time. – Starr must have made quite a bit of money out of it. The takings must have been about £15 or more – one third for Red Cross – £10 for Meredith, from which he was going to give 6d to the weed – & the violinist was a good deal of a musician and gentleman. – £9-19-6 for Meredith. – I want my money back – my 1/2[d].[1]

Meredith Starr of course was a gift, making a fool of himself with sublime unconsciousness of absurdity – though Lady Mary seems embarrassed. She was however used to being pointed at. Her father was an alcoholic ticket-of-leave clergyman, never allowed a parish and banished to Cape Town by his aristocratic family; where a coloured lady took pity on him, and first cared for, and later married him – to the horror of the white community. Their reactions became somewhat more complex when he suddenly inherited the title of the Earl of Stamford on the untimely decease of an elder brother. Lady Mary, looked down on as a half-caste at home, was sent overseas to finishing school, and must often have wondered who she was.[2] But Meredith was a 'natural', an occultist hippy and faddist fifty years before his time. Another Lawrence letter described how 'They fast, or eat nettles, they descend naked into old mine-shafts and there meditate for hours and hours, upon their own transcendent infinitude: they descend on us like a swarm of locusts, and devour all the food on shelf or board' (iii. 158). Not altogether fool was Meredith, who somehow always did rather well out of his eccentricities.[3]

Lawrence, then, has the gift of a clownish plot to follow and 'produce', with stage directions adequate to such comedy of embarrassment. He had a fine eye for incongruity. The 'Weed' in Lady Mary's cotton kimono was a given, but the costume of the 'occult form' of the Angel of Destiny, though also given, is effectively delayed. The language has a pleasing exactitude: the portmanteau 'yowling', Lady Mary singing not only faintly but 'blankly'; the rhythmic intensification of the action words in 'The Bells', and in the exotic dances. The weed's gesture is nicely observed

– and the bathos of 'the love of your lily-white feet' beautifully timed. Gift or no, the whole shows to advantage the charade-lover's (and dramatist's) powers of observation and staging. For Esther Andrews there would also have been the extra pleasure of the familiar made exceeding strange: the sudden appearance of Frieda's black silk shawl, the camp-bed and Lady Ottoline's gift counterpane (which owing to her extraordinary handwriting, was always known as 'the countrypair' in which guise it had first been announced to them).

One or two features of characteristically Lawrentian humour are worth pointing to, however. The verbal wit of 'recites his own grandeur' comes from playing off two unlikely words against each other – with an aptness perfectly capturable in reading. Lawrence's humour however is very often *oral* – which is why it can often be missed. For example: 'Unfortunately the Cornish *couldn't* laugh, they were too pained' needs a comedian's pause on the ambiguous last word, to give the secondary hit at Cornish 'nearness' time to come through. (As they would say in Aberdeen 'Bang goes saxpence' – and one remembers the Leith man congratulating Harry Lauder with ''Twas all I cuid dae tae keep frae laughin' oot loud'.) Similarly, it is only when one 'does' the gloom of William Henry out loud, in a lugubrious accent with drawn-out vowels, that one 'hears' what Lawrence wanted. There is abundant evidence of his power of comic mimicry: how he would take off Pound, Yeats or a soulful lady playing the harp, or himself in all sorts of absurd situations, till people were helpless with laughter. It always adds to the pleasure of his humour to 'do' it aloud – of which the sublime example is probably the shouted argument in the car on the way down the mountain in 'The Captain's Doll', which some silent readers miss altogether. This letter also shows how his humour thrives on bathos – a technique which makes *Mr Noon* a notable example of 'The art of Sinking' in prose. Lawrentian humour is also very often spiced with a soupçon of malice. His pen is sharpened here by his sense that Starr had involved *them* in his tom-foolery – and was to do so even more in the correspondence which followed in the *St Ives Times*, in which Starr named Lawrence as a major modern artist (along with other undoubted but controversial artists like Epstein), but then fulfilled the Starry art of the bathetic by climaxing the list with the name of Aleister Crowley as the greatest of all.[4] Moreover Lawrence in 1917 could not afford to waste one and twopence. One could say 'it takes one to know one' – except of course that this was one of the lowest points in the whole of his career, when no publisher would touch *Women in Love*, he could sell nothing, and was growing vegetables for subsistence. Very soon he would be expelled from Cornwall – the letter comes near the nadir of his 'nightmare' of the war. People who accuse Lawrence of lacking humour very easily forget how little he had to laugh about in the period which saw his major work – but this letter is one proof that he could laugh at the worst of times. Another is the letter he wrote a few weeks later, when a tempest destroyed his gardens with their months of work, and laid waste the 'fecundity' he had described with such pride. He met the disaster, as he often did, by humorous exaggeration.

> It rains and rains, and it blows the sea up on to the land, in volleys and masses of wind. We are all being finely and subtly sea-pickled, sea-changed, sure enough 'into something new and strange'. [He was a habitual misquoter.] I shouldn't be a bit surprised to find one morning that fine webs had grown between my toes, and that my legs were slippery with sea-weedy scales. I feel quite spray-blind, like any fish, and my brain is turning nacreous. I verily believe I am being metamorphosed – feel as if I daren't look to see. [Bert-Caliban is a nice thought.]   (iii.156)

One advantage of writing about humour in the letters is that it allows one to point to something in the grain of his temperament, more spontaneous than worked-up set pieces like the Starr concert, or the comedy in the fiction and the poems. The letters are full of well-crafted jokes, of course. One smiles at a comic character created wholly as a voice: like the splendid Miss Fisher of Taormina at her tea-party, with someone practising the piano on the floor below: 'Can you bear it *another* instant?' – 'What Miss Fisher?' – 'Why that AW-ful noise!' – Did you EVER! I hate the place. I simply HATE the place. And I hate the PEOPLE – Oh my! – And the flies! Aren't the flies simply AWful!' (iv.101). Or – a more august example – when, after 'gaily ringing our last shilling for the empty heavens to hear it', Lawrence thinks it about time for a miracle to stop the war: 'the Lord suddenly shouting out of the thunder' – as at the end of the book of Job, presumably – '"Fous-moi la paix, la bas" like a man just wakened up' (ii. 611). Or one smiles at someone transmogrified in an image like his old mentor Edward Garnett, suddenly heard from in 1921, after a long silence, and with the news that Bunny had married. Edward presumably flirts with his new daughter-in-law? 'Because I always think of you when a hornet hovers round the jam pots after one has made jam. Only you're all Badger-grey instead of striped. But a humming wasp all the same' (iv. 100). Or the touch of malice in deflating the sentimental or pretentious, as in the counterpoint of voices in the account of the 'famous' Taormina violinist, recently returned to the island, who 'played "The Rosary" con moltissimo expressione, till I thought his fiddle-strings were turning thick as salsiccia with emotion. Poor darling, his wife has lately died. She used to accompany him on the piano, with so much *feeling*, said Giuseppina May, that, poor thing, she was nothing but a shadow. And now she isn't even that' (iv. 101–2) – the worst bathos of all. But always there is the humour turned on himself, as when Nellie Morrison exclaimed that he was the very image of the St Francis in Achsah Brewster's painting, and that the Buddhistic Brewsters simply must meet him. Two 'opposite' images collide with the utmost incongruity. 'Nellie Morrison is an ass who would say a pudding on a dish looked like Buddha, if you crossed the spoon and fork in front to look like two cross-legs. Your St. F needs a good *schiaffo* [a clip on the ear], and a pint of Chianti. Never ate enough' (iii. 720). In the same spirit, Baroness von Richthofen's 'little son-in-law' pleads for her help against her two daughters, made aggressive by gobbling '4 chickens', and guzzling '4 litres of peach-punch' in Zell-am-See (iv. 63); and Signor Lorenzo assumes that Grazia, the old woman downstairs in Fontana Vecchia, terrified that the ghost of 'her poor dead Beppe' might appear at All Souls, 'comes sheltering under my wing because, I suppose, she thinks I'm such another tyrant and nuisance, such as he was' (iv. 109). And always there is the comedy of incongruity: as when in a Taormina hotel he watches 'Dr Rogers from Cambridge hypnotising Danish damsels with fox-skins over their shoulders and glaucous eyes across the lunch table, over poached eggs' (iii. 496) – a grotesque visual rhyme.

What I would also like to show, however, is how (over a six month period) the spontaneous humour in letter after letter, written without revision, not only shows up most of the characteristics of Lawrence's humour, but also reveals it as – quite simply – a constant of his temperament.

The controlled anticlimax is always there – a comedy of adjustment and proportion – and, often, a comedy of timing. As he elaborates a British cliché about 'hanging on like a bull-dog, because you've shut your teeth in the rear of this damn craven life' one begins to sense, in the overdoing, a deflation coming, that yet does not destroy its essential optimism. 'In the end one pulls it down, I think, and has a triumph. (Mine hasn't turned up yet)' (ii. 29). There's a nice double-take image there, about DHL with his teeth endlessly shut! An even better example allows his voice to swell in characteristic cadence as he outlines his 'working philosophy': 'the only stable happiness for mankind is that it shall live married in blessed union to woman-kind – intimacy, physical and psychical, between a man and his wife. I wish to add that my state of bliss is by no means perfect' (ii. 70–1). Sometimes the 'swell' is beautifully disguised, so that the puncturing comes as a greater surprise. 'We sit by lamplight and drink beer, and hear Edgar on Modern Capitalism. *Why was I born?*' (ii. 63).

Always, too, there is a playfulness of language. Cynthia Asquith's baby (not yet troubled), the 'fat and smiling John' met at Kingsgate, becomes known as 'the jonquil with the golden smile' (ii. 89). Edith Hopkin, out of school and working in a bank now, is referred to as 'that young fellow' (ii. 56), or 'that haughty Enid' (ii. 58). Bunny Garnett is invited to Kingsgate with a promise of happiness: 'et nous voilà, trois lapins dans les salades' (ii. 32). That cries out for a cartoonist's pencil . . . the incongruous shapes would be pleasing. Sometimes the humour needs time for the double- or even triple-take. He announces that he has discovered the missing story 'Witch à La Mode' he has been pestering the Garnetts about: it was in amongst Frieda's intimate underwear. But he has had to change its name in order to 'get it out' (ii. 36) – the modish witch Frieda having imprisoned it, presumably, because it had its origins in his attempt to seduce Helen Corke. (With pleasant decorum, the new name he chose for it was 'Intimacy'!)

Surprisingly often in his work, a major scene will rest on the revivification of a cliché, to release underlying meaning that has got obscured by being worn too smooth. (An extraordinary passage in *Aaron's Rod*, for instance, when Aaron is robbed, explores what it means to go hot and cold all over.) But in the letters he often simply enjoys playing about with clichés. Having once written that Ezra Pound seems keen to take him under his wing, Ezra's editor becomes a 'wing-chicken', another 'tenant of Pound's wing-cover' (ii. 27, 26). This easily extends into parody, where the absurd expansion of a cliché becomes a way of pointing a criticism. He is irritated that a baker's bill has followed them to Irschenhausen, but the response comes pat. '"Cast thy bread upon the waters", I cried to the baker, "and send thy bills out after it."' But then, as the cliché is concretised, the Georgian Muse descends with a vengeance: 'Far down the dancing Danube, and over Hungaria's restless plains, my baker's bill on its bobbing course, goes seeking the golden grains. – Ask Mr Marsh' (who had criticised *his* rhythms) 'if *that* isn't perfect Flecker-rhythm. *The Golden Journey to Samarkand*. You knew it climbed Parnassus *en route*?' Of course, by contrast, his own rhythms 'go cackling round like a poultry farm' (ii. 62).

Comic self-deprecation is also a constant. 'I'm the sort of weedy plant that takes badly to removal' (ii. 33). Or, mindful of the Gospel according to St. Matthew, if Constance Garnett were to have 'a little drawer in which I, poor hole-less fox and nestless sparrow, – could leave my MS, I should once more call blessings on your wise and venerably translating head' (ii. 37). A little earlier in the same letter he had called her 'you Newnham Missis' (ii. 36). From Bavaria, he laments at having been lost to sight among a horde of young Germans buying ginger-bread fancies for their girls: 'I never got a look in. I am born to be elbowed out' (ii. 63).

More seriously *and* more comically, he will use humour to proportion things that otherwise could be painful. There are many jokes about his rumpuses with Frieda. Sometimes the joke lies in a word, and an aside. 'Frieda and I have quarrelled just as arduously as ever. You'll come to my funeral?' (ii. 30). Or it might be an image, as when, Lawrence having rowed Mrs Pearse back from Fiascherino to Lerici after giving her tea,

Frieda wanted to help on the return journey, and they 'fell out so fright-fully – we were rowing one oar each, – that the boat revolved on its axis, and seriously thought of diving under water out of our way. So today Madam must walk, whether she will or no' (ii. 120). Or he will work up a comic frenzy, to Cynthia Asquith.

> You say we are happy – per Bacchino! If you but knew the thunder-storms of tragedy that have played over my wretched head, as if I was set up on God's earth for a lightning conductor, you'd say 'thank God I am not as that poor man.' If you knew the slough of misery we've struggled and suffocated through, you'd stroke your counterpane with a purring motion, like an old maid having muffins for tea in the lamplight and reading Stanley in Africa ... We are the most unfortu-nate, agonised, fate-harassed mortals since Orestes and that gang. Don't you forget it.   (ii.107).

He had a nice outsider's eye. Suddenly the Oxbridge Eddie Marsh's admiration for Horace gets a miner's son's rejoinder: Horace is 'a mellow varsity man who never quite forgot Oxford' (ii. 105). (Lawrence liked Marsh, and admired Horace, and yet a tone is caught.) And W.L. George, who had achieved huge popular success with a novel about a prostitute, is quite affectionately pinned down in his absurd Mills-and-Boonery. (Again this needs to be viva voce.) '"Ah – did you see it – the snowy white neck – the beckoning of a curl – wait – wait –" – This in the Strand as an ordinary girl goes by' (ii.108).

That eye for incongruity is everywhere. Sometimes it is sardonic, as in the contrast between Switzerland and Milan: the one in which the 'only excitement' is 'that you can throw a stone a frightfully long way down – and that is forbidden by law'; the other 'with its imitation hedge-hog of a cathedral and its hateful town Italians all socks and purple cravats and hats over the ear ...' (ii. 88). On occasion, the sardonic eye with its touch of Lawrentian malice can suddenly modulate into another perspective altogether, as in the response to Waterfield, the well-to-do artist who had hired a castle in Aulla and entertained them there. Having felt he must praise Waterfield's pictures to his face, Lawrence relieved his feel-ings behind the painter's back: 'the artist gentleman painted in the manner of various defunct gentleman artists – their ghosts haunted his canvases like the ghosts of old dead soldiers his castle hall. And the servants crouched in a corner of the great dark kitchen, making polenta cakes –' (ii. 128–9) The malice drops away; and incongruity makes a deeper proportioning point. Sometimes there is just the joy of incongruity for its own animated sake. The church in Tellaro was (and still is) so perched on the rocks at the edge of the sea that 'once in the night the church bell rang – and rang again. The people got up in terror – the bell rung mysteriously. Then it was found that the bell rope had fallen over the edge of the cliff in among the rocks, and an octopus had got hold of the end, and was drawing it.' A tall story of course, but (says he) 'quite possible' (ii. 123). Unforgettable, too, is his picture of Irschenhausen after rain, when the normal world is suddenly animated in wholly fresh ways: 'it rains – oh Lord! – the rain positively stands up on end. Sometimes one sees the deer jumping up and down to get the wet out of their jackets, and the squirrels simply hang out by their tails, like washing…' (ii. 63).

Lastly, of course, there are the more elaborate 'turns', in the letters, as in life. There is 'Lawrence and the post-master' where, being short of money as so often, and waiting anxiously for promised cheques to arrive, he drags off every day to the post office at Tellaro, and after a half-hour scramble over the rocky path round the headland, 'I get only a broad smile and a wave of the hand that implies a vacuum in space, and a "niente, signore, niente oggi, niente, niente".' That is of course if he had managed to *find* the man, who on this occasion was helping the priest decorate the church. 'So when the post-master is forced to follow at my heels up the cobbly track, humbly to deliver me my letter, I am justified' (ii. 86). Better still, there is 'Lawrence and the pianoforte', made all the more fortissimo by having, this time, to get to Lerici and then take the workmen's steamer all the way across the Gulf to La Spezia, to try to arrange delivery of a piano on which Frieda had set her heart, but which will have to come in a rowing boat from Lerici to Fiascherino since there is no road. If he had only caught Rugi Gulielmo alone! – but unfortunately there was an audience for the man's excuses:

'Ecco – un pianoforte – it's not like a piece of furniture – if it was a piece of furniture – hé, va bene – but a pianoforte – hé –' I loathe and detest the Italians. They never argue, they just get hold of a parrot phrase, shove up their shoulders and put their heads on one side, and flap their hands . . . Now I shall have to go tomorrow, and pay a regiment of facchini to transport that cursed pianoforte.

   'Take it up tenderly
Lift it with care
Fashioned so slenderly
Young and so fair'. . .[5]   (ii. 108)

Or, there is sheer fantasy, as in the dressing-down he imagines Marsh is to give to W.H. Davies who (Lawrence thinks) is 'really like a linnet that's got just a wee little sweet song, but it only sings when it's wild. And he's made himself a tame bird'. So Marsh, the most mild-mannered of men, is to excoriate the ex-super-tramp, for his own good of course:

'Davies, your work is getting like Birmingham tinware; Davies, you drop your h's, and everybody is tempering the wind to you, because you are a shorn lamb; Davies, your accent is intolerable in a carpeted room; Davies, you hang on like the mud on a lady's silk petticoat.' Then he might leave his Sevenoaks room, where he is rigged up as rural poet, proud of the gilt mirror and his romantic past: and he might grow his wings again, and chirrup a little sadder song.
(ii. 92)

What humour is (or what is humorous) seem questions impossible to pursue sufficiently humorously – and tastes in jokes notoriously differ. But that Lawrence had a sense of humour, ingrained, and constant, admits I think of no doubt, though there are periods of his life (more miserable than June to December 1913) when it appears more fitfully. We know that his comic turns could make listeners helpless with laughter. The letters however tend not to be worked up to that extent; and are mostly rather playful than side-splitting. But though Lawrence was notoriously liable to fall into rages, the evidence shows that, in the full sense of the term, his sense of humour was good-tempered, proportioning, as well as delightful.

Notes

1 Published, with grateful acknowledgement to and by kind permission of the owner, who wishes to remain anonymous. The text of the whole letter will appear in *The Selected Letters of D.H. Lawrence*, ed. James T. Boulton (Cambridge: Cambridge University Press, 1996).

2 R.R. Langham-Carter, 'Lord Stamford's Tangled Affairs'. *Familia, Quarterly Journal of the Genealogical Society of South Africa*, xi, no. 1 (1974), 8–13, 16; and ibid., xi, no. 3 (1974), 78–80; also Lawrence Green, *Growing Lovely, Growing Old* (Cape Town: Timmins, 1975), pp. 178–82; and with thanks to Barry Smith, who brought these to my attention.

3 A much less sympathetic picture is drawn by the waspish minor poet Robert Nichols (1893–1944), in annotating a letter of Philip Heseltine to him from Dublin of 14 December 1917 (British Library Additional Mss. 57794, 24): 'Reference to Black Magic would be presumably to Meredith Starr. I seem to remember that Philip later introduced me to some sort of imposter of that name ... a fellow with long hair, bulbous rings etc., & an infernal gas bag.'

Meredith Starr later published *Atma Jnan: The Garden of the Heart* and *The Future of the Novel* (a collection of interviews with well-known writers, not including DHL) and a book of poems. Later still he founded a successful residential centre or 'secular retreat' devoted to 'Constructive Psychology', which moved from a Devonshire farmhouse to the much larger Frogmore Hall in Hertfordshire.

4 *St. Ives Times*, 31 August 1917, replying to outraged correspondence in the issue of 24 August.

5 This adapts 'The Bridge of Sighs', ll. 5–8, by Thomas Hood (1799–1845) ['Take her up tenderly, / Lift her with ...'].

~ 9

Lawrence to Larkin: A changed perspective

John Bayley

For Larkin, as for Lawrence, most writers were frauds. The pair of them were exceptions, because of the way they saw things; and being exceptions constituted their originality as artists. The relationship between them is thus a surprisingly close one, although it also reveals the change in perspective between Modernism and the 'Movement', between the literary renaissance of the earlier part of the twentieth century, and the disillusion that followed the Second World War.

It also demonstrates a paradox: Lawrence the prophet at one in his hatred of fraud with Larkin the solipsist. The writer who is not a fraud must needs be vicious in his honesty.

In a letter to his friend Harry Chambers (9 October 1963) Larkin made a remark about the writer Paul Potts, author of *Dante Called You Beatrice.* For Larkin the book was 'quite a testament, though I should run a mile from him the author in reality'. He goes on to 'wonder if he is as noble & generous & sensitive as he suggests?' Larkin continues, somewhat significantly: 'I've always taken comfort from D.H.L.'s "You have to have something vicious in you to be a creative writer."'[1] Significantly, because it is typical of Larkin's outlook to put the word 'vicious' and the word 'comfort' side by side. (Barbara Pym, whose novels Larkin greatly admired, and to whom he wrote many letters, is also fond of using the word 'comfort' with a deadpan comic overtone. She suggests that women are in particular need of it, no matter how 'sharp' 'the nicest women' may be.[2])

A degree of viciousness, at his own expense, is essential to the writer if he is to be not 'truly great' (comic overtone again – see the poem 'Fiction and the Reading Public', written in February 1950 and published in 1954 in *Essays in Criticism*[3]) but a true original. In his own extremes of self-consciousness Larkin could well have formulated what was implicit for him in Lawrence: a writer's seriousness must consist in not taking himself seriously. A true original can never be a fraud, in the sense that the 'truly great' usually are. One reason is that 'originality is not an ingredient of poetry, it *is* poetry', a remark by Clive James about which Larkin comments 'I've been feeling that for years' (*SL* 506). 'One never gets any better at this lark,' he observes to Robert Conquest, in a letter the same month, referring to his failure to get on with his poem 'Aubade' (*SL* 505). If one got any better one would stop being original: one might even become 'truly great' – a fate not only banal but in every sense deadly.

For to be dead in the sense of the illustrious dead, who lie in Westminster Abbey, and in their tomes along library shelves, is, so to speak, a fate worse than death for the real writer, as opposed to the 'truly great' one, at whom must be directed a barrage of jokes and ironies. The poet's real life, real originality, is a matter of his never having any firm ground to stand on, never building up a bronze monument to withstand time, and to give the poet the confidence for new monumental building in the same style – new deathless works. T.S. Eliot tells us that the poet, his 'shabby equipment always deteriorating', must prepare himself time after time for a new 'raid on the inarticulate';[4] but the tone in which he writes, and the 'wise old author' formality of his utterance, make the statement less than convincing. Such sentiments can be, or at least sound like, a form of self-protection, quite different from Larkin's terse knowledge that one never gets any better at this lark, or Lawrence's ability to scrap whatever it was he was writing, like so much waste paper, and start all over again. For both the business of writing begins to look, as it does when it is a matter of tombs and tomes, like an enormous joke, the ultimate and most basic joke.

Both for Lawrence and for Larkin – and it is the reason for the latter's deep and enduring admiration for his elder – the point about life and fun was immediacy. Nothing can be preserved, and nothing should be. The point about a true joke is not only its sudden and complete originality but its non-preservation. It does not and cannot last; but, as Larkin

sometimes implies, the only function and success of art – more specifically of a poem – is to give the appearance of its doing so. Lawrence's
hatred of the monumental in architecture and culture resembles
Larkin's contempt for the preserved body of 'Eng. Lit.' which he was
required to study for his University course. The literature he likes and
responds to – 'thrills to', as he puts it (*SL* 35) – has, like Lawrence's books,
the constant element for him of the unpreserved, the non-serious. He
suggests that Lawrence cannot be serious if he tries; and that what is so
marvellous about *Lady Chatterley's Lover* is that it is wonderfully and
liberatingly laughable ('parts of it made me laugh deeply' *SL* 144) – when
it is being, for Lawrence's more engaged and responsible critics, something which is unfortunate because it might be laughed *at*. His critics
wish to spare Lawrence's ego and save his face, in a way that he never did
himself. Like successful performers in a music-hall, both writers depend
on the 'them/us' aspect of humour. The reader, like the audience, must be
inside the act. There is no question of impressing him, or winning him
over. Essential that he should be already with the author as he goes into
his routine: otherwise detachment can lead to hostility or indifference.
We all laugh at 'them', and recognise them at once, whatever form 'they'
take.

This aspect of humour has its unattractive side, particularly to *bien
pensants*. Much ink has been spilled, after all, on the question not only of
what might seem the unintended comedy of Mellors's sexual frolics with
Connie, but also on Lawrence's unfairness to Sir Clifford Chatterley, to
Michaelis and even to Mrs Bolton. These characters are all very much
'them', in their different ways, although Mrs Bolton is a brilliantly if
unsympathetically observed character. Lawrence's contempt for
Chatterley for having been wounded in the war seems especially gratu-
itous, and indeed odious; but it is very much a part of the unflinching
'us/them' world, in which we must be with him completely, or stand dis-
approvingly outside – becoming one of 'them'. There was no doubt
where Larkin stood. Not for him the critical qualifications and dis-
approvals – he was wholly a Lady Chatterley man. And it is all the more
significant that Larkin's view of his war – the Second World War – should
have been much the same as Lawrence's of the earlier conflict. Larkin's

own friends may have taken part, but they got no credit with him for doing so: on the contrary, they had every chance of finding themselves becoming 'them' in the process.

Larkin's resentment of the war was of a piece, as time went on, with his resentment at governments (Mrs Thatcher's the exception), immigrants and the Welfare State. He assumed, indeed took it for granted, that Lawrence would have been with him in all such matters. And it is significant that it is the later Lawrence, the Lawrence of *Lady Chatterley's Lover* and *The Plumed Serpent*, to whom Larkin seems to have felt especially close. The reason for people's likes or dislikes, in life or in art, as he tells his friend J.B. Sutton in July 1949, 'are fishy enough to fill the North Sea, and certainly not ethical or even respectable'. The point about 'us' is that we can be as silly, or as perversely paradoxical as we please, and only 'they' might be stuffy or censorious enough to lift an eyebrow. 'Life is chiefly an affair of "life-force"', and yet 'I refuse to believe that there is a thing called life, that one can be in or out of touch with.' A propos of the 'life-force', he remarks to his correspondent that it may sound 'Lawrentian':

> but where I differ from Lawrence is that to me this energy is quite amoral, not particularly 'pure', & entirely selfish. Nevertheless I shall not abandon D.H.L. – we are too similar for that, and besides no one who has really thrilled to Lawrence can ever give him up . . . I find myself falling in step with Lawrence's moods as if I were falling in step with you on the road down to Canley brook.   (*SL* 154)

The difference Larkin admits between him and his writer hero is a difference in name only: in fact it is clear that he feels all these characteristics are Lawrence's too – how could they not be? Nor is Larkin wrong about this, from the point of view of his own sympathy and identification with Lawrence, which even extends to a perhaps unconscious identification with the tone of many of Lawrence's letters to friends of his youth ('falling in step with you on the road down to Canley brook').

But of course the key factor is 'thrilling' to Lawrence. For the young aspirant of the age he was *the* great liberator and exemplar, and it made no difference that, as Larkin put it, 'his exhortations leave me cold' (*SL*

154). It was not Lawrence's teaching that enthralled the discontented and rebellious young of that post-war time, of whom both Larkin and Kingsley Amis were representative, but his status as the great symbol of frustration and irritation, subversion and anger, and yet, and above all, humour and clowning. That was the Lawrence they worshipped and admired; and Larkin admired with the kind of discernment one would expect, even though he made no attempt to assess or criticise his hero systematically or responsibly, and would have scorned to do so.

From our point of view the side of Lawrence in which Larkin was most interested, and on which in his own letters and comments Lawrence was himself most interesting, was the detachment of the comedy hero. This is more significant even than the fact that Lawrence was the liberator from the claustrophobic lifestyle and ideology of the provincial middle class, and its inhibitions about sex and the body. Lawrence could be seen as wholly iconoclastic, and irreverent about all the beliefs or conventions that pressed upon the young, and which irked and hampered their sense of themselves and of their lives. That meant that for Larkin he was not only irreverent, but, in the most basic and down-to-earth sense, selfish and irresponsible. His reverence for life, and his unique sense of life and of living things, was not cosmetic or hypocritical, but for Larkin it was of a piece with his actual refusal to take the ordinary man's share in life. Whatever his claim and status as preacher, his status as individual amounted in the end to a total irresponsibility. His famous rages against society and social evils obscured this to some extent, but not intentionally. Lawrentian irresponsibility is a natural phenomenon, like the sun or the rain, which his more devoutly correct admirers may prefer not to notice, but which was in no way concealed or equivocated by the man himself. So it seemed to Larkin, and it was this that constituted Lawrence's enormous appeal for him.

Yet there is a certain obvious irony in the fact that while Larkin himself, and with his own connivance, is imaged by the critically correct as the poet and man who refused to become an adult, Lawrence was for his older admirers, and for Leavis in particular, the exemplar of spiritual adulthood, enlightenment and maturity. For Larkin this enlightenment becomes something rather different, though no less impressive. In a letter to his friend J.B. Sutton of December 1946, in which he says he has been reading Lawrence's letters once more, he adds that it 'gives me great comfort to know that he existed and his work still exists – a sort of touchstone against the false' (*SL* 131). The word 'comfort' again, and the suggestion of a triad or trinity of Lawrentian forces – comfort, comedy – total non-falsity – constituting a somewhat different ground of Lawrence worship than the one on which Leavis had taken his stand. For Larkin, Lawrence is solitary, funny and comforting, and sees through everything: and though it would be obvious to point out that this is how Larkin saw himself and his work, and is making Lawrence in his own image, it is none the less important that Larkin's Lawrence worship should also have been so spontaneous and so acute.

In the same letter he suggests that Middleton Murry got Lawrence wrong. Murry's inbuilt falsity went with solemnity, earnestness and lack of humour, and it is these characteristics which must have exasperated Lawrence. Larkin's opinion here is sensibly judicious. 'It looks to me as if it were the war in particular and *the failure to establish contact with people in general* that was the root of the trouble. Not sex at all. But this needs thought' (*SL* 131: my italics).

Crying in the wilderness was not Larkin's thing; and he suggests it was not Lawrence's either, but that there was rather some more homely and ordinary way in which Lawrence was cut off, or self cut off. The admiration underneath here may well be for an artist who succeeded and survived by being cut off, and whose art flourished in those conditions. *A Girl in Winter*, Larkin's most ambitious attempt in fiction, makes what virtue it can of the state of cutoffness, and indeed succeeds marvellously well as an extended prose poem. But Larkin was already feeling anxiety that he would not be able to write another novel, anxiety that went with the obstinate urge to press on with one somehow. In the same letter he continues: 'I keep burning a small fire of determination to write another book. I want it to be long and fairly involved, but with few tricks: a man's life, no less. An immense subject, and I quail before it. But *it will be done*' (*SL* 131). *Sons and Lovers* may well have been the model. 'If Lawrence had been killed after writing that book he'd still be England's greatest novelist', he had written to Sutton much earlier (*SL* 32). Larkin would now abjure the poetic devices of *A Girl in Winter*, which was indeed full of its own kind of native tricks. But although one or two novels in a more overtly Lawrentian vein were begun, they remained no more than fragments.

It may be that 'a man's life' was not the kind of work to be encouraged by Lawrentian inspiration. For one thing it cannot help sounding a little pompous, which would be as unthinkable for Larkin as for Lawrence. As Larkin sensed, Lawrence's comedy outsider status – a 'that'll show the buggers sort of feeling', which made Larkin 'chuckle' (*SL* 146) – is not compatible with being on the inside of an individual man's or woman's life, and writing about it in the way that Larkin wished to do. Consciously he may have had in mind for his novel an older novel, of the kind that produced a Henchard, a Lydgate or a Dorothea Brooke. He once remarked that the novelists he admired and wanted to be like are Lawrence, Hardy and George Eliot. The second pair could give him no help. But *A Girl in Winter*, in its, and his, own way a masterpiece, is subtly but deeply indebted to the later Lawrentian models, and above all to Lawrence's characteristic play of scenic rather than verbal humour.

Indeed the more one reflects on *A Girl in Winter*, and the more one recalls its most memorable moments, the clearer it becomes that although Larkin has transformed for his own purposes those scenes from Lawrence which make up what Leavis called a 'dramatic poem',[5] the comparable scenes in his own novel are deeply influenced by the Lawrentian example. The significant difference is that the message Lawrence's poetic drama builds into those scenes has been either discarded – it seems deliberately – or changed, even reversed. Larkin like Lawrence naturally adored the specific and the actual, in terms of beasts, birds and flowers, clothes, habits, food. *The Rainbow* and *Women in Love, Aaron's Rod, Mr Noon*, are all sprinkled with such glittering little nuggets of peerless actuality. Lawrence himself would have instantly noted such details in *A Girl in Winter* as the clear soup joggling about in the white plates of the dining car, as Katherine and Robin Fennel eat their lunch while journeying up from Dover to his home.[6] A detail fixed in life, and silently offering this kind of artist's mysterious but also hilarious baptism.

It is in the nature of Lawrence's dramatic method to charge such moments with his own kind of significance; and this grows ever more marked in the later novels, the ones to which Larkin seems to have particularly responded. Even in *Women in Love* the dramatic significance of many such actualities is made abundantly clear. An obvious example would be the chapter 'Moony', or the unforgettable rabbit, which tears round and round its grass enclosure with what seems mindless and mechanistic fury, and which gives a deep scratch to Gudrun's arm.[7] In addition to its dramatic symbolism, that episode is a striking example of Lawrence's silent scenic humour.

Larkin's silent humour is related, but subtly different. The soup joggling in the plates suggests the silent agitation of the young, as they converse politely with each other, but nothing is made of this. Larkin likes his tableaux to stop being acted before, as it seems, meaning can be established. Humour is never used, as Lawrence uses it, for the dual purpose of promoting 'doctrine' and letting that doctrine be tacitly criticised, or even mocked (without, however, being discredited) from a rival centre of awareness. In 'The Captain's Doll', Alexander Hepburn and Hannele are coming back from an excursion in the mountains, and are trembling on the edge of a ferocious quarrel; they have, however, to return in the same open charabanc.

> "I think," said Hepburn, "I may as well finish what I had to say?"
>
> "What?" cried Hannele, fluttering in the wind of the rushing car.
>
> "I may as well finish what I had to say," shouted he, his breath blown away.
>
> "Finish then," she screamed, the ends of her scarf flickering behind her.
>
> "When my wife died," he said loudly, "I knew I couldn't love any more."
>
> "Oh—h!" she screamed ironically.
>
> "In fact," he shouted, "I realised that, as far as I was concerned, love was a mistake."
>
> "*What* was a mistake?" she screamed.
>
> "Love," he bawled.
>
> "Love!" she screamed. "A mistake?" Her tone was derisive.

"For me personally," he said, shouting.

"Oh, only for you personally," she cried, with a pouf of laughter.

The car gave a great swerve, and she fell on the driver. Then she righted herself. It gave another swerve, and she fell on Alexander. She righted herself angrily. And now they ran straight on: and it seemed a little quieter.

"I realised," he said, "that I had always made a mistake, undertaking to love."

"It must have been an undertaking, for *you*," she cried.

"Yes, I'm afraid it was. I never really wanted it. But I thought I did. And that's where I made my mistake."

"Whom have you ever loved?—even as an undertaking?" she asked.

"To begin with, my mother: and that was a mistake. Then my sister: and that was a mistake. Then a girl I had known all my life: and that was a mistake. Then my wife: and that was my most terrible mistake. And then I began the mistake of loving you."

"Undertaking to love me, you mean," she said. "But then you never did properly undertake it. You never really *undertook* to love *me*."

"Not quite, did I?" said he.

And she sat feeling angry that he had never made the undertaking.[8]

This scene does indeed give the impression of not being 'put into words'. The comedy leaps straight out of the page, that is to say, with all Lawrence's amazing gift of freshness, doing its job with incomparable swiftness and certainty. A job, none the less, is what it is doing. And scenic humour in Larkin is in its own way unemphatic, yet played down and presented with just as sure a grasp of what a certain kind of wordlessness requires.

At this point Robin ran down the steps carrying a folding-camera. Mr Fennel, who was wearing a panama hat, stepped forward.

"Now give that to me. I'll be the man who presses the button."

"Oh, but we want you in the picture," exclaimed Jane, coming forward.

"Not a bit of it. Just you all get together. Ladies at the front, gentlemen at the back. Yes, round the seat will do."

"Is it all right for the sun, sir?" said Jack Stormalong anxiously, looking as if he would like to take the camera into his own hands.

"I've taken dozens of photographs," said Mr Fennel firmly, "without bothering about things like that. The secret is to hold it steadily."

"It'll do," said Robin, aside.

"You might hold it straight as well," said Jane. Mrs Fennel was in the middle, with Katherine on her right and Jane on her left. "If you'd wait a moment, I'd put some proper shoes on," she said. "These aren't really fit to be seen."

"My dear, posterity won't be interested in your shoes, presentable or not. Now let me see. I can't see anything at all. Where are you?" He swivelled the camera plaintively. "Wave something."

Jack waved a hand.

"Ah. Yes, that's got it, thank you. The next trouble is going to be Jack's head. I'm afraid your head will be out of the picture, Jack."

"Well, that's a comfort," said Jane.

"Wait a minute. Nil desperandum. I'm afraid we shall have to dispense with the ladies' feet—you needn't have worried about your shoes, my dear."

"Perhaps if you stepped back, sir——"

"No, this will do very well. Now then. That's got it. Everybody smile. Remember this is a special occasion—where's the thing, the button on this thing? Where—ah. Now then."

And so the image of them standing and sitting in relaxed attitudes in the evening sun was pressed onto the negative for all eternity.[9]

Meticulous in its aimlessness, the dialogue seems recorded both by the camera and by the writer's deadpan humour. Like the shouts and gestures in 'The Captain's Doll', it moves without effort into comedy, not only by being banal in itself but by seeming incongruously to imitate the silence and fixity of the finished photograph, preserved 'for ever' between 'matt black pages', as in Larkin's poem 'Lines on a Young Lady's Photograph Album' (CP 71–2). Both writers succeed by presenting comedy, through their art, as if there were no suggestion of artifice about it. It becomes part of the natural – and, in Larkin's case again, the comforting – order of things, like the landscape of cold into which the

---

relationship. Some at least of Lawrence's sexual prophecies have become the sexual clichés of today. And yet there remains an element of special pleading in Lawrence's art, in 'The Captain's Doll' and in *Lady Chatterley's Lover*, which Larkin was well aware of, and which he also may have perceived as justifying itself by means of comedy: the sort of consciously mocking Lawrentian humour which he particularly appreciated, and which at the same time is different from the natural and implicit element of humour in which both his own art and Lawrence's swim, as it were by nature. Humour as a weapon of special pleading is not the truest humour; nor does Lawrence really resolve a problem which his art can affect to dispose of in so easy a fashion.

> I do think D.H.L. went deeply into it all. But I don't think he drew any conclusions that are really dependable. – I mean he never resolved the quarrel between the necessity & beauty of being united with a woman one loves, & the necessity of not being entangled or bullied or victimised or patronised or any of the other concomitants of love & marriage. It's funny how Mellors never really swears love, or even *wants* love: whenever Connie tries to fix him with her eye, a 'mocking grin' comes over his face, or some such. It's no good, he just doesn't want it. This is enormously important, I think, & Murry is wrong when he treats it as just something L. just dreamed up to 'avoid' love – it is something that is '*true*'. (SL 151)

Mellors's, or Lawrence's, 'mocking grin' is the male's natural defence; as Larkin is well aware, however 'true' it may have been to his own personal feelings. But Larkin is well aware that the famous independence of the sexes which Lawrence advocated is in important ways paradoxical: it does not appear to go with what Larkin calls Lawrence's 'yarning on about how contemptible freedom is'. Children, as Larkin sees, are the real issue here. He has had the idea, he says, of showing in an article how Lawrence's beliefs are in opposition to the way he actually lived, and are illustrated 'ONLY BY THE CONTRARY' (Larkin's capitals): '. . . he's always yarning on about how contemptible freedom is – but by golly-wogs try giving him a salaried position, or suggesting he should join the Army! But the absurdity of it all struck me like a fist in the knackers – like

heroine of *A Girl in Winter* finds herself sinking at the end of the novel, 'as if icefloes were moving down a lightless channel of water'. 'Yet their passage was not saddening. Unsatisfied dreams rose and fell about them, crying out against their implacability, but in the end glad that such order, such destiny, existed. Against this knowledge, the heart, the will, and all that made for protest, could at last sleep.'[10] The passage seems to be imitating a 'profound' piece of writing, which in a sense it is: and in some curious way the reader's knowledge of this adds both to the quietness of the comedy and to its underlying sense of comfort and authority. For the ice landscape is not symbolic, as it is when Gerald dies an alpine death at the end of *Women in Love*. It seems very probable that Larkin had that passage in mind when he wrote the end of his novel; but if so he gave it a quite different dimension, subduing whatever looming 'protest' or meaningfulness it might have into the rich, insistently banal comic texture.

For Larkin, what is funny is simply and naturally part of the artist's imaginative process; and he makes a revealing comment in a letter to his friend Patsy Strang in February 1954, not long after the appearance of Kingsley Amis's *Lucky Jim*. In effect he damns that novel, in spite of his enthusiasm for its humour, by separating that humour from imaginative process. 'And of course the Kingsley humour I think quite unrivalled, quite wonderful. It's in the general thinness of imagination that he falls down' (*SL* 223). There is no such thinness of imagination in *A Girl in Winter*, a work of art of essentially the same kind as the Lawrentian masterpieces, although on a different level. *Lucky Jim* is an artful piece of comic farce, in the most deliberate and thus most superficial sense: nothing more.

It remains to consider the detachment of comedy in the cases of Lawrence and Larkin. Lawrentian and Larkinian comedy may seem saturated in the rich juices of living: and yet at the same time there can seem about both something best apprehended by the outsider, the individual not instinctively and unconsciously rooted in life. Protesting too much, and too repetitively, Leavis continually emphasised the 'living nature' of Lawrence's achievement, the fact that 'Life for him is everywhere life'.[11] In one sense this is obvious: in another it becomes under examination

interestingly ambiguous. For there is a sense in which the concept of 'life' will only be meaningful if we are able to seem to look at it from the outside: we are, in fact, not so much 'living' ourselves, as the clients and users of 'life' as art.

In a letter to Sutton, Larkin makes the point from another angle, in his mildly droll way. 'I refuse to believe that there is a thing called life, that one can be in or out of touch with. There is only an endless series of events, of which our birth is one and our death another' (*SL* 154). He was making the same point ten years or so later. 'Life is a funny business. The only way of getting shut of your family is to put your neck into the noose of another one. Such is nature's abhorrence of a vacuum. Life doesn't wait to be asked: it comes grinning in, sits down uninvited & helps itself to bread & cheese, & comments uninhibitedly on the decorations' (*SL* 286).

In view of the attitude and preferences expressed both in his poems and his letters, it was natural that Larkin would examine with some rigour his literary idol's credentials not so much as a life-enhancing artist – the truth of that went without saying – but as a man who was himself supposedly 'rooted in life'. Larkin begins his enquiry by suggesting that Lawrence required from life what he required from women: something that suited him and from which he could remain detached; something, officially, without what Larkin calls women's need for 'emotional haberdashery' (*SL* 158). By offering and demanding a thing they call 'love' women blackmail men and force them into feelings of guilt and dependence. All this is fraudulent, and writers who endorse it are frauds. Lawrence is not the only one who is not: Larkin came to have a great respect for the novels of Henri de Montherlant for the same reason. De Montherlant, he argues, is not a misogynist, but a writer who cannot g along with the usual cant about women and love.[12] Incidentally he is al a very funny writer.

Both Lawrence and de Montherlant may well turn out to have b prophetic in their attitudes. Feminism today endorses something m different, in the relation of the sexes, from the view held by Lawren also by de Montherlant and Larkin. Something, that is to say, inv sexual freedom, dignity and independence in regard to a stabl

trying to argue away the sun – so I desisted' (*SL* 166). Larkin saw, of course, that contradictions of this sort are irrelevant where Lawrence's art and writing are concerned. But he goes on to remark on what was (to him) the oddity of the fact that Lawrence never mentioned in his letters or elsewhere the possibility of being a father. Hardy did, and he was 'the most reticent of men'. 'I should have thought that D.H.L., one of the least reticent of men, would have made some mention of the position' (*SL* 166).[13]

The interest of the point is Larkin's own identification with Lawrence's attitudes at this time of his life, at least as they seemed to be. Larkin saw Lawrence not as a role model but as a predecessor in all the problems of being an artist, and a husband and father – problems that were pressing upon Larkin acutely at the time. He suggests that Lawrence wanted a woman just to 'sit still & back you up' (*SL* 158). But the trouble was that women 'want children: they like scenes: they want a chance of parading all the emotional haberdashery they are stocked with. Above all they like feeling they "own" you – or that you "own" them – a thing I hate' (*SL* 158).

The answer, he supposed, was that 'we all have love, if we choose to use it' (*SL* 159). But he expresses this in a characteristically comic metaphor. 'Want some ten pound notes? Go round giving people ten pound notes' – and you'll get some back. But this 'doesn't explain where you got the £10 notes from in the first place' (*SL* 159). In terms of theory, even Lawrentian theory, the problem was a non-problem, as Larkin saw very well. And yet the example of Lawrence haunted his own practical problems: and his boundless admiration for the other writer was something that he felt could inspire him too.

Women in Love had inspired *A Girl in Winter* by contrary means. The heroine of Larkin's novel had accepted non-participation in life as thankfully, or at least as fatalistically, as Lawrence, through the characters of Gerald and of Gudrun, had rejected it. And yet did Larkin feel that something in the Lawrentian comedy – in Lawrence's 'mocking grin' – put him as much against life as on its side: and hence that as an artist in comedy he was himself treading faithfully in his master's footsteps? That seems possible, even likely.

He certainly felt that the nature of participation in life – the problem of living and being – was his subject, no less than it had been Lawrence's; and that the undercover bond between them was the core of the secret comedy involved. Lawrence's hilarity was what he responded to most deeply in the other artist, the hilarity which is always in the background of the Lawrence letters. 'John Thomas and Lady Jane / Were caught larking in the rain' (vi. 313). It was clear to Larkin, as it has not been to many of Lawrence's more earnest readers and critics, that *Lady Chatterley's Lover* was inspired above all by Lawrence's sense of comedy: that sexual liberation was above all a question of being joyous and amused by life. Larkin's way of being joyous and amused in such matters was to be gloomy, querulous and pessimistic; but with him these are life-enhancing qualities, in their own way a response to life no less vivid than Lawrence's own. In both cases what is significantly affirmed is a deep underlying irresponsibility. The 'mistake' that the Captain affirms – the pretence of love ('I realised that, as far as I was concerned, love was a mistake') – also determines the personality of Mellors, who makes no mistakes by the simple expedient of throwing up everything he does as soon as he seems to be becoming too involved in it.

> Sometimes you hear, fifth-hand
> As epitaph:
> *He chucked up everything*
> *And just cleared off,*
> And always the voice will sound
> Certain you approve
> This audacious, purifying,
> Elemental move.　　　　　　　　　　　　　　　　　(*CP* 85)

Larkin's 'Poetry of Departures' expresses his own sense of the ironies of attachment and detachment, as he had found them in Lawrence. Both of them, as Larkin was aware, led paradoxical lives: in one sense rooted in their relationship and ways of life, but in another and more secret sense, restlessly and remorselessly independent. They had to live like that, if they were to be the kind of artists they wanted to be, and were.

Even Larkin, whole-hearted admirer of Lawrence as he was, and, significantly, of the aspects of Lawrence which others have passed over or disapproved, perceived and understood the impossible situation which Lawrence had got himself into at the end of *Lady Chatterley's Lover*. The novel could not 'move on', as all Lawrence's other books do with a natural irresponsibility, from the sea to Sardinia, from Australia or Mexico back to Europe. There is an odd sense in which all Lawrence's novel plots end like that of Larkin's in *A Girl in Winter*, in a kind of acceptance of the life or the death force, the relief and solitude of departures, and the new promise of negations. One life, one writing – that was how it had to be; and it was a life determined by the freedoms that the writing – in Lawrence's case – may even seem to be doing its best to deny.

Such a denial is in its own way the root of the comedy, as Larkin saw. Connie may be going to have a child, but Mellors will be away and will not have anything to do with it, and neither will the writer or the reader. The novel does not end, but abandons itself to the secret limbo in which Lawrence's characters – the ones he approved as well as the ones he disapproved of – have their only real existence. Ursula and Birkin, no less than Mellors or Paul Morel, find themselves launched, like Larkin's Katherine, on to a negativity which, in Lawrence's case, affirms its own positiveness without the means to prove it. Neither Connie nor Ursula can in fact have a child in the context and intimacy of Lawrence's art, because Lawrence himself cannot conceive of the process, and its fulfilment. It exists only at the end of the rainbow.

Larkin perceived all this is in Lawrence, as his hero figure, and in his own way he himself exploited it. Like Lawrence at the end of *Lady Chatterley's Lover*, he was defeated in his attempts at fiction by the efforts that he made to be positive, and to write a novel with a conventional kind of plot and sequence – that of 'a man's life, no less'. This was not how things could be managed. Creation could only be achieved by means that were negative, and for that reason fundamentally aesthetic. For Lawrence too, the aesthete as comedian and creator came to predominate, in his later work. And for both writers the aesthete has to be also the amused or derisive bystander. Anthony Powell, himself, a great comic writer, has observed that Mellors as a character is seen wholly aesthetically. He reminded Powell of the ditty with a double entendre that Mary Pickford used to sing in the music halls. 'Everything he does is so artistic.'[14] That would apply to love-making and washing the dishes, as well as to the clothes Mellors wears, and the ways he rears baby pheasants. Mellors could hardly be expected to do anything that did not seem to involve his own aesthetic awareness of himself, because that is the way it is necessarily seen from outside, by the reader.

And the same applies to Larkin. The brides and bridegrooms of his poem 'The Whitsun Weddings' are involuntary players in an aesthetic comedy, watched with awed amusement by the fascinated outsider. As in the poetic series 'Livings', the act of being human, and fitting into some normal human occupation itself becomes a strange, and quietly outlandish, aesthetic display, a source both of poetry and of comedy. The marvellous and distinctly Lawrentian image that ends 'The Whitsun Weddings' – 'an arrow-shower / Sent out of sight, somewhere becoming rain' (CP 116) – shows comedy turning in Larkin to its familiar final resource of aesthetic wistfulness: the humdrum matters of birth, growth and death must take place elsewhere, not in the focus of the poem.

That wistfulness is alien to Lawrence, and to his triumphant powers of aesthetic seizure and definition. A Larkin joke, however – and Lawrence's too – is aesthetic in its completion, like Birkin throwing stones at the reflection of the moon, which in Aspects of the Novel E.M. Forster called one of the finest aesthetic scenes in English fiction.[15] Many of Lawrence's achievements in creation, and all of Larkin's which they so greatly inspired, have in the end the dimensions of an arty joke. Neither artist can help implying that art *is* a joke, which is bound to have to be appreciated outside, and beyond, the involuntary process of living. Life 'doesn't wait to be asked', but a joke has to wait to be seen. Larkin's poem 'Spring' has the line 'And those she had least use for see her best' (CP 39). Perhaps the time has come to admit that to be on the side of life is also to be on its sidelines; and that this was the joke in Lawrence that Larkin saw best, and was best inspired by.

Notes

1 *Selected Letters of Philip Larkin 1940–1985*, ed. Anthony Thwaite (Faber & Faber, 1992), p. 359: subsequent references will appear in the text in

the form (*SL* 359). It has not proved possible to trace the source of the DHL remark.

2 Barbara Pym, *Less than Angels* (Jonathan Cape, 1955), p. 180.

3 Philip Larkin, *Collected Poems*, ed. Anthony Thwaite (The Marvell Press and Faber & Faber, 1988), p. 34: subsequent references will appear in the text in the form (*CP* 34).

4 'East Coker', *Four Quartets* (Faber & Faber, 1944), p. 22.

5 Leavis's first use of this phrase appears to have been in his title 'The Novel as Dramatic Poem (I): *Hard Times*' in *Scrutiny*, xiv (Spring 1947), 185.

6 Larkin, *A Girl in Winter* (Faber & Faber, 1952), p. 75.

7 *Women in Love*, ed. David Farmer, Lindeth Vasey and John Worthen (Cambridge: Cambridge University Press, 1987), pp. 240–3.

8 *The Fox, The Captain's Doll, The Ladybird*, ed. Dieter Mehl (Cambridge: Cambridge University Press, 1992), 148:39–149:34.

9 *A Girl in Winter*, pp. 161–2.

10 Ibid., p. 248.

11 See e.g. F.R. Leavis, *Thought, Words and Creativity: Art and Thought in Lawrence* (Chatto & Windus, 1976), p. 94: *D.H. Lawrence: Novelist* (Chatto & Windus, 1955), p. 90.

12 Larkin, 'The Girls', *Required Writing* (Faber & Faber, 1983), p. 260.

13 See DHL to Frieda, 15 May 1912: 'I want you to have children to me – I don't care how soon. I never thought I should have that definite desire' (i. 40–3). This letter was, however, not in the edition of DHL's letters Larkin would have been reading (*The Letters of D.H. Lawrence*, ed. Aldous Huxley, Heinemann, 1932).

14 *Memoirs* (Heinemann, 1982), iv. 72.

15 (Harmondsworth: Penguin Books, 1962), p. 147.

Index

DATE DUE

			Printed in USA

HIGHSMITH #45230